THE
SOCIAL REVOLUTION
IN AUSTRIA

THE
SOCIAL REVOLUTION
IN AUSTRIA

BY

C. A. MACARTNEY

Sometime Scholar of Trinity College
Cambridge

CAMBRIDGE
AT THE UNIVERSITY PRESS
MCMXXVI

CAMBRIDGE
UNIVERSITY PRESS

University Printing House, Cambridge CB2 8BS, United Kingdom

Published in the United States of America by Cambridge University Press, New York

Cambridge University Press is part of the University of Cambridge.

It furthers the University's mission by disseminating knowledge in the pursuit of
education, learning and research at the highest international levels of excellence.

www.cambridge.org
Information on this title: www.cambridge.org/9781107425835

© Cambridge University Press 1926

First published 1926
First paperback edition 2014

A catalogue record for this publication is available from the British Library

ISBN 978-1-107-42583-5 Paperback

CONTENTS

THIS book, if it had a sub-title, would be styled a "study in changing values." Its subject is one which is devoid of striking incident, but should not lack interest in a world so feverishly occupied with readapting its own values to changing circumstances.

Everyone knows something about the nationalist movement among the non-German races of the old Habsburg Monarchy, and is aware that most of these races took the opportunity afforded them by the war of 1914–1918 to throw in their lot more or less openly with the Entente, which rewarded them by confirming their independence.

The ideas of Englishmen are not as a rule so clear about modern Austria. They underestimate the absolutist character of the old régime, the cleft which separated the Dynasty and ruling classes from the ruled in all parts of the Monarchy. It is seldom realised that the essentially dynastic policy of the Habsburgs ended by creating among the German subjects an opposition hardly less strong than that of the Czechs or Croats. If it had happened—and it might once have happened—that war had found Germany and ourselves grouped against Austria-Hungary and Russia, our sympathies for the different peoples of Central Europe would have been startlingly other from what they are to-day.

The modern State of Austria is not a mere political rump, but the product, although distorted and maimed, of active and self-conscious forces within the country. It is true that these forces could not have created the present Republic, but for the often unwilling co-operation of the neighbouring nationalities and the inevitable effects of the war. They took advantage of a situation, rather than created it. Yet if this limits their achievement for good or ill, it does not take away their interest.

The chief moving force in this case was the Austrian Social Democrat Party. The history of the world from 1917 onwards has been that of the struggle between Socialism and the forces opposed to it. It is a subject which is perhaps the most important of our time, and that to which the least clear thinking has been applied. The words "socialism," "communism" and "bolshevism" are not rightly understood by one in a hundred who takes them in his mouth. In practical form they are indeed susceptible to description only, not to definition, just as, to take the opposing ideologies, one definition of "monarchy" would not cover all the manifestations of that form of State even in twentieth century Europe.

Socialism is a system which must take widely different forms according to local variations of history and conditions. It is not a matter to be advocated or condemned as a whole, since every State of Europe to-day is socialised at least in some minor details of its system, and none, not even Russia, has succeeded in socialising anything like the whole. It is hardly possible that, with the general growth of population and the increase of industry, the impulse towards Socialism, where it can be usefully applied, will not continue to increase. It would, therefore, be natural to suppose that all thoughtful men would be anxious to examine seriously and impartially what experiments have already been made, with a view to considering how far and in what manner their lessons may be applied to other conditions.

Such is, however, not the practice of most citizens, nor even of most politicians. As a rule, taking the most extreme form of Socialism which has yet been attempted, and that which grew up under the most abnormal and un-European conditions—the bolshevik experiments in Russia—they either laud or decry it blindly.

This work has attempted to give an impartial survey, from the widest point of view, of what Austrian Socialism is, what it has attempted and what accomplished. In the writer's opinion, such a survey has little practical use if it is confined to lists of figures and economic calculations. It is necessary to look further, to see what were the conditions which gave birth to this particular form of the world movement, how far they helped and how hindered its development, and further, what was its effect on the non-Socialist classes of society. For this reason, less than half of the book is devoted to the Socialist Party itself, the remainder bearing on it only indirectly, but being necessary, in the opinion of the writer, to bring the efforts of that party into focus.

No attempt whatever has been made to lay down the law whether the teaching of Marx, or of any other Socialist leader, is theoretically sound or desirable, and I have tried to eliminate every expression of personal opinion on this point. I have concerned myself solely with results, and here I have done my best—a very difficult and probably a very thankless task—to set down these results with absolute impartiality. It is an attempt which has not, so far as I am aware, been made hitherto, in Austria or elsewhere.

Austrian Socialism must always differ widely from our own. In the first place, it is far more essentially political. Its early history forced it into bitter opposition to the great political forces which made the old Habsburg Monarchy —the Church, the Dynasty, and the Army. Treated by all three as a hated outcast, it naturally became violently republican, atheist, pacifist. None of these three qualities, unless perhaps the last, appears to me to be necessarily inherent in a theoretically perfect form of Socialism, and it is well to understand the conditions which made them inevitable in Austria. Secondly, it was much more nearly and directly influenced by the example of Russia than our parties have ever been. Thirdly, it has been obliged to devote itself very closely to the complex racial problems of Central Europe. Fourthly, the non-industrial classes with which it has had to deal, both landowners and capitalists, differ very widely from the corresponding classes in Great Britain. In the case of the former, the obstacles in the way of its extension are much greater than they are with us; in the case of the latter, the frequent incompetence and dishonesty among Austrian capitalists may perhaps inspire an exaggerated sympathy for the alternatives offered by Socialism.

I have not attempted to lay before the world any new or startling facts about Austria-Hungary. I have made my account of conditions before the war rather fuller than I should otherwise have done because no work has yet appeared in English, so far as I am aware (and few in German), which adequately covers this ground.

A bibliography of the principal works consulted will be found at the end of the book. The chapters dealing directly with Socialism have been kindly read by Dr Fritz Brueghel, librarian to the Arbeiterkammer of Vienna, who has passed the facts there stated as correct. I cannot expect any person actively engaged in politics in Austria to agree

with all the opinions passed in a work which strives after
impartiality.

I am indebted to many friends for kind help and suggestions, and would like to express my especial thanks to
my friend, Dr Siegfried Pollak, of the Oesterreichische
Volkszeitung.

All opinions given in this work are my own purely
personal views, gathered during a sojourn of some five
years in the Austrian Republic. No other person is in any
way responsible for any opinion expressed here.

C. A. MACARTNEY

March 1926

CHAPTER I

THE DYNASTY

CENTURIES of patient acquisitiveness had assembled under the personal sway of the House of Habsburg the most heterogeneous collection of subjects which Europe could show. The process of accumulation had been varied and gradual; the set-backs almost as numerous as the advances. Treaties, campaigns, marriages, barters had all played their part. If the campaigns were often disastrous, the marriages were the more brilliant by contrast; and perhaps the almost uniform incompetence of his generals was one of the brightest gems in the Monarch's diadem. At any rate, it was one of the factors which permitted him the unique and stately boast of having lost in his day more than an ordinary king had ever dreamed of possessing.

For that venerable Dynasty was not as others. Something more august than the ordinary—something holy, as its old title was not abashed to call it—clung about it. One of the political ideas which permeated Europe for many centuries was that the Habsburgs must rule; where and what was an open question, which each generation answered as its circumstances dictated. "Austria," the incorporated seat of the Habsburgs' will-to-power, changed its frontiers every decade; it was indefinable, it was almost a poetic idea. In fact, one of the most agitating problems of the reign of Franz Josef, and one that was never solved, was how his domains should be entitled, how displayed on the Imperial and Royal coat of arms. But the Pragmatic Sanction—in its essence a purely family arrangement, the establishment of an entail—was a most practical fact, the power of the Habsburgs a stern reality which was not affected by the fact that it identified itself, now with the throne of Spain, now of the Netherlands; now with the hegemony of Germany, now with the rule of Northern Italy; and lastly with a mainly Slavonic realm in South-eastern Europe, with aspirations over the Balkans. It was the peculiar fortune of the Habsburgs always to find some-one to whom their rule was profitable, whether exercised over the person concerned or over his neighbours.

The real core of the Habsburg dominions, as became ever more apparent through the centuries, was the Danubian Basin. What lay outside that natural unity was an excrescence. The Dynasty would have stood more firmly had it recognised this fact, had its insatiable ambition not continually pushed it to foreign conquest which was expensive and difficult to hold, certain to be lost. The Netherlands, the Italian provinces (Trieste, the maritime outlet of the Danubian Basin, is an exception), the German hegemony vanished one by one, leaving the surviving lands exhausted by the efforts to retain the impossible. Galicia, the Bukovina, and Dalmatia remained, it is true, to the end; but recognised as "outsiders" and enjoying a prac-tical, if not legal, special position.

But in the Austrian hereditary provinces, the lands of the Bohemian Crown and of the Holy Crown of St Stephen, the Habsburgs' footing was secure to the last. Here they had received tasks which were higher than the task of administering the internal affairs of some northern or western realm. They were the guardians of the marches; the bulwark of Europe against repeated and frightful in-vasions of the Ottoman, the sword of Christendom against the Turk, the shield of the Catholic Church against infidel and heretic, north, east and south.

To guard the gate of Europe towards the east, to educate and civilise the rude peoples over which their shadow was cast, was a task, which, if well performed, justified extraordinary pretensions. The nations of Central Europe rallied round their defender, and the military State which arose out of the common need for defence was fully powerful enough to preserve the prestige of the Habsburgs as the successors of Caesar and the staff of Saint Peter. The Catholic Church was their mighty ally; by its aid they were enabled to break the power of the Estates which represented local autonomy in their provinces, and weld them into a military and foreign-political unity.

After the Turkish flood had ebbed back to Belgrade, Central Europe was exhausted. Its old aristocracy had perished, or at least had been terribly weakened, in the Turkish and religious wars. The Habsburgs of the eighteenth century, Maria Theresa, the greatest of them all, and her son Josef II, the enlightened despots, enjoyed a breathing space in which they could deepen and renew the idea of their Dynasty. They were no longer satisfied with unity against the enemy; they aimed at an internal unity, at creating a homogeneous State which should be their personal possession.

Thanks to their efforts, an unity was achieved which was far in advance of anything dreamed by their predecessors. The power of the Estates was reduced to a shadow, except in Hungary; and a competent and loyal bureaucracy took over the administration of the Habsburg domains in obedience to the exclusive will of the Monarch.

Both these great rulers necessarily availed themselves of the Germans, by far the most cultured and competent of their subject races, in their reforms, and Josef II believed it possible to create an Austrian nation, German in thought and feeling, throughout his dominions. He very nearly succeeded west of the Leitha; in Hungary he failed, and when he died, leaving his work unfinished, his successor found a changed world.

The first date which marks the decline of the Habsburg Monarchy is that of the Peace of Karlovitz, January 26th, 1699, which sealed the victory of Austrian arms over the Turks. A second is that of the fall of the Bastille in Paris, July 14th, 1789. From this day on fresh ideas were growing up within the peoples, struggled for nigh a century and a half against the idea of Habsburg autocracy, and at last overthrew it.

The Habsburgs readapted themselves geographically, after the Napoleonic interlude, but not spiritually. The Emperor Franz and Metternich found a new vessel into which to pour the old dynastic ideology: under them Austria represented the spirit of autocracy and reaction. While the French revolution shattered the old belief in the Divine Right of Monarchs; while Protestant Prussia gradually wrested to herself the first place in Germany; while the power of Turkey decayed and that of Russia grew; the Habsburgs remained as the champions of things as they had been before 1789.

The petty oppression, the stupidity, perhaps most of all the financial incompetence of Metternich's long era, called forth a general revolt. Every class and every nation had cause of complaint. The Magyars, the Italians and the Poles chafed against the new restraint; the Slav nations awoke to memories, at first faint and doubtful, of national consciousness. The peasants, still semi-serfs, groaned under their burdens; the workmen were thrown into misery by the unemployment consequent on the introduction of machinery.

A revolution in which every nation and every class took part was frustrated by its very complexity. Mutual hatred and jealousies were so strong that the Crown, which still commanded a traditional awe and the loyalty of most of the army, was able to reassert its authority after a few months.

The peaceable Emperor Ferdinand, who had been persuaded or terrorised into granting a Constitution, a measure of liberty for Austria, and semi-independence to Hungary, was removed from the throne by the victorious generals and the boy Franz Josef elevated to his place.

For two or three years Franz Josef felt his way back from Liberalism. As soon as his position was strong enough, he suspended the Constitution which he himself had granted and re-established the era of absolutism.

The system which Franz Josef's counsellors evolved for him during the first and supremely important decade of his reign was that which remained the real government of Austria up to 1918. The later appearances of Constitution and Parliament obscured this truth until in 1914, some months before the outbreak of the world war, Count Stürgkh, the Minister President, quietly sent Parliament packing, so that Franz Josef's reign ended as it began with naked absolutism.

Franz Josef's absolutism was the most thorough-going that Austria ever experienced. All previous monarchs, if they gradually centred in the hands of their bureaucracy the upper instances of power, left local administration and the affairs of the peasants to the patrimonial Courts of the feudal nobility. Franz Josef was the first Habsburg to abolish these privileges of the nobles and to introduce a system of absolute bureaucracy and centralism through his whole Empire, including Hungary.

To aid him in this difficult and, as time was to show, ultimately impossible task, he built up a system which achieved a durability and efficiency which one cannot but admire. The foundations on which he built were a loyal army and a loyal bureaucracy, both of them international in origin but German in tone and usual language; a sub-servient Catholic Church, inspired with ideals of inter-national authority by the Grace of God; and a privileged aristocracy.

The net of Austrian bureaucracy was extraordinarily widespread. It included, besides what we ordinarily think of as State officials, most of the railway employees, nearly all of those in charge of education (even the professors of the University of Vienna were appointed by the Emperor, not always with reference to their scholastic abilities), the important forestry service, and even the members of the two great theatres in Vienna and Budapest. Local government only gradually attained a certain measure of autonomy, and never reached anything like such freedom as our town and district councils enjoy. The bureaucracy was an enormous system in which branches, departments and posts were endlessly multiplied, and which invaded the private life of the individual to an extent hardly con-ceivable by an Englishman.

Much has been written against the Austrian bureaucracy, often wrongly and unfairly. Even from the point of view of the outsider it was alert and liberal if compared with the

Serb, the Russian or even the Italian. In one respect especially, it was an example to the Continent: corruption among its members was almost unknown. Its technical efficiency was, moreover, of a high order. Better work has probably seldom been done for a State than the work of the Austrian railway, road and river engineers, or, to take another instance, the modernisations accomplished by Austrian officials in the provinces of Bosnia and the Herzegovina were nothing short of amazing.

As a rule, too, the members of the bureaucracy were kind, polite and helpful towards the general public so long as their superiority was unquestioned—a matter in which radical reforms had been introduced since 1848. Against all this it would be ungrateful to dwell too heavily on the defects of the system, on the multiplication of offices, the amazing obscurity of the official jargon, the slowness and deadening of initiative caused by the hierarchical system. A machine which had to deal with such an extreme complexity of affairs was necessarily slow and cautious. The extreme inactivity which is often displayed, the baffling silence and oppositional attitude, were not so much due to antiquated and superfluous regulations, although there were enough of them, but to the essential character of the system.

The bureaucrats were not the servants of the public, but of the Emperor. The first organs created by the Habsburgs to assert their own authority against that of the Estates were known under the generic name of "Polizey," and this character never left them. They were essentially police, the Monarch's line of defence against the people, which all the later Habsburgs always felt in their hearts to be potential rebels. Thus the actual police, acknowledged or secret, played a peculiarly important rôle in the bureau-cracy, and its powers were extended to deal with matters to which, in England, a policeman is quite indifferent, and to deal with them by methods which we should hardly tolerate. To take a single example: everyone in Vienna lives in flats, and each block of flats has a porter. The house doors are always locked at ten at night, and until after the revolution of 1918, no inmate of a house possessed a key to that door. If he came home after lights out, he had to ring until the porter opened to him in person. All porters were police agents. After the revolution, it may be noted, they themselves struck against the system, and tenants are now allowed keys.

The bureaucracy was well situated. Pay was good, in-surance against sickness and old age admirable, and this at a time when such measures were almost unknown for the private individual. The social standing of its members was high, on a par with that of the fighting forces. With these it was closely connected, most of its lower grades being actually filled from the ranks of the time-expired N.C.O.'s, and thus imbued with the loyalty, discipline, respect for authority, contempt of the *pékin* and lack of imagination proper to soldiers and servants of an autocrat. The higher ranks were similarly filled with youths who had been destined from their childhood up for this career, and knew how to value its secure, comfortable and honourable conditions.

This great body served its master faithfully. For many decades it formed a real bond of union among the varied races of the Empire. Austria did not exist but in the person of the Monarch; but as his servants, the bureau-cracy felt itself Austrian, and did truly, if thinly, incorporate that elusive idea. True, it was German as well, but in speech and culture, not in political feeling; the German nationalism was as suspect to the Emperor as any other form of nationalism.

Very much the same may be said of the army, which helped Franz Josef on to the throne and was by him reorganised and set on a pedestal on which it had never stood before. Previous to 1848 the Austrian army had not enjoyed a special regard. It was a necessary implement of government, but neither well paid, greatly esteemed, nor particularly efficient. A large number of its officers were not Austrians at all, but Germans from various small States of the Deutscher Bund. Among the rest, the strongest contingent was Serb and Croat, drawn from the Military Frontier which guarded the marches of Austria and Hungary against the Turk and the plague.

After 1848 the army was thoroughly reorganised and became, like the bureaucracy, an "Austrian" factor. It too was German in tone and speech, for no other language was conceivable as an universal instrument of command. But it might not be German in sentiment, and indeed was mobilised twice in the early period of the reign against German adversaries. Franz Josef's officers, like his civil servants, were asked to give a strictly personal loyalty. They were Austrian, and thus a-national. In general it may be said that the officers, until the last years, and many of them throughout the final revolution, conformed to this exacting standard. They were greatly favoured and greatly trusted. They enjoyed a position apart. Everything was done to secure their comfort and good repute, and to mark them off from the inferior civilians. A great deal of the actual government of the country rested in their hands.

Their senior generals filled high positions of State, and became the trusted advisers of the Emperor. In the frequent intervals of martial law in the provinces, the military carried out the administration, which lay almost entirely in their hands in Bosnia and the Herzegovina.

The third great prop of the Dynasty was the Catholic Church. The connection between Church and Monarchy was rooted in the deepest antiquity; it went back to the ideas of the Holy Roman Empire. In spite of their frequent quarrels, inevitable where the pretensions of both were so wide-reaching, Pope and Emperor always looked upon each other as traditional allies. In the Counter-Reformation each rendered the other invaluable services, and it is most remarkable how, even up to the present day, the anti-dynastic movement in Hungary, Bohemia and elsewhere was identified with the non-Catholic population, while the Catholics of the Tirol and Croatia were the Emperor's most loyal subjects.

The enlightened despots, especially Josef II, while always remaining good Catholics, did much to modify the overwhelming political influence which the Counter-Reformation had given the Church. For them the Church was a servant, not a master. In the first half of the nineteenth century, religion in Austria, like everything else, lost its deeper feeling, became soulless. Franz Josef, again, was the man to restore it to its old place. Deeply influenced in his youth by his mother, a bigoted Bavarian, and by his tutor, later Archbishop of Vienna, he was at once genuinely pious and keenly alive to the political value of the help which Catholicism could give him.

At the beginning of his reign, when the boy-Emperor was still completely under the influence of his mother and tutor, Franz Josef allowed the Church to attain a power in Austria greater, perhaps, than she had ever enjoyed. In those days, before he had become sadly disillusioned, he still dreamed, it seems, of reviving the world Empire of Charlemagne. With Catholic support the dream seemed not impossible. Both in Italy and in Germany the forces of Catholicism and Protestantism were fairly equally divided, and a strong coalition of Pope and Emperor might yet triumph over Prussia and Sardinia. These ambitions, no less than the feelings aroused by his narrow escape from the hand of an assassin, prompted Franz Josef to embark on a grandiose foreign policy, and to conclude a Concordat for his own domains which made Papistry unlimited lord over the spiritual and intellectual life of his subjects. After his fine ambitions had failed, and he himself had attained to greater mental independence, Franz Josef cast off the leading strings which he himself had imposed, and abolished the Concordat.

But later on the alliance was renewed, and at the end was again very close. The chief members of the Imperial Household were unaffectedly clerical. The Archdukes were always brought up by clerical tutors, Franz Josef himself was very deeply influenced by his confessor. In later times, too, the political interests of Church and Monarch once again became obviously identical. The German nationalist movement for union with Prussia openly styled itself "away from Rome." Socialism was an equal enemy of altar and throne, and the growing nationalist movements identified themselves ever more with the national religions. Important, too, was the part played by religion in the rivalry with Russia. The priests of the Greek Orthodox Church were the chief proponents of the Pan-Slavonic idea which grew ever more menacing in the Balkans. The Catholics among the Southern Slavs were pro-Austrian; the Orthodox styled themselves " Serbs," identified themselves with the free Serbian State, and looked to Russia as their natural protector. Hence the storm of wrath which descended from Vienna on the head of Ferdinand of Bulgaria when he baptised his son Boris into the national Church of Bulgaria.

The universal Catholic Church, the Austrian supernational army, and the Austrian bureaucracy—these were the three pillars on which Franz Josef founded his Monarchy. With their help he proposed to maintain an edifice which was politically, socially and financially an oligarchy. For if Franz Josef was a despot, he was no leveller. All power was his, by the Grace of God; this was for him a commonplace which he never questioned; but he made a great difference between subject and subject. Franz Josef was a child of the revolution. He never forgot the early impressions of 1848, the horror and disgust which had seized the Court at the spectacle of revolutionary Vienna, the barricades and the swarming masses of those unkempt, half-starved figures which were seen in those days for the first time outside their foetid warrens, the proletariat. A child of the revolution, but only of the deep hatred which it aroused in the minds of those against whom it was directed. He reigned for sixty-eight years, and always thought of the people as a revolutionary mob.

So Franz Josef's reign was not merely autocratic, it was also—what is not always the same thing—feudal. There were three classes which occupied a privileged position, enjoying the favour and backing of the Crown, in return for their support of its dynastic policy. These were the

old land-owning aristocracy, the industrial and commercial German or Germanised middle classes, and the
great Jewish financiers. A close analysis of the way in
which Austrian policy, internal and foreign, was jockeyed
in the interests of one or the other of those classes, or two
of them in combination, would lead to amazing conclusions.
Here, however, we have only space for a word on the subject of the most influential, the landed aristocracy.

The nobles of Bohemia, Hungary and Poland are among
the richest in Europe. The estates of their leading members
are of staggering acreage; their castles of a splendour
which must be seen to be believed. Unfortunately, the
class as a whole, with hardly a single exception, has failed
to grasp, even faintly, the idea of service to be rendered
in return for privilege. The children and grandchildren of
men who enjoyed on their vast estates the powers and incomes of princes, the nobles have seen nothing in the
national and democratic movements of the nineteenth
century but financial and social disaster for themselves,
and have uniformly thrown themselves on the side of
reaction. At heart as selfish and idle as any race in Europe,
they were forced into politics by the knowledge that they
could only save their obsolete position by identifying themselves with the policy of the Monarch, by surrounding his
person and building up a wall between him and the real
world. In this they succeeded admirably, favoured by
Franz Josef's personal dislike of contact with the middle
or lower classes, and personal distrust of parvenu ability.
Although gradually forced by the increasing need for
specialised brains out of the technical Ministries or the
specialist branches of the army, they still maintained a
solid phalanx of their representatives in the branches of

public service in most direct contact with the Monarch;
that is, the posts of Minister President and of Minister of
Foreign Affairs. The appointments in these posts were
always made by Franz Josef in person, and almost always
from among the higher nobility; and this all-important
fact goes far to explain both the weakness and the extraordinary artificiality of Austrian State policy under Franz
Josef.

Small as these influential circles were in comparison
with the growing and struggling masses of the people, they
have yet placed their imprint on the whole of Austrian life.
They affected the very character of the people, and apparently permanently; for events since 1918 have not
changed the Austrians in the slightest from their former
selves: charming, impressed by titles, frivolous, good
mannered and irresponsible. They could hardly learn to
be otherwise in a State where everything, up to 1914, was
thoroughly feudal, a system of castes and interests to which
modern ideas were abhorrent and to be suppressed as
rapidly as possible; a system run on bureaucratic, military
and clerical lines, neither by nor for the people. The
liberal-thinking individuals among these circles themselves
often rebelled against the dead level of conservatism to
which tradition bound them. For the liberal spirit has
never been lacking in Austria, even in the highest social
circles. But they were powerless to alter the general tone,
and a singularly unhappy fate appeared to dog the foot-
steps of the would-be innovators, even when they were of
the Imperial Family.

The absolutist form of the State which, for Franz Josef,
was the natural and only right system, lasted for a decade.
During that time, Austria was plunged into one venture

after another, in pursuit of the chimaera of glory for her ruler. In Germany, Austria challenged the growing ambitions of Prussia and forced her to withdraw. In Italy, Radetzky defeated the arms of Piedmont. Then the tide turned. The Crimean War ended in a humiliation. A fresh conflict with Sardinia, at this time in alliance with France, resulted in the loss of Lombardy. The ambitious foreign policy, the militarism and bureaucracy, emptied the State coffers. The discontent of the peoples grew too dangerous to be longer ignored. Franz Josef was obliged to return to Constitutionalism, how unwillingly may be judged from the words in which he addressed his Ministers:

...His Majesty demands from all his Ministers the solemn promise that they will protect the Throne with full energy and single application against the extortion of further concessions, whether by pressure from the Parliament or the Diets, or by revolutionary attempts on the part of the masses.

In particular, his Majesty deigns to insist that the competencies of Parliament, as described, be strictly regarded, and that any attempt on the part of that body to interfere in the conduct of foreign affairs, in military affairs and the matter of the Command of the Army, meet with the most determined refusal...[1].

But the Emperor's humiliations were not yet at an end. His centralist policy had not crushed, it had only provoked the nationalist movements which were growing stronger, year by year, in every part of the Monarchy. The Federalists of Austria proper and the Liberal Party in Hungary rejected the Constitution. In 1866 a fresh and most disastrous conflict with Prussia deprived Austria for ever

[1] Protocol of the Emperor's address to his Ministers delivered on February 26th, 1861, two days after the granting of the so-called "February Patent,"

of her status in Germany. Taking advantage of Austria's embarrassment, the last of the Italian provinces freed themselves of her yoke. At the same time the Magyars, the most active and powerful of all the subject races, utilised the moment of Austria's weakness to conclude with the Monarch the bargain known as the "Ausgleich."

By this famous and peculiar agreement, the Empire was divided into two equal halves: the "lands of the Hungarian Crown" and its adjuncts, that is, Hungary proper, Transylvania, Croatia, the Military Frontier and the Banat; and the remainder of the Empire, which, for lack of any comprehensive and inoffensive term, came to be known as "the kingdoms and provinces represented in the State Council." The person of the Monarch remained common to both, and common were further the foreign affairs, the military and naval forces and such financial matters as touched the realm as a whole. Each half, however, voted separately as to the number of recruits to be supplied and the conditions of service. The three Ministers for these departments acted jointly for the whole realm, and were responsible to delegations from the two Parliaments, which met in Vienna and Budapest in alternate years. These delegations deliberated separately, communicating only in writing, unless these exchanges of notes brought no agreement. Only when both delegations were agreed could any measure receive the sanction of the Monarch.

Every ten years a contract was drawn up determining the economic relations between the two parties, customs, common railways, etc., and especially the two cardinal questions, what proportion of recruits for the common army each was to supply, and what quota of expenses for the common budget.

This arrangement, as it turned out, was thoroughly unfortunate, so much so that it is hard to understand why Irish leaders desired to model their relations with England on it. Every "agreement," when it fell due, became the signal for the most violent disputes. The uncertainty as to what these agreements would be was disastrous for trade and industry. Neither party could be satisfied. Austria certainly not, since she invariably came off the worse in the bargaining, owing to her own disunity; while the Hungarians were perpetually dissatisfied with their position, as leaving them still short of complete independence.

It was a very wearisome warfare which these unloving bed-fellows waged, turning to a large extent on technicalities, such as the phrasing of titles. The ruler was bound at his coronation to swear an oath of fidelity to the Constitution, so that the Emperor Franz Josef, who had pledged himself to the agreement, could do nothing to alter it. In later years, however, it was known that the Archduke Franz Ferdinand was considering an alteration when he should have the power to make it, and the expectation of this—of which more anon—was an added factor to envenom the last years before 1914.

In any case the dualist Constitution of 1867 settled the Magyar question for a certain time. The Habsburg Monarchy had now attained its final form, except for the difference made by the occupation and later annexation of Bosnia and the Herzegovina.

In Hungary, the dominant Magyar race occupied the central Danubian plain, while a kindred race, the Szeklers, were settled in large numbers in Transylvania. In the mountains of the north, the population was mainly Slovak —an ignorant and backward peasant race, akin to the

Czechs. In Transylvania, besides the Szeklers, there were German colonies, while the bulk of the peasant population was Rumanian. In the north-east the Ruthenes, or Ukrainians, had spilled over the frontier from Russia. In the south were Orthodox Serbs; in the south-west Croats.

Alone of all these nationalities, the Croatians enjoyed a sort of Home Rule under a Lieutenant, or Ban, appointed from Budapest. A delegation of forty members from the Croatian Parliament attended and voted at the debates in Budapest on matters concerning both nations. In purely local affairs, the Croatian Parliament was autonomous. The arrangement was just as unsatisfactory as the dualist compromise and as obscure legally; and offered as many loopholes for oppressions and chicaneries. So long as it lasted, it was the incessant aim of the Magyars to break the Croat independence; the Croats resisting, now by compromise, now by appeals to Vienna, now secretly to Belgrade.

In the western half of the Monarchy, the Germans occupied the Alpine districts from the Swiss frontier to the edge of the Hungarian plain, and the Danubian basin. Slovenes, a race akin to Serbs and Croats, were settled on the southern mountain slopes down to the Bosnian frontier and the sea. Italians lived in Trieste and the maritime cities of the Dalmatian coast, Serbs and Croats[1] in the rest of Dalmatia. In the provinces of Bohemia and Moravia the central districts were Czech, the fringe to south and north German; the population was in general almost inextricably mixed. The Czechs were the more numerous,

---

[1] Serbs and Croats are one race and speak one language, but write it, the Serbs in Cyrillic, the Croats in Latin characters. The difference is one of religion and culture. The Serbs are Orthodox, Byzantine and Russophil; the Croats Catholic and Western in their orientation. The influence is strong enough often to obscure the underlying unity.

the Germans the wealthier and more advanced. In Galicia the western half was Polish, the eastern Ukrainian. In the little Bukovina, Ruthenes, Germans and Rumanians lived together in exceptional amity.

The Jews, the most, and the gipsies, the least, influential of all the races, were scattered throughout the whole Monarchy.

Bosnia and the Herzegovina were populated by Serbs and Croats. The rough proportion of nationalities in the Monarchy was as follows (in millions)[1]:

Austria proper...	...	9·2	Germans
		6·0	Czechs
		4·3	Poles
		3·4	Ruthenes
		1·2	Slovenes
		0·7	Serbs and Croats
		0·7	Italians
		0·2	Rumanians
Hungary	... ...	8·6	Magyars
		2·8	Rumanians
		2·0	Germans
		2·0	Slovaks
		0·6	Serbs
		0·4	Croats
Croatia and Slavonia...		2·1	Serbs and Croats
		0·1	Germans
Bosnia and Herzegovina		0·4	Croats
		0·85	Serbs
		0·85	Serbo-Croat Mahomedans

Or, grouped on broad racial lines: 11 million Germans, 8 million Czecho-Slovaks, 4½ million Poles, 4 million

[1] Official figures of 1900. The Magyar figures are certainly too high. For one thing, they reckoned Jews and gipsies as Magyars.

Ruthenes, 3 million Rumanians, 8½ million Magyars, 6½–7 million Southern Slavs, 0·7 million Italians. More broadly still:

11 million		Germans
8½	,,	Magyars
3½	,,	Latins
23	,,	Slavs

The Constitution once granted, the voice of the people once admitted to a hearing, almost the whole of public life in the Dual Monarchy was now occupied, to the extreme detriment of its material interests, with the inter-racial warfare of those nationalities. In Austria proper and in Hungary, however, the conflict took a widely different appearance.

In Hungary, the Magyars, a sublimely selfish and un-scrupulous race, were also by far the most civilised of the nationalities concerned. Only one other race—the Jews—had attained an equal level of culture, and the Jews were few in numbers and had obviously no intention of con-testing Hungary with the Magyars for their national home. The Magyars therefore conciliated them, helped them to power and riches, and got from them in return the support of their financial and journalistic influence.

As regards the remaining nationalities, the Magyars, who had managed to neutralise their absolute national minority by a franchise which gave them a substantial majority of voters—the more so as voting in Hungary was open—pursued a policy of the frankest oppression, carried through with a cunning which was equal to its ruthless-ness. The Slovaks, Rumanians and Ruthenes simply did not make their voices heard at all. The only nation which was able to put up any sort of opposition was that

of the Southern Slavs, and even here the Magyars kept
their ascendancy secure for a long time by playing off the
Orthodox Serbs against the Catholic Croats.

Matters were different in Austria proper. The Dualist
system had been based on the premise that the Germans
should keep the ascendancy in Austria, the Magyars in
Hungary, and that these two races, in alliance, would be
strong enough to break the Slav opposition. But the pre-
mises proved incorrect. The Germans had neither the
political skill nor the selfishness of the Magyars. The heart
was taken out of them by the disastrous campaign of 1866,
when Austria ceased to be a German State, still more when
all Germany, thanks to Bismarck's policy and the successful
Franco-Prussian war, consolidated itself into one nation
—without Austria.

Meanwhile, among the Slavonic nations, but chiefly
among the most advanced of them, the Czechs, the
nationalist movement grew with astonishing rapidity.
From hordes of helpless peasants, first the Czechs, then
the Southern Slavs, grew into organised nations; developed
middle classes of their own, gave birth to a national consciousness which gradually pervaded every class of their
societies. As they developed, it became less and less
possible to rely solely on the Germans for the control of
the military and administrative service. The Emperor was
forced, rightly and inevitably, into making linguistic concessions. The Germans resented this curtailment of their
privileges and began to form an opposition. The crown
was put on their discontent by the occupation of Bosnia
and Herzegovina, which gave the Monarchy a definitely
Eastern and Slavonic orientation. Then Count Taaffe,
Austria's Minister President for many years, inaugurated

the policy of treating all nationalities with equal favour,
or equal injustice: playing one off against the other and
reserving for the Monarch the position of *tertius gaudens*.

The position of the Monarch was still comparatively
strong; for besides the advantages of inner lines, he could
still rely on the loyalty of the army and civil service, the
Catholic influence, and the steady support of one nation
—the Poles. The Poles, alone among the Austrian nationalities, never developed an irredenta. They had no real
hope of a revival of the Kingdom of Poland, an ambition
which was obviously unattainable, considering the strength
of Germany and Russia, except in the case of a world war.
They therefore gave their whole support to the Austrian
Government in return for practical, if unacknowledged,
autonomy in Galicia and a free hand against the Ruthenian
minority.

With this backing, the Emperor and Taaffe were able
to look with equanimity on the struggles of the remaining
races, of which the most bitter and most important was
that of Germans against Czechs in Bohemia and Moravia.

The battles were almost always fought on the linguistic
question, and were followed out into the minutest detail,
in a way which seemed to the outsider as ludicrous as it
was incomprehensible. It was difficult to understand how
vitally important the trivialities were to the parties engaged,
not in themselves, but because every tiny decision was
pounced upon to prove that such and such a village was
no longer purely German, but mixed German and Czech,
or that the Slovenes, or Italians, or Ruthenes, had or had
not the right to exist in some border district. So, to the
amazement of onlookers, the foundations of Empire rocked
with debate as to what language should be used to print

the name of some slum street in Prague, what printed on
railway tickets issued in Vienna for destinations in Bohemia. A Government fell on the question of a Slovene
school in Cilli, and Ruthenian passengers broke the head
of the Polish booking-office clerk in defence of their right
to take a ticket to Peremysl, rather than Przemysl, a town
whose existence they denied.

Legislation was divided between the central Reichsrat,
or Parliament, and the provincial Landtage, or Diets. It
was the habit of the minority of the day to make work in
the Reichsrat impossible by turning its grave sittings into
a menagerie without the trainers. *Vox populi vox Dei.*
Deputy Kotlař, a Czech, spoke in German for thirteen
hours and thirty minutes without resting. Soon after,
Deputy Baczynski, a Ruthenian, broke this record by
twelve minutes. Deputy Lechner, a German, who had not
to wrestle with a foreign tongue, achieved the figure of
thirty-six hours—a truly remarkable effort, since he is
said to have been always to the point throughout. Deputy
Lisy, a former Master of the Watch, brought his cavalry
trumpet into the People's Forum and blew on it sonorously
while motor horns tooted, whistles shrieked, desks banged
and inkpots hurtled through the air.

Among the Czech Deputies, there were two who dis-
dained such methods: spoke to the point, or sat in silent
dignity. One of them was named Masaryk, and later he
did more perhaps than any single man to bring about the
ruin of the Habsburg Empire and its Parliament.

Meanwhile, in the provincial Parliaments, "the lesser
fleas bit the little fleas." There were few of these in which
at least two nationalities were not represented, so that if
the Germans or the Czechs found their government

majority turned into a farce in Vienna by the obstruction
of their adversaries, they revenged themselves in Prague
by making the local Diet equally helpless.

Under the circumstances, one cannot but feel a certain
sympathy with the old Emperor when he remarked to
Field-Marshal von Hötzendorf, "Believe me, this country
cannot be ruled constitutionally." As a matter of fact, the
effort was never seriously made. It was always possible,
and became an ever more frequent practice, to close the
provincial Diets altogether, proclaim martial law, and rule
by the unimpeded efforts of the bureaucracy and the military. For the central Reichsrat, a special paragraph—
no. 14 of the Constitution—provided that "in cases of
urgent necessity, where the consent of Parliament could
not be obtained," the Ministry, on its joint responsibility,
could pass practically any measure it desired, with ' provisional validity." This paragraph was actually applied
seventy-six times in the course of eight years, and thirteen
budget estimates alone were forced through under it in
the face of a recalcitrant Parliament.

In the light of this paragraph it will be seen that Austria
was, at the best, constitutional only in name. The ultimate
control rested after all with the Crown alone, and with the
Ministers and provincial governors appointed by the
Monarch. So long as they could rely on the bureaucracy
and the army, the bear-garden which called itself Parliament might be indifferent to them.

Towards the end of the century, however, there were
signs that even these trusted staffs were growing rotten.
Civil servants and officers were after all men, common
soldiers enlisted for two or three years cannot in that time
exchange the hot ideals of their brothers, their fathers and

their friends for an abstract loyalty to a figure which was growing ever more remote, more impersonal; the civil servants especially found it humanly impossible to avoid identifying themselves with their respective national movements, the more so as part of the consistent policy of the different nations was to put its own nominees into the administrative posts. As time went on, the civil service lost most of its "Austrian" character, became increasingly Czech, Polish or Italian. The process was most advanced among the Poles, who were quite frank about it; least among the Germans, who retained to the last much of their traditional feeling towards the Emperor.

Another process which tended to weaken the dynastic feeling was the gradual—very gradual—advance of democracy. In a country founded on privilege, it was inevitable that this should be so; that the masses of the people should feel less warmly towards the Monarch than the privileged classes who owed to him much of their wealth and position. The rise of the Austrian proletariat to political power was very slow. It was opposed, tooth and nail, by the privileged classes, only assisted, ironically enough, at times by the Monarch himself, who, in the sublime impartiality which he attained in his later years, conceived and carried through the scheme of breaking the opposition of recalcitrant nobles or middle classes by extending the suffrage. The poorer classes were entirely without representation in the earlier years of Franz Josef's reign. In 1882 the three electoral categories of landed proprietors, town chambers of commerce and rural districts were extended to give the vote to all citizens paying direct taxation to the value of five gulden a year or over. In 1896 a fifth electoral class, of the people, was added, without privilege and electing about one-sixth of the total number of Deputies. Finally, in 1907, after a prolonged and stormy agitation extending over many years, and after the Czar of Russia had set the example, general suffrage was introduced.

As a matter of fact, the Austrian Social Democrats— who were far stronger in the German districts than else- where—if no friends of the Emperor or his autocratic system, were not a disruptive force. They believed in the possibility of an Austria, a "super-national State"; but on a federative and truly constitutional basis. In this they were in agreement, not only with the conservative and Catholic Germans, but with the "Old Czech" Party which headed the Czech national movement during the first half of Franz Josef's reign. Palacky it was, the most famous of the "Old Czechs," who uttered the often-quoted, over- quoted dictum that "if Austria did not exist, it would be necessary to invent her." An all-important change came when the "Old Czechs" were replaced by the "Young Czechs," whose most important leader was Kramař.

Kramař was a man of great wealth, great ambitions and international connections—his wife was a Russian. He was the soul of the Pan-Slavonic propaganda inside the Austrian Empire. He and his party were the first to work methodically for the break-up of the Monarchy; spinning secret threads to Paris and St Petersburg, preaching to the Czech nation the doctrine of independence under the Russian aegis.

As the Czechs grew more openly disloyal, a similar party formed among the Germans themselves. The extreme German nationalists, most of them Protestants who com- bined hatred of the Dynasty with hatred of the Catholic influence, began to agitate for separation of the German provinces of Austria from the rest and their annexation to Germany. Even the most loyal of the nations had turned away, in part, from the Monarch.

Yet, at the beginning of the twentieth century a curious period of quiet settled on the weary national struggle; a sort of truce as though quarrels and rivalries were hushed up in the presence of the age and sorrows of the Monarch. People said: "When Franz Josef goes, that will be the end of things," and seemed to wait for his going.

For the Emperor Franz Josef was old; he was the oldest figure in Europe. He was older than dualist Hungary, older than the rise of the Slav nationalities, older than German liberalism, older than the whole new aspect of his Empire which had turned its back on the West to face the Balkans. He had a store of memories and experiences which not one of his subjects could match. He was the father of his peoples in a way that perhaps no ruler will ever be again. He was their Emperor, and their fathers' fathers had looked on him for salvation in the dark days of Metternich; the descendant of the greatest Dynasty in history, the finest figurehead in the world, yet no empty figurehead, but a power as great as his most famous ancestors; and a very old man. So political parties schemed and plotted, but the people, his subjects, the peasants or the small shopkeepers, whose souls felt the need of reverence, found it here; and when the aged man with the muttonchop whiskers drove out in the streets of his own city his people lined the pavements and did homage to him as to a god. Even in Hungary, where for many years a large proportion of the population had been openly agitating for independence, a final, prolonged crisis was succeeded by a sort of armistice at the last.

But the Emperor Franz Josef had, as he said himself, an "unlucky hand." His foreign policy was a record of one unbroken sequence of failures. So at the very end, after losing Italy, losing Germany, losing Rumania, he lost his own realm in grasping at two little, semi-barbarous Balkan provinces.

The Habsburg Monarchy fell at last over the Southern Slav question.

The principality of Serbia had sailed a stormy course, ever since its launching under the rival dynasties of Karageorgević and Obrenović. Milan Obrenović, who ruled it in the latter part of the nineteenth century, was a dissolute rapscallion, principally remarkable for his debts and his family scandals. Under King Milan, who was permanently in need of money for his private ends, Serbia became little more than a vassal of Austria-Hungary. In his foreign and financial policy alike, he did little without advice or orders from Austria, which rewarded him by saving his country from the consequences of a disastrous campaign against Bulgaria.

Milan was, however, as he said himself, the only Serb who was friendly to Austria. His people, estranged by his despotic methods and iniquitous family life, rallied round the Radical Party, a party representing the interests of the small peasants, strongly Russophil in sympathies and partly anarchist in origin.

Milan was succeeded by his son Alexander, a youth who by an unfortunate marriage more than carried on the traditions of his august father. In 1903 a band of conspirators murdered Alexander and his wife under disgusting circumstances, and raised Peter Karageorgević to the throne.

The new king was a very different man from the old. A soldier and a man of great personal simplicity of life, he entered politics as a "people's king." A popular and democratic Constitution was introduced and freedom of press, assembly and speech guaranteed; a new and democratic era began.

King Peter was the man of the Radical Party, and this party, whose utterances were violent and provocative to a degree, set about freeing Serbia from the economic bondage to Austria-Hungary. At the same time, they were exponents of inflated Pan-Slavonic and Pan-Serb theories, masters in the art of secret intrigue, and suspected by the Austro-Hungarian Government of tampering with the loyalty of the Southern Slavs within her frontiers.

About this date things began to move in the other Southern Slav districts. In Macedonia there was a revolution, in Croatia, which had suffered for many years under an extraordinary tyranny of Magyar corruption and oppression, the Ban Khuen-Hederváry retired and the country gained a breathing-space.

In 1905 the Magyar Parliament came into its last and gravest conflict with the Crown. In the same year the Croats and Serbs of Austria-Hungary combined for the first time in a coalition, and endeavoured to exploit the situation to their advantage by combining with the Magyars against the Crown.

Two years later, after having estranged themselves from Vienna, they were again in conflict with Budapest, and the new Ban, Baron Rausch, suspended the Croat Diet altogether and ruled as an absolute sovereign in a conquered country.

Meanwhile, the Monarchy had turned on the principality of Serbia, largely in the interests of the Hungarian landed magnates; made impossible conditions for the renewal of the commercial treaty; and when these were refused, forbade the export of Serbian livestock into the Monarchy altogether—a measure which meant complete ruin to Serbia.

Austria-Hungary determined to complete its work. In 1908 the occupied provinces of Bosnia and Herzegovina were annexed. The Magyars gave their consent for the price of an "electoral reform" which took the last vestiges of independence from the non-Magyar nationalities in Hungary.

The Monarch and the Magyar nobles had thus succeeded, in an astonishingly short space of time, in turning the most loyal races of the Monarchy into the most dangerously discontented. The feeling of Yugoslav unity received a great impulse. In Serbia, Montenegro, Bosnia, Herzegovina, Dalmatia, Croatia, Southern Hungary and Slovenia the Southern Slavs rallied together to form one *bloc*, united by none knew what secret threads[1].

Everyone knew that the situation could not last for long. It must be solved, either by a war with Serbia and her final

---

[1] In the trial of the assassins of Sarajevo, one witness, a peasant, feigns idiocy and replies "I don't know" to almost every question.

President: Do you know the Kingdom of Serbia?
Witness: Yes.
President: Do you know that there are circles there which want Bosnia and Herzegovina to be incorporated with Serbia?
Witness: I read of it in the indictment; I never heard talk of it.
President: Have you heard that Austria and Serbia are now at war?
Witness: Yes, I have heard that.
President: Do you know what "annexation" means?
Witness: Yes. It means "war." (Laughter in Court.)
President: My friend, you are not such a fool as you make yourself

suppression, or by a reorganisation of the relations with Hungary. But Franz Josef, who was too old for changes, could not in any case make a change here, for he was bound by his oath to the Compromise of 1867.

So all eyes were turned on another figure—a burly, broad-shouldered man with an impenetrable forehead behind which lurked none quite knew what plans; the heir to the throne, the Archduke Franz Ferdinand. Only so much was known, that he waited impatiently for his day, and that when it came, it would bring great changes which would hardly pass without a storm. A man of energy and ambition, even of a devouring ambition, who had waited long to show his capabilities. The Catholic Party had great hopes of him; they saw in him the strong ruler and pious Catholic who would crush separatism and heresy with a high hand and bring back the days of old. Others murmured and feared. Especially the Hungarians saw in him a bitter enemy, and nerved themselves for the coming struggle.

It is highly interesting to speculate what would have happened in Austria-Hungary had Franz Ferdinand come to the throne and the situation been allowed to work itself out without foreign interference. He was generally credited with the intention to transform the dualist system into a trialist by creating a great *bloc* of the Southern Slavs. The alteration, impossible for Franz Josef, would have been equally impossible for the new ruler, once he should have taken the same oath. A recently published document shows that he did not indeed really propose, at least at first, to set up a trialist system. He did, however, intend to utilise the interval between his accession and his coronation in Hungary to proceed strongly against separatism there, using the Croats to support him as had been done in the days of 1848. It was a plan which might, with luck, have succeeded or might have precipitated the Empire into civil war. At the best, it must have resulted in years of dissatisfaction and dispute, since a predominance of the Slav agricultural Catholic circles would have been hardly less objectionable to the German-speaking industrial districts than to Hungary.

In any case it was destined never to be put to the test. Outside influences had grown too strong among all the Slav nations of the Monarchy. If one party was willing to try once again the old plan of combining with the Dynasty against its fellow-subjects, there was another which believed that a decisive stroke would suffice to demolish the whole fabric of the Dual Monarchy. So it happened that Franz Ferdinand's hour, so long in coming, in the end never came. An assassin's bullet stretched him low, leaving the old man behind, as though Heaven itself willed that none should thwart that aged, omnipotent figure. And the old man lived yet three more years, and died in his turn; and again two years, and the fabric of his Empire crumbled and collapsed.

CHAPTER II

THE PEOPLE

Such was the régime, such the rulers in Austria; not by any means deserving of the almost unlimited abuse which has since been heaped on them, for they meant well and often did very well. But they were essentially narrow, oligarchical, reactionary, pledged to the support of a system and a theory which had outgrown its use. It is not surprising that, when revolution swept away the army and titles, of the three great people's political parties which succeeded to the administration, two were called Socialists and the third descended from those who called themselves Liberals.

For as the people gradually made themselves heard, it was only natural that each new class signalised their arrival into politics by more or less of rebellion, although the complex Austrian conditions made it possible for the forces of conservatism to recapture them later to some extent and use them as a force against later comers. The revolution of 1848, the turning point of Austrian inner political history, brought its chief benefits to the middle classes. It was the "bourgeois" revolution, generally compared by Austrian writers to our Cromwellian movement. It had a second, perhaps predominant tendency which falsifies the comparison, for it was strongly nationalist. Its leaders were mostly imbued with the idea of cutting off the dead weight of the Slavs and Magyars and joining on with the New Germany, which it was hoped that the revolution in Berlin and elsewhere would bring to birth. The hope was not realised. The disastrous war with Prussia in 1866 finally quenched Austria's German ambitions and turned her face to the East. The Emperor found in the Polish magnates the secure staff which he sought, and leaned more and more on the Slavs. The occupation, then the annexation, of Bosnia and Herzegovina made Austria predominantly Slavonic. The German nationalists of the day protested vainly against these measures, which more than any act of the Habsburgs estranged them from their rulers. From this time on they were often in the opposition, some of them (the anti-clerical party which called itself "Los von Rom") were avowedly enemies of the Dynasty. But the principles of none of them—they were split into innumerable different groups—went beyond those of Liberalism. They had tasted power, and were not excluded from it on principle. Their revolutionary days were over, for they enjoyed full political rights, and this privilege, not yet extended to the masses, kept them *ipso facto* from extremes. Their chief political interest was one which was not social, and did not survive the dismemberment of the Monarchy, lying as it did in the guarding and extension of German rights against those of other nationalities in Austria as a whole, and particularly in the provinces with mixed populations, the chief of which were those composing the present Czechoslovakia.

The Christian Socialist party, which represents to-day the bulk of the peasant, clerical and middle-class interests, started with a fine swing. It has moved a long way to-day from its original standpoint, which was indeed one formed on momentary conditions. It was born under peculiar circumstances. In 1882 the suffrage had been extended to all persons paying annual direct taxes of five gulden (ten shillings). This wide-reaching measure put a great political power for the first time in the hands of the peasants and the small dealers of Vienna. The middle-class parties of the day were disunited and discredited. The new electors sought a leader of their own. Just at this moment, however, the previous liberalism had been showing unexpected and unwelcome effects. The Jews, admitted for the first time to the status of citizens, had gained an extraordinary position in a few years and had already got into their hands nearly the whole finance and commerce of the Monarchy. Unluckily for them, the first-fruits of their leadership had been the stupendous "crash" of 1873 on the Viennese Stock Exchange, in which a period of feverish speculation had been succeeded by a financial disaster without parallel. Anti-Semitic feeling was running very high. The German Nationalists had formed a new and vigorous party on the programme of freeing Austria from the Jewish and from the Slav influences. As a programme it had points; as a catchword unbounded possibilities, which were quickly understood by one of the most remarkable figures of last century's politics—Dr Karl Lueger.

Lueger was a man of humble birth, a Viennese through and through. He was a demagogue of genius; a man of warm and kindly heart, of remarkable personal appearance and extraordinary abilities. "Bonny Charley," as he was called, became the idol of Vienna. No more popular cry could be raised than the protection of the "small" man against the Jewish exploiter, nor was any man better suited to raise the cry and make it popular. At first, naturally, the Government looked askance on him. He was too new, the interests which he represented were too anti-oligarchic to please the Court. But Lueger was too adept a politician, and too truly Viennese to be a real revolutionary; nor was revolution part of his plan. The first great success of his party was in the municipality of Vienna, where it became supreme and Lueger himself, after several failures, was elected burgomaster. Afterwards, the organisation was extended to the country. The peasants had still no leaders except their priests, and the interests of the priests and the anti-Semitic party were too nearly akin to permit them to quarrel for long. After some twenty years of existence, the party fused with that of the Clericals and identified itself largely with Conservatism and even dynastic interests.

To-day, for all its name, it is really the equivalent of our Conservative party.

There remains the third great party of to-day—unquestionably the most interesting in Austria, and one of the most interesting of the world, the Austrian Social Democrat Party. During the revolution and the years immediately following it, the Social Democrats formed the real kinetic force. What has been changed in Austria, for good and for ill, has been their work. In order to understand Austria to-day it is necessary to examine in some detail this party, which differs widely from our own Labour Party. We make no apology, therefore, for devoting nearly the whole of this chapter to a sketch of its origin and development.

Until the nineteenth century was well on its way, there was practically no Labour movement, as such, in Austria. Industry developed slowly, and was nowhere on a large scale. The country was mountainous, the large towns few, the level of general education low, Austria itself lay far to the east of the great industrial centres, and bordered on the purely agricultural and sparsely populated districts of Russia, Hungary and the Balkans. The highly developed systems of Church and State co-operated to teach the workman submissiveness and conservatism, and few questioned the parental authority thus asserted. The measures of centralisation of the previous century had broken down the remains of the guilds and local rights, leaving the workmen entirely without political rights. They had been protected, to some extent, by Imperial decrees of various dates; for the Habsburgs were by no means malevolent rulers, and the social legislation of Maria Theresa, for example, was remarkably advanced for its day. But despotism moves slowly, and when in the first half of the nineteenth century railways were built, industry began to grow up and a real industrial proletariat came into existence for the first time, their conditions were miserable.

Their condition (wrote Violand of the workmen of 1848) was very bad, as the masses of immigrants from Bohemia continually depressed the wages, thus increasing the working day to 14, then to 16 hours. If a crisis arrived, and some factory closed down, even if a labour saving machine was introduced, great numbers were faced with death by starvation, and many succumbed to it. They had no remedy for their misery; workmen's associations were strictly forbidden...the result was unlimited moral decay...the long hours led to fearful stupidity and, among the weavers especially...to frequent insanity.... Conditions were growing steadily worse....Moreover the workmen were treated by the authorities as a rabble, a herd of cattle.

In the revolution of 1848 the workmen played a considerable part. But it availed them little. The peasants were liberated, the middle classes increased their power; but for the proletariat this proved but an exchange of one master for many. In some ways they were indeed worse off after the revolution than before it, since the subsequent reaction was on the watch for new sedition, and ruthlessly crushed any trace of a popular movement. The employers, meanwhile, had strengthened their position, and reached the stage of Manchester politics. In 1868 it was stated by an official commission that in one spinning factory the men were at work from 5 a.m. to 9 p.m., and after this were not allowed to leave the factory, but slept by their machines. The engineer of a Prague machinery works calculated that his workmen only lasted ten years.

Meanwhile the proletariat was growing in numbers and slowly coming to self-consciousness. In Germany the teaching of Marx and Lasalle was taking root and the seeds of modern Socialism were being sown. Austria was at first no ground for them; Lasalle, in an early visit, met with a completely chilling reception. The early demands of the Austrian workmen's leaders were indeed modest to a degree. They were not yet in a state even to make a proper beginning; for the simple right of free meeting was forbidden to them. In 1863 they put forward a request to be allowed to form a workmen's union. It was refused. "The experiences of Germany, especially Prussia," wrote the official concerned, "have shown that such movements, however they begin, tend to flow over into subversive politics, and it seems likely that the same thing would happen in Austria."

Nevertheless, the right was granted on January 1st, 1866, and immediately a crop of "Vereine"—word dear to the German heart—sprang up. The Labour movement had now taken definite form, and was come to the parting of the ways. It had to decide on its attitude to the Government. There were two courses open, and each had a faction in favour of it. The one followed the good old lines of Austrian politics. The workmen themselves, by "self-help"—through savings-banks, co-operative stores and productive societies, and such like—were to improve their lot as far as might be within the bounds of the existing State. It was a programme congenial to the Austrian workman, who by nature and upbringing is modest in his wants, respectful of authorities and averse to disputes, and a little wisdom, even a little kindness on the part of the authorities, would have enabled them, by encouraging this party, which at first was in a majority, to gain a lasting control of the Labour movement.

But the Government of the day was stricken with blindness. It scented sedition everywhere, and the most modest requests of the workmen were met with unvaried refusals. Disheartened, they left the leadership to the second faction.

This other party, which styled itself "State-help," was the father of the modern party. Its programme was far more radical than that of its rivals, and, unlike that, really threatened existing institutions. It accepted the doctrines of Lasalle, thus binding itself up with the international Labour movement; and its political programme included the intervention of the State to protect the workman, and to reform society as a whole; State-help for the workmen's co-operative societies; direct and universal suffrage; and separation of Church and State.

The Government had practically forced the workmen to this course. Now when it was too late, it awoke with a start. A hurried series of secret appeals were issued to employers and local authorities to encourage and help the

"Self-help" party. But the latter had abandoned the struggle. Those who still hoped for help from authority sought it in political parties which were not exclusively Labour—among the Liberals, the Democrats, and later the Christian Socialists. The Socialist Party and the State were now, and were to remain, declared enemies. At first, the workmen pressed their advantage home. They were grown conscious of their own strength, and in 1869 a vast body of demonstrators paraded the streets of Vienna to demand the right of combination. In the following year it was granted, and the old provision under which all strikes had been illegal vanished. The workmen proclaimed a victory; the State smarted under a defeat.

The hostility with which it regarded the workmen was undisguised, and soon after it assuaged its smarts by arresting their leaders *en masse*. An excuse was provided by the fact that these had recently attended the meeting of the German Social Democrats in Eisenach, and had officially adopted their programme as their own. This the public prosecutor designated as "tantamount to high treason," and on the strength of it the leaders were sentenced, one to six years' imprisonment, three to five years each and a large number to lesser terms. Many of the workmen's organisations, the forerunners of the trade unions, were dissolved by law, and the whole movement crushed as far as the authorities could crush it.

A long term of lean years followed. Although a year later a new and liberal Government released the prisoners and the organisations revived, they were weakened by the great financial crash of 1873, which hit employers and employed alike, and the trade unions in fact reached their lowest ebb in 1874 and 1875. Personal rivalries between the leaders condemned the party to incapacity; hardly were they healed, when it was split again on a question of theory.

A considerable fraction of the workmen, especially in the non-German districts, was permanently embittered by the attitude of the Government. "We can hope for no more reforms from the ruling classes," wrote their organ, "and therefore it is no use fighting for universal franchise." And again: "We want no milk-and-water lightening of work, we want total liberation." An increasingly strong anarchist tendency grew apparent, and manifested itself in political crimes. Murders were committed, and workmen and police came into bloody collision in the streets of Vienna. The Government retorted with all vigour; it is an unprofitable controversy to decide how far its senseless severity bears ultimate moral responsibility for these crimes. Vienna and the neighbouring districts were under martial law for two years; 300 persons were expelled from them. Juries were suspended for such offences as had "anarchist and subversive motives." Any offence, however small, which was suspected of a connection with the anarchists was most cruelly punished. It was the darkest hour of Austrian Socialism, the hour when it was both weakest and least worthy in itself, and in bitterest conflict with the rest of society. But as so often, the darkest hour preceded the dawn. At this crisis, when the old forms of Socialism seemed to have failed altogether, the whole movement was reformed and renewed by one of the most remarkable and most justly venerated figures in Austrian politics.

Dr Victor Adler, scion of a rich bourgeois family of Jewish extraction, had entered politics as a German

Nationalist. He was already one of the leading figures of this tendency of thought, and had in fact been one of the men who had recently drawn up the new Nationalist programme. This movement seemed to him, however, too narrow and lacking in real ideals and social aims. He became a convert to the cause of the people and made it his own.

His was a strange figure to find among the despised and hated Socialists. "No one really knew him," wrote a friend thirty years later, "or quite knew what he was after or what he wanted. We looked on him as a rich, liberal-minded bourgeois, who had been disgusted by his own class and came to us out of sympathy with us and anger with the rest." Perhaps anger with the rest really was at the back of his conversion; at any rate, he saw in the people's movement a task more worthy of his gifts than the barren defending of one nation against another. But that movement to be strong must be united. The first step was to reunite the various factions. This task he took on himself and laboured at it, in the face of inconceivable difficulties, for three long years. As became his past, he was an upholder of parliamentarism. Secret societies had had their day and proved useless. Socialism must be a regulated movement, working in the open, and aiming at acquiring universal suffrage, when it could force through its demands by regular methods and force of numbers. He was not in a hurry, for he was a man of long view; nor in favour of violence, for in his personal character he was goodness itself. His watchword was slow and sure progress, strengthening the people step by step till they should be in a position to impose their will.

In 1889 he had accomplished the first step. The "radical"

or anarchist party, which formerly had been in the majority, was converted to his views. At a meeting attended by Kautsky the various factions were formally united and the Social Democrat Party in its present form was born.

From now until 1914 the party moved steadily forward under Adler's leadership. The tasks imposed on it were very different from those which confronted our Labour Party during the same years. The need for social legislation is much the same all the world over, and the programme adopted in 1889, with subsequent modifications, did not of course differ materially from that of the national and international organisations of the world. It included full and legally authorised freedom of combination; a maximum eight-hour day; the prohibition of night work, except in special cases; of child labour under fourteen years; of female labour when it was especially harmful to the female constitution; a full Sunday rest; inspectors appointed by the workmen's organisations; and State insurance against incapacity, old age and sickness.

Many of these reforms were not brought about until after the revolution, one or two are outstanding. Nevertheless, on the whole Austria was not backward in social legislation. Even before Adler began his work, during the very period of unprecedented severe police repression, many valuable measures had been carried through. It has always been the habit of Austrian legislators to give with one hand while taking away with the other, and their harshness towards the lower class proceeded rather from fear than unkindness. The compunction of Parliament and the Crown itself had been awakened by the state of things which the agitation of the 'eighties revealed, and this, combined with the agitation of the new Christian Socialist

Party, had produced a period of lively interest in social reform, so that in 1891 Adler himself declared that "Austria had the best legislation for the protection of the workman in the world after England and Switzerland." If this interest flagged afterwards, it was because the growing intensity of the national conflicts pushed it into the background.

The difference as compared with affairs in England lay in the political situation. Until 1895 the workmen were entirely unrepresented in Parliament; they did not receive anything like a liberal franchise until 1907. And up to the fall of the Monarchy, they were fighting a battle against a system which was always really, often avowedly, hostile.

For up to the last the Monarchy never looked on the workmen as members of the State, but always as subjects. The Austrian State was the Dynasty. It might take as allies the higher nobility and the Church; old and august powers like itself. The workmen were beyond the pale; subjects whose duty it was to be loyal, whose reward for loyalty would be acts of grace, reforms graciously granted.

Against this idea stood Adler's programme:

What to-day is called "social reform" springs mainly from fear of the growth of the proletariat movement, the hope of convincing the workmen of the goodness of the moneyed classes, and the recognition that the increasing misery of the people will in the end affect its physical capacity....These State measures side-track the real issue and do not touch the real heart of things. Modern social reforms must therefore never be carried through by the exploiters, but always by their victims. So long as the capitalist system lasts, social reform can do no more than set bounds to inhuman conditions.

As a summary of the Governmental point of view, these remarks were entirely just. The workmen had to become

free and equal members of a Parliamentary State, before
they could even begin their real work, and a long political
struggle lay before them. When the congress of 1889 laid
down that "to achieve our aims, all suitable measures
which are consistent with the people's natural feeling of
justice are admissible" it must be remembered that the
state of things at this time did indeed violate every natural
sense of justice.

The party's line of development had to be adapted to
these circumstances, for mere growth in numbers, so long
as the franchise was denied, was not sufficient in itself.
Nevertheless it was a necessary preliminary, and in fact,
once the party was united and properly led, it grew with
amazing rapidity. At first it had a formidable rival in the
Christian Socialist Party; but this was soon altered. For
the 'nineties brought about a second great period of economic expansion in Austria, and on comparatively new
lines. The old typically Austrian days of home-workers,
one-man businesses and small, easy-going trade were beginning to pass. A great organised industry of large businesses and factories on strictly capitalist lines was springing
up. These new factories, with their hundreds of organised
hands, provided the material for the Social Democrat
Party. The Christian Socialist Party found little hold
there. The diminishing numbers of small tradesmen allied
themselves with the peasants, then with the clericals, and
came more and more into opposition with the actual
industrial proletariat. Over the latter, whose numbers
grew apace, the Social Democrat Party had soon established
what was a practical monopoly. Its strength was only
revealed in the first elections on the general suffrage in
1907, when it returned 87 members, almost all out of the

German and Czech districts, out of a total Parliament of
501—an amazing achievement under the circumstances.

But ten years elapsed before 1907, and during those
years the party had to make its force felt elsewhere than
in Parliament. The instrument which lay to hand was that
of the trade unions, and it was in these, or in close connection with them, that most of the work of these years
lay. A Socialist historian quotes with indignation the
comment of a Government official that "trade unions
and workmen's educational associations are not primarily
of a specialist educational character but intended to
accustom the workmen to the idea of a class association
and therefore political, even when not contrary to the law
of justice and dangerous to the State." Yet the remark is
obviously just, and indeed the same author's whole work
is concerned with proving its justice. Until the arrival of
the suffrage the party organisation and the trade unions
were almost identical. The utmost care was devoted to
developing and training them, to increasing their numbers
and bringing them under Socialist influence. In fact,
the trade unions system was extraordinarily advanced in
Austria, even before the war, and almost exclusively Social
Democrat. Even though only a proportion of the members
of the trade unions are organised Social Democrats, the
party can count on the votes of nearly all of them in an
election, and on their support in most matters of policy.
Even under the aegis of Adler, whose sense of justice and
statesmanship certainly far exceeded that of most of his
successors, the party made every effort, while organising,
centralising and unifying the trade unions movement
and levelling up hours and conditions, to get rid of all
elements which were not purely Social Democrat. Into

this campaign a great deal of ruthlessness and unfair dealing had been introduced. Whatever emanated from a hostile or even a neutral source was boycotted; only what was socialist was allowed to be good. Thus, for example, when the (then Christian Socialist) municipality of Vienna proposed to set up a central labour exchange, the Social Democrats howled down the scheme, proposing instead to set up an exchange of their own for the whole of Austria —a promise which to this day they have not fulfilled. Then, as now, they were ready to bring any pressure, fair or unfair, to bear on individual workmen to force them into their organisation. Yet, if many times they set party advantages before the real good of their followers, it is only just to state that they were following the invariable example of every political party or power, from the Dynasty downwards. This connection of the trade unions with the party is to-day, from the outsider's point of view, one of its least agreeable features. It is largely responsible for the exaggerated materialism of the party's ideas. The leaders of the big trade unions of manual labour have an excessive influence on policy, especially where they represent essential industries; they are able to force through the material interests of their followers at the expense of the general public, and, many of them being persons of somewhat incomplete wisdom and judgement, do so with disastrous results. It is a relic of the days when the "direct action" of the trade unions was almost the only weapon available to the party, and one which Adler was obliged to keep in continual use.

As soon as he had the trade unions organised, a series of strikes began, and continued over the turn of the century with unceasing frequency and violence, and they did not fail of their effect. Up to 1869 strikes had been illegal, and the idea that they were in some sort criminal died hard. Even thirty years later, soldiers from Bosnia or Transylvania were often enough sent by the Government to quell by arms, if need be, the strikes which broke out in a Czech or German-Austrian factory or mine. But their persistence gradually brought the Government to a truer idea of the Labour movement. In later years, the intervention was not always on the side of the employer. Even before suffrage was extended to them, the workmen had begun to force their way into the position of members of the State, a power to be reckoned with and no longer to be bloodily suppressed.

The last victory was that of the suffrage, which might have been the prelude to quite a new state of things. As it proved, however, the year which saw its attainment was the culminating point of the Social Democrat movement under the Monarchy. The last years before 1914 were darkened for all by the shadow of impending conflicts. Not only the foreign situation, but the relations with Hungary, and of the Austrian nationalities among themselves, took up the time and energies of the Government. The Social Democrat Party itself, which had based itself throughout on the broadest principles of internationalism possible, was weakened by a national split, in consequence of which the majority of the Czech party broke away from the Austrian leadership. Thus the Socialist movement was forced to remain stationary for a while, and only the war and the revolution brought its sudden and unlooked for development.

It was destined in after years to lose much of its original character, much too of what was most worthy of sympathy in it. In the days when Adler led it, it was not necessary to believe in the theories of Marx to sympathise with the struggles of the Austrian proletariat. True, the party had officially adopted those theories, but it had never reached the stage which infallibly incurs the hostilities of non-Socialists—it had never come, that is, within even the remotest distance of being able to put them into practice. In those days it could only struggle courageously, against heavy odds, to secure a measure of tolerable economic conditions for the often very wretched working-classes and a measure of political liberty which lagged far behind what the same class had long enjoyed in more advanced countries. It was almost a fight for the right to exist—for the right, at any rate, to decent human treatment—to be looked on no longer as "a rabble, a herd of cattle." For the thoroughly feudal ideas of the Austrian aristocracy had been quickly assimilated by the Jewish capitalists, the successors to part of their power, and the purely social motive, one might almost call it the fight for good manners, had always played a great part in the Austrian Labour movement. Nowadays it would be hard to say which side nas come out with less credit; neither has distinguished itself, nor shown ability to rise above demagogy and petty rudeness. Then the Socialists certainly came off more creditably, if only because they had more excuse for their lapses. Adler was anything but a demagogue, neither was he a mere doctrinaire. In the nature of the things, he often found himself engaged in very bitter conflicts. The Socialists played a lone hand. They were different from all other Austrian parties. If a national party grew troublesome, one made it some cultural or linguistic concession, or more often made half a dozen of its leaders into Hofräte; and

M 4

there was peace. With the Socialists it was not so. They were always in opposition. There can be no man of any prominence of the older generation in the party who has not seen the inside of a prison; Adler saw it many times. One of his closest helpers was murdered in the street by a fanatical opponent; and the threat of summary and condign punishment was always hanging over them all. They replied with what means they had; with strikes and demonstrations, sometimes on a truly grand scale. Yet Adler himself said with perfect justice: "I never begin any demonstration until I know where it will end." As, in the early days, he had converted the party of violence to his own policy, so he continued to keep the movement to the end intensely practical, moving forward step by step, without ever going aside from the ultimate end. From the point of view of a Marxian theoretician, all that he accomplished in these years was preparatory, for, as we have said, he was never near establishing the supremacy, far less the dictatorship of the proletariat. What he did do was, partly to ameliorate their physical lot, but far more to weld them into one body, to give them unity and self-consciousness, and to compel a hostile Government to look on them as a free force within the State, not merely as a body of rebels.

Its history gave the Austrian Social Democrat Party certain qualities peculiar to itself. One or two of these we have noticed already. Very prominently, the close organisation and ultimate connection with the trade unions and excessive dependence on their often narrow and materialistic point of view. The bitter tone too, the savage abuse of the old Monarchy and its system, are easily understood when we learn how long and difficult was the struggle for political rights which accompanied the economic battle. Indeed, the party leaders are generally in essence more politicians than economicians, often too—such is the school through which they have passed—far more politicians than statesmen.

This is not to say that the leaders neglected the theoretical study of Socialism. Indeed, they developed it to a remarkably high pitch. Adler himself had leanings towards the theories of the Fabian Society. He was in personal touch with many of them, and at one time a Fabian society was actually founded in Vienna, one of its members being the distinguished agriculturist, Dr Michael Hainisch, who later became the first President of the Republic. The centre of the intellectual life of the party lay, however, in the small group, many of them of Semitic origin, who were connected more or less closely with that remarkable publication the *Kampf*. This group represented much that was best in Austrian political thought of the day. Austrians are always strong in theory, and especially Viennese Jews enjoy nothing so much as political speculation of an ingenious, slightly unpractical and rather idealistic type. Of all parties before the war, the Social Democrats offered the best openings to this type of mind. Quite apart from the fact that most of the other parties were anti-Semitic, none of them could make such a ready appeal to idealism, none of them tilted so regularly against exactly the same forces as had been for centuries the enemies of the Jews. For the connection between Jewish intellectualism and Socialism is entirely natural in a country ruled on such lines as Austria was.

This group of intellectuals came into power with the fall of the Monarchy, and in later chapters we shall try to give an estimate of their doings. One of the immediate consequences of their access to power was a considerable divergence of views between the leaders and the masses of the party—a divergence which in 1919 very nearly led to a total shipwreck. For these leaders were in most instances not workmen and had no personal experience of factory life. Much capital was made out of this by the opposing political parties; but not quite justly. The workmen themselves could never have produced a sufficient number of well-educated and far-seeing men to lead their cause and it was no less just because its spokesmen were capitalists or Jews. Nor was the Jewish influence really apparent. If anything, the tune of the party was rather German-Nationalist, for it never quite lost the marks of its leader's origin.

The theoretical labour and research of the party reach a high level. The worst qualities in them—especially prominent since the war—are their doctrinaire materialism, the blind and thoroughly reactionary way in which they cling to the holy words of Marx. The best is their zeal for education. In this respect they have really accomplished much and it was a work which needed doing, for the general level of education in Austria has been, and still is, very low.

These two qualities—materialism and zeal for education—appear at first sight to form a strange contradiction. They are reconciled only when we understand the great point on which Austrian Socialism differs from British.

The key to the riddle, as indeed to most riddles in Austria, lies in the position of the Church. Without Austrian clericalism, Austrian Socialism would be entirely different. It should have appeared from the preceding pages that the main interest of the party did not

lie in the fight against capitalism. It was not until 1919
that capitalism could be attacked at all, and then only
with the greatest reservations. The political struggle came
first, and this was directed against the Monarchy, and
against the Church.

Of these two, the Monarchy was less important. It was
hated for what it involved, rather than for what it was, for
although Socialism usually adopts a Republican programme,
there is no particular theoretical reason why it should do
so. There is bound in any case to be some ruler and representative figure-head, whether king or president. It is
different with the Catholic Church.

Our own Constitutional Monarchy, or Czarist absolutism, or the old rule of the Turks in Europe, with all
their differences, are alike in principle. They require from
their subjects a certain standard of behaviour, be it obedience to the laws, abstinence from political intrigue, or the
prompt payment of taxation and rendering of military
service. Once these demands are satisfied, they are well
content that their subjects should be happy each in his
own way. But the Catholic Church and Marxian Socialism put forward far greater claims. Indeed, not only in
the extent of their claims, but also in their character, they
are bound to clash violently. Each claims to regulate not
only conduct, but thought. Each lays down a world system
and insists on orthodoxy. The Catholic must believe in
God and the Pope, the Socialist in matter and Marx. Nor
do the disciples of Marx claim for him a less absolute
infallibility than cardinals do for the Pope. If one likes to
push the parallel a little further one might add that both
systems put their trust in a holy book which was written
for times and conditions which are not universally true

to-day, and, incidentally, in a tongue unintelligible to the vulgar—a criticism the truth of which must be admitted by any honest man who has tried to read either the Epistle to the Hebrews or *Das Kapital* in the original. Both tend therefore to come under the influence of intellectual oligarchies, and to spend much of their time in quite arid discussions of doctrine, and both readily breed heresies, which give rise to the most envenomed disputes.

The Catholic Church of Austria is the real enemy of Socialism. She is the living representative of the old order. She was the chief stay of the Monarchy, but more powerful even than that, for she has outlived it. She is the upholder of conservatism, loyalty, piety, respect and obedience, the supporter, incidentally, of country against town, and Gentile against Jew. Until her hold over the spirits of the people has been weakened, Socialism, the very reverse of all this, cannot move. The Catholic Church, too, was and is an active political force; she does not confine herself to stating her ideals, but compels their acceptance by her flock with terrible threats of hell-fire. Therefore we find that even to this day the real battle of Austrian Socialism is directed against the Church; its domains are that ground which has been wrested, or reclaimed from her; its campaigns, marches and countermarches along this dangerous frontier. For under these circumstances the Socialist maxim that "religion is every man's private affair" is already a direct challenge, since Catholicism admits of no neutrality. Nor do many of the Socialists attempt to adhere to it. If at times they remember its existence, it is only to point out the impossibility of following it. In fact, they carry on a continual warfare against the Church with a tenacity equal to that of their adversary.

This circumstance really determines the whole character of the party and accounts alike for the best and the worst in it. On the one hand, the interest in education is not quite so altruistic as it seems. While it is perfectly true that Socialism has done a great deal in the way of schools, educative associations, lectures, exhibitions, and opera performances for the working classes; that it runs an admirably conducted library of Socialism and an excellent bookshop, and itself publishes a high number of educational works; yet all this is not untinged with politics. Often—not always—"education" and "progress" consist of nothing better than vulgar and envenomed attacks on the clergy, as the representatives of the rival educational system; for the Church until very recently had entire charge of all education in Austria and still possesses most of the influence in secondary education, and has not lost it all in primary. The textbooks and lectures are marred by hateful propaganda which, far from enlightening a child's mind, can only acquaint him too early with bitterness and coarseness. This anti-clerical campaign is generally vulgar and not infrequently absurd; for in their eagerness to reject what the Church approves, and *vice versa*, the Socialists are apt to accept anything that is "modern," such as atheism, psycho-analysis, crematoriums or easy divorce, and to devote endless panegyrics to them all without, we must suspect, having learned or thought anything at all about them except that the priests dislike them.

On the other hand, these newspaper and electoral campaigns—the repellent vulgarities, for instance, of the *Arbeiterzeitung*—are not entirely gratuitous. It must not be forgotten that they are directed against a foe which is exceedingly strong and well able to return tit for tat and which has not always in the past proved itself particularly scrupulous about its own use of the power which has lain in its hands.

Here, for the present, we will leave Austrian Socialism. It was a movement which, before the war, would hardly fail to inspire sympathy among impartial observers. The workmen, when it took up their cause, were ill off economically and practically disregarded politically. In the face of enormous difficulties and an united opposition such as could hardly be found elsewhere in Europe, it wrested for them not only physical advantage, but the tardy recognition of their rights to citizenship. It could hardly hope for more unless a singular chance should arise. Such a chance arose in fact, and all unexpectedly; the war of 1914 found the party unprepared, wavering, without unity of policy. It was at first frankly unequal to the crisis. But events continued to fight for it and bore it to power in 1918 on the back of an almost automatic revolution.

CHAPTER III

DISSOLUTION

THIS work will make no attempt to follow the intricacies of the diplomatic or military events which marked the opening, the long course and disastrous close of the European war in what was Austria-Hungary. Such details can be sought in the official publications of many countries, and in the memoirs in which nearly every leading politician and general has set forth with greater or less success his apologia. We should rather be tempted, did space allow, to present the history made in these years in a series of portraits. Each of the really significant figures of the time had a twofold character: the human personality, and the idea (and in some cases a negation of ideas) which he represented. It seems, too, that the idea often purposely chose weak and humble vessels, as though to shine through them more plainly, endowing them with a force greater than their own. For the character of our portraits undergoes a continual and remarkable change. Men are accounted mighty in their day and are cut violently off, or perish miserable and unnoticed, if their ideas were too small for the time or ill-fitted to it. And again, poor and weak creatures devoid of either wealth or birth or circumstance are exalted by the ideas of the time and set by them, almost in spite of themselves, in the high places.

Striking indeed is the procession. Its head is glorious, dragon-fanged with field-marshals, armed with diplomats, coruscating with crowns, orders and jewels. Its tail wags uncouth and awkward, one joint anarchist, the next pro-

fessorial, yet swinging with mighty effect, right and left.
But a giant canvas would be needed to paint even the chief
of all those portraits. At the beginning must stand the old
Emperor, the aged man in his tower of ivory wherein for
years now he had been preparing his retreat from the
world he had ruled so long. Now his poor old eyes blink
from its windows at a tumult not known for many decades
nor rightly understood. Round him the guardians of the
tower: Berchthold, the world-wise diplomat; Conrad von
Hötzendorf, soberly weighing the chances of war, now
or a year later, in terms of armies of millions of men;
Stürgkh, brushing aside a people's will to rule it with less
confusion; Tisza, beating with his fist on the table and
crying to the rebels "perhaps we are doomed, but before
we fall we shall still be strong enough to crush you."
These few men and their like, brought up to high position
and a great responsibility, tower above the world for a
term of years. Nations and armies are pawns in the game
which they play. Then, suddenly, the foundations uphold-
ing them totter. One here and there goes crashing down.
Some of the pedestals have fallen for ever; others are
vacant. New men ascend them, but men of a different
type, wraiths of the old. On the chief throne sits a young
man, dazed and bewildered, desperately anxious always
to do the right thing and inexorably condemned always
to do the wrong.

> A stranger and afraid
> In a world he never made.

And then there are no players any more. The pieces on
the board come to life and move, mysterious and sinister,
of themselves. New figures guide them. Karolyi, the

renegade Count with the hampered speech; Adler, the touzle-haired doctor, the mildest man who ever murdered; Kramař, but now awaiting twenty years of prison for high treason; Radić, a stomachy little Croat peasant; Masaryk, a gentle, incorruptible professor, exiled in Switzerland; Jaszy, a journalist; Deutsch, a Jewish army-subaltern; Korošec, a genial priest. Somehow, these men had set themselves in contact with the ideas which flowed between the two queer poles of the world: the pale autocrat of the Kremlin and the spectacled professor of the White House. Their ideas and ideals, persecuted for years, became now suddenly omnipotent, and before the men who embodied them crowns and dynasties and armies went down.

In Austria-Hungary, as in every other country engaged in the war, the years 1914–1918 fall into two phases, one of enthusiasm and courage, and one of doubt, despondency and weariness under too heavy burdens. These phases, easy to discern in England, were far more marked in Austria, even as every evil of the war, casualties, starvation, high prices and profiteering came more quickly and in greater measure. And the second, lighted for us by the hope of ultimate victory, was for them intolerably overshadowed by the certainty of defeat, which weakened every bond of loyalty till the last was gone, and a final, hurried *sauve-qui-peut* brought complete collapse.

If perhaps the less said the better about the real designs which led the Austrian and German rulers to force on the war, at least the occasion for Austria was a good one. The murder of the heir of the throne and his wife, on the edge of the Balkans, made it seem a war of righteous vengeance on a nation of barbarous murderers—the more so since this conception of Serbia had been systematically propagated for years. More important, it was a war against Russia, against a huge and dreaded power embodying all Eastern savagery, despotism and imperialism in the name of the Czar. It was one in which Austria stood side by side with her blood-brother Germany, and it was one to avenge the honour of a venerable and beloved monarch.

Thus a large proportion of the peoples of the Monarchy hailed its outbreak readily enough. The Germans, fighting with Germans against Slav encroachment. The Hungarians, facing their secular foes in the Balkans. The Poles, expectant of a national liberation which only Russia's defeat could give them. The clericals of all nations, rallying to their Emperor.

Both Czechs and Southern Slavs proved, too, more amenable at first than Austria's enemies had expected. Though there was much disaffection among the former, yet a minority not to be ignored and all the German-Bohemians were loyal; nor were the rest as yet convinced that they could do better for themselves than to stand by Austria and win a price for their support. For Wilson had not yet spoken, and the shares of small nations were not quoted high on any market.

Among the Southern Slavs it was only in 1918 that the idea of autonomy under the Habsburgs was finally rejected. For them the main point was that they were fighting their ancestral enemy, Italy, and for this reason the Southern Slav troops were throughout among the most loyal in the whole Empire. Moreover, nearly all their provinces were under martial law, many of them the actual theatre of war; so that an open display of disloyalty was impossible.

One party, recruited from all the nations, must, had it carried through its principles logically, have opposed the war. This was the Social Democrat Party, the most powerful among the Austrian workmen and in the districts of the great ammunition factories. July 1914 caught them in the middle of preparations for a great international conference. When the clouds were gathering, and again on the day when hostilities commenced, they entered solemn and formal protest against the war, and washed their hands of bloodguiltiness or responsibility. When, however, this had proved quite ineffectual to arrest the march of events they changed their tone and the startled readers of the *Arbeiterzeitung* were presented with a dashing article entitled "Deutschlands Tag," and another a month later headed "Nach Paris."

The Austrian Socialists, like most of their colleagues in all continental countries, had thrown in their lot with hardly any exception with their country at war. Perhaps, after Professor Trotter's explanations, it would be safe to ignore the volumes of ratiocination with which they subsequently explained away this attitude and say simply that the nation to-day is still for good or ill a unit of herd instinct and stronger for almost every man than that astral shape the International. The feeling must have been the more powerful because many of the leaders had begun their careers as German Nationalists. Possibly, too, they were not deceiving themselves when they declared that the danger of an invasion by Czarist Russia outweighed all others. Certainly this fear in the years when it was continued and imminent was a great cohesive force in the Empire.

The declaration of war found Austria unexpectedly strong and united, the more so because the elements of strength and unity were at that moment alone potent. The

army and officials had the undivided control of affairs,
under a set of men who had little use for Parliament's
confusion of voices. Tisza in Hungary was renowned for
a strong man. In Austria the Minister-President was
Graf Stürgkh, who since entering on office in 1911 had
continually been at war with Parliament and in March
1914 had dissolved it without ceremony. His enemies
accused him of having done so in order to have a free hand
in the war whose coming he foresaw. In any case, a free
hand, as he had now, was assuredly what he desired.

Thus Austria entered the war and continued it for over
two years under what was practically an absolutistic régime
conducted by Stürgkh, the permanent officials and the
military. The private citizens ceased to count. Parliament
was not called together, and the press, the second voice of
the people, was stifled by a rigorous military and civil
censorship. The Austrian censors were not merely passive
like our own; they were a constructive force. Opposition
papers were supplied with patriotic articles, with a hint
at the wisdom of printing them—and they printed them.
A clerk was sentenced to death (commuted to five years'
imprisonment) for distributing translations of " I did not
raise my boy to be a soldier " to a few clients who he said
in his defence were in any case spinsters and past the
marriageable age. Martial law was established not only
in many provinces in or near the theatres of war, but also
in those provinces where sedition was to be expected. In
such districts, the control was directly military and even
stricter than the civilian.

The war brought a very large proportion of the inhabitants of Austria into the service of the State. The already
vast civil service was increased; the private railways were

put under State control. The armed forces absorbed the bulk of the remaining men of military age and the munition factories, which sprang up in great numbers and quickly took over much of the industry, were controlled by officers and practically part of the army. This was true at least as far as the workers were concerned. They were put under the strictest discipline, and any who proved unamenable to it were sent to the front forthwith.

This summary method, so different from our own, had interesting consequences, of great subsequent benefit to Socialism. In England after the war the idea of class-warfare was strongly counterbalanced by the rival feeling of difference between those who had fought and those who had not. The sentimental bond between the ex-private soldier and the officer who had shared his perils and miseries in the line was often stronger than that between the poor man who had gone out to fight and his mate who had stopped behind, drawn good wages and endangered his own former comrades in the trenches by strikes. In Austria it was not generally so. The workmen in the munition factories were better off than the soldiers in the line, but still suffered hardships and were semi-militarised. On the other hand, the upper classes produced a high percentage of *embusqués* and ornamental officers who over-crowded the lines of communication and staffs, while even those at the front insisted on such exorbitant preferential treatment in the matter of leave and rations as to engender not fellow-feeling, but envy and hatred in the men under their command.

One class stood apart from all the rest—the farmers. Here again the Austrian conditions afford a peculiarly interesting example of how an economic asset can turn out a political calamity. For the old Monarchy—it was one of its most boasted *raisons d'être*—could approach the state of an economic unit. Its agriculture and industry were so balanced that both the import and export of necessaries was small. In time of war this circumstance, while relieving the Government of a great anxiety, did not fail to create internal dissension. For the farmers were no small minority, as dependent as every one else on the general fate of their country; they were a body strong enough to dictate, and to defy the rest of the population in the defence of their own interests. And this is what in effect they did. The crisis began in 1915 when the granary of Galicia had been ravaged, and other food-producing districts were all beginning to feel the pressure of shortage of human and animal labour, deficiency of machinery as the old wore out and could not be replaced, and lack of fodder and fertilisers. Not all the Government measures could restore production to its previous level, nor persuade the farmers to sacrifice their own interests. Early in 1915 Hungary, the great agricultural country, took the fatal and decisive step of closing her frontiers against Austria. Henceforward she released for export only small quantities of foodstuffs, and those at extortionate prices. At one blow, the conditions in Austria were reduced from bad to miserable, and the cleft between the two halves of the Monarchy widened to a gulf never again to be bridged over. Later, certain relaxations of the restrictions were allowed, but only at the secret price of a further change of the quota of common taxation in favour of Hungary. It was the clearest proof of the deepening differences between the countries. The Austrian farmers followed suit in a small way, shutting themselves off, as far as possible, from the ever-gaping maw of the town. The restrictions with which they surrounded themselves were one of the chief causes of the loose construction of German-Austria after the war.

Thus the first two years of the war present a curious picture. The armies were loyal and undefeated; the powerful bureaucracy and military authorities in concert conducted the affairs of the State smoothly; criticism was silenced; it might appear to the superficial observer that all was going well. Yet all the time, the universal evils of war were raging. Prices were rising enormously, profiteering was rampant. The food situation was bad, the conditions at the front indescribable. The supply and administrative services were inefficient; rations bad, hospitals scanty and ill supplied, water often failing, boots and uniform a farce; transport deficient; vermin beggaring description. The gulf between Austria and Hungary and between the agricultural and urban districts of Austria was widening. A mighty Nationalist agitation was spreading in the Slav provinces, which had already begun to form committees abroad and treat secretly with the Entente. But of all this the country heard nothing, unless it marked the number of arrests made and sentences passed by military courts, which (juries being suspended) appeared to be going systematically through the Slav Deputies of Parliament. The early war enthusiasm had long since vanished; for some on the appearance of the first *communiqué* issued by the General Staff—perhaps the most truly original piece of literature which the war produced in any country (it began "Lemberg is still in our possession")[1]—

[1] Unless one may count the words with which the King of Saxony abdicated: "Macht Euch Eure Dreck alleene!" he cried in his broad Saxon dialect to the representatives of the people, and left them to do it.

for others when the first transports of wounded from the front returned to whisper something of the truth from their agonised lips. But discontent or discouragement found no voice. They sank oppressed before the mighty and despotic figure of Count Stürgkh who straddled over all.

Suddenly, in October 1916, Stürgkh fell under an assassin's bullet and the picture changed.

Dr Friedrich Adler, the son of the great Socialist leader, is the true type of a fanatic. Mild in manners and character, violent in mentality, he sucked in the doctrines of Socialism with his mother's milk. Throughout his childhood his father was for him the greatest figure in the universe and that father's ideals of pacifism and internationalism his *summa bonorum*. When war broke out, he saw, appalled, that not only his father, but practically all his comrades, defended what for him were detestable things. Victor Adler regarded the war as a Crusade against Czarism; Renner as a defence of the "Supernational State"; Austerlitz, the editor of the *Arbeiterzeitung*, opened its columns to chauvinism. Friedrich Adler had the child's view which understands no compromise. He protested still that this war, and every war, was abominable, but he found himself solitary, cast out, stigmatised as a detriment to his party.

He brooded long over the spectacle of his colleagues acquiescing in war, censorship, and the suspension of Parliament and juries. At last it seemed to him that only a sensational protest would call the attention of the world to this state of things, and that the only practical form which it could take would be the assassination of the man in whom the evils found their incorporation.

Accordingly, having put his affairs in order, he went at noon on October 21st, 1916, to the restaurant where Count Stürgkh lunched. He lunched himself, sitting three tables off from his intended victim, having observed it to be a trait in his family to act more coolly on a full stomach. Another long wait followed because other guests and waiters were about, whom his bullet might have struck. At last the occasion arrived; he walked up to Stürgkh's table and emptied a revolver into him at point blank range, crying "Down with absolutism! We want peace!"

Adler's trial was not held until six fateful months were passed, which had changed the whole situation drastically. After only a few weeks the aged Emperor had followed his Minister to the grave, and that venerable figure which had been the only thing common and constant to so many peoples through an almost fabulous length of stormy years had disappeared at last in the greatest storm of all. The new men who came to the rudder of State were of a different breed from the old. Gone was the strength and majesty, the tradition and the serene assumption of authority so little questioned because itself so unquestioning. The new Emperor was a young man, nervous, kindly, well-meaning, but no match for his awful difficulties and heavily burdened by having an Italian and unpopular wife. The successor of Stürgkh, the autocrat, was Körber, one of the best Ministers whom Austria had ever known; yet chosen for his moderation in an hour when autocracy was needed if it ever was in history. Körber's numerous followers were nonentities. The Foreign Minister was Czernin, clever, but nervous and obviously oppressed by his burdens. Everywhere the old rigidity was breaking up. In Hungary a stormy agitation for universal suffrage beat against Tisza, last sturdy representative of the ancient régime. Socialism was growing stronger, and Karolyi was gaining recruits for his unceasingly preached gospel, that the war was lost and that it was essential to give him the Government and let him make a separate peace to save what could still be saved. In the Slav provinces, the Nationalist movement was making giant strides. The Poles were as good as lost. As early as 1915 they had been promised their Polish kingdom under a Habsburg crown. But it seemed now that even this would not content them. The Czechs had set up a Government abroad and offered the crown of Bohemia to the Grand Duke Nikolaus. Their whole country was rotten with sedition. So, too, with the Southern Slavs, although their aspirations were complicated by having to deal with Hungary even more than Austria.

And in every province, from Vorarlberg to the Bukovina, dislike of the German alliance was growing ever more acute. With few exceptions the races of the Danube basin are lazy, easy-going, averse from exertion, followers of the primrose way. It is this character which has allowed them to revolt so little against an absolutism which does the job of governing for them, be it only not too oppressive. But the yoke of Stürgkh and yet more the yoke of the German allies were too oppressive. They called for too great and too sustained sacrifices, ever more apparent as rations were reduced again and again and not only the necessaries but also the little comforts, the evening café and the newspapers vanished one by one; and to what end?

To what end? No one for two and a half years had dared to ask or answer that question. In the spring of 1917 suddenly it was asked and answered from a million of throats.

On March 15th, 1917, the Russian revolution broke out and changed the face of things. The revolutionary government sealed the fate of Austrian hopes of retaining Poland by promising the Poles its support in the erection of an independent State; simultaneously, agitation increased everywhere. In Russia a new gospel was being preached of freedom and equality, the end of militarism and war and despotism and misery. It was preached and heard and carried into the heart of Austria by the thousands of her prisoners of war released from captivity to return to their homes. And a second voice was raised in the far West. America entered the war—surely no one could doubt its issue now—and its President proclaimed that every nation should have the right of self-determination. Thus fatally it became clear that the defeat of the Central Powers was the necessary preliminary if the hopes of the bulk of Austrian subjects were to be realised.

Thus when the first Austrian Parliament since 1914 met in May 1917 the Slavs were already far advanced towards open revolution. The Polish club demanded an "independent and united Poland," insisting that the Polish question was one for international consideration. The Czechs declared that it was necessary to "transform the Monarchy into a federal State of free and equal national States." They spoke in the name of the "Czecho-Slovak people"—a direct challenge to Hungary, whose frontiers included the Slovak districts. The Southern Slavs demanded the "unification of all districts of the monarchy inhabited by Slovenes, Croats and Serbs into one independent State, free from any alien national sway, resting on a democratic basis under the sceptre of the Habsburg-Lothringen Dynasty." This again challenged Hungary.

There remained the Hungarians and the Germans of Austria. Perhaps in other circumstances the uproar of the Slavs would have drawn them more closely round their German Emperor. But now they too were divided and unquiet.

Three great parties divided the political votes of the Germans: the Christian Socialist, the Social Democrat and the bundle of parties grouped together under the name of German Nationalists. The first-named, recruited mainly from the strenuous Catholics of the Alpine provinces, was still entirely loyal to the Dynasty. But the Dynasty itself was unhappily committed to a policy unsympathetic to it—the German alliance. If the war was carried out to a logical and successful end its result must be "Mitteleuropa," the subjugation of Austria under Prussian tyranny. Thus the party most loyal to the Crown found itself in opposition to the Crown's official policy, and a wave of pacifism swept over the most faithful defenders of the country.

The German Nationalists were in precisely the opposite position. Their programme was one of reaction against the influence of the Church, the inefficient semi-oriental methods current in Austria, and the waxing preponderance of the Slavs. They had come into open conflict with the Crown on the occasion of the annexation of Bosnia and Herzegovina, and of all other political concessions to the Slavs which reduced their own old-time predominance. When in May 1917 the Slav deputies put forward their claims and the Emperor listened, still more when a month later the Kaiser Karl, well-meaning as ever, amnestied the Czech leaders sentenced to long terms of imprisonment for high treason, the Germans saw themselves betrayed. It was worst of all a year after when the Kaiser made his unlucky effort through the medium of Prince Sixtus of Parma to conclude a separate peace with the Entente, betrayed the German alliance and denied his treachery on an oath which every child knew to be perjured. Henceforth they saw but one salvation—to sweep away the ill-fated, decayed Monarchy and incorporate the Germans of Austria into honest, strong, efficient, western, modern, German Germany.

Where the very Conservatives were turning against the established order, it was not likely that the Social Democrats would remain passive. Indeed, Adler's trial, which took place in the days immediately preceding the convocation of Parliament, was the turning point in their history. The six months between his "demonstration" and his trial had made an understanding of his action possible. No dwindling hope of victory in war could now encourage the workmen, no fear remained of barbarous Moscovy or of Cossack troops galloping through the cherry orchards and acacia-shaded beer-gardens which surround Vienna. From the East came no more terror, but the hope of liberation; and against this promise of milk and honey Austria could offer only a pittance of black bread, a bitter substitute for coffee, rare tobacco which looked and smelt like beech leaves and here and there a mouthful of bad mutton which from some dim ancestral prejudice the Austrian rejects, though he be dying of starvation. Against the long hours and harsh discipline in the factories, the ever-imminent prospect of the trenches, the soul of the workman turned within him. And Friedrich Adler, standing his trial for murder, spoke for two days winged words:

"The state of justice in Austria awoke in me a feeling of shame to be an Austrian.

"In you (the judges) I see not an organ of law, but only the organ of a criminal government.

"We are not citizens in Austria, but only subjects.

"I have always been a revolutionary...the idea of revolutionary tactics is again on the order of the day.

"The revolutionary programme is truly that of the workmen.

"If to-day we really must kill and be killed, then, logically, murder can be no privilege of the rulers. We also have a right to use force."

And on hearing his death-sentence: "Long live revolutionary international Social Democracy!"

His words woke echoes both in the general public and in the Social Democrat Party. His own supporters, the left wing of the party, had hitherto been a small minority. But in the annual conference of October 1917 they were already strong, growing in strength and obviously possessed of the future. Now, too, they were enormously reinforced by the return of Dr Otto Bauer, the most brilliant political thinker in the party, perhaps in Austria, from captivity in Russia. At this conference they produced a programme which in principle was that of the Independent Socialists of Germany. It demanded that the party work actively for a peace without annexations or reparations.

But the left Socialists went further. Dr Bauer had always maintained, against the views of Renner, that Socialism must give the greatest possible freedom to nationality. He was clever enough to see the break-up of Austria coming and the importance of making friends and not enemies of the Nationalist leaders. Accordingly, he put in the programme a clause declaring the necessity for each nation to summon a Parliament which should be sovereign in itself, and be empowered to settle common affairs by agreement.

This position was too advanced for the majority in 1917, which contented itself with a resolution in favour of a democratic federation of national States for Austria-Hungary. From this time on, however, the influence of Otto Bauer and Friedrich Adler was gradually gaining against the more conservative leaders until it practically controlled the party. The Austrian Socialists became an active revolutionary force working hand in glove with the Nationalist leaders for the abolition of the Dynasty, the break-up or the transformation of the Monarchy and the end of the war.

Indeed, most people in Austria, from the Emperor downwards, were now pacifists and would gladly have given up the wretched struggle but for the awkward attitude of their formidable allies. Save us from our friends! The Germans had by now taken charge of the military situation. Austrian divisions, and even smaller units, were thoroughly well shuffled in with German troops; German officers ordered Austrian soldiers about with their own inimitable, implacable, intolerable efficiency. The Germans were confident of victory and determined to fight to the last. If Austria had thrown up the sponge she would promptly have been invaded and occupied by Germany and become the theatre of war between Germany and the Allies. She groaned, and went on fighting to a chorus of continuous bickering between the diplomats and the generals of the allied but not affectionate States.

Pacifism began to be preached openly. Lammasch, a mild and learned professor of international law, made three great speeches in favour of peace in the new Parliament. Peace without annexation was an imperative necessity, and could and must be obtained from Wilson. The

Socialist leaders attended the conference in Stockholm, and on their return met to proclaim it now "twice, a hundred times the duty of all Socialists to do everything to put an end to the war."

Conditions in the beginning of 1918 were miserable past belief, and especially in the industrial centres. The farmers, themselves in great embarrassment, withheld their stocks. The German and Hungarian provinces were only yielding half the harvest calculated, the Slav provinces only one-third. The Government fixed rations and maximum prices, but actually these were regarded only by the very honourable or the very poor, who died in consequence. Everyone else swarmed out of Vienna into the country and exchanged commodities for food, which was brought back in pockets or rücksack, or bought at enormous and soaring prices. It was each man for himself, and each parish, district and province for itself. A hasty peace was concluded with the Ukraine in the hope of tapping its food supplies; but owing to bad communications and bad management this source, of which much had been expected, yielded practically nothing.

In January 1918 the workmen's flour ration was once again curtailed and the industrial town of Wiener Neustadt struck. The strike spread to a number of towns in Austria, then to Vienna, then to Hungary. It was on a grand scale, approaching the character of a small revolution. Bosnian and Rumanian troops were called in to put it down. But it had been well organised and the Socialist leaders were able to put forward a series of demands for peace without annexation and the democratisation of governmental machinery to which the Foreign Minister was forced to give his solemnly pledged assent.

The industrial situation was indeed getting extremely serious. In Berlin there had been great strikes, and the name of Spartakus had been heard, doubtless for the first time, in the poorer quarters of that unclassic city. In Austria, the Social Democrat leaders, even those of the left, were finding their followers increasingly hard to control. For the first time the Communists were beginning to take a hand. The Kaiser feared for his personal safety.

In 1918 too, for the first time, the army began to be seriously affected. Up to this date it had remained almost entirely loyal. Only a few—but a minority—of the Czech troops had deserted to the enemy and formed themselves into legions side by side with the Entente. But now the fearful conditions and the weakness of the units began to tell. Vienna was full of deserters in hiding. A mutiny broke out in the fleet at Cattaro. The sailors deposed their officers and hoisted the red flag. A squadron sent down from Pola suppressed the rising, but the Socialists in Vienna were strong enough to intervene and save most of the mutineers from execution. A Hungarian, a Slovene, a Czech, a Serb battalion mutinied, refused service, and murdered their officers.

Yet up to the last the open disaffection among the fighting men was small. In general, they stuck to their posts well and military discipline was still strong while civilian had ceased to be. It was in the Hinterland that the collapse spread. The Poles had lost their last regard for Austria when Czernin concluded peace with the Ukraine and agreed to incorporate Eastern Galicia with the Bukovina into a separate province. That these districts are to nearly seventy-five per cent. inhabited by Ukrainians was a detail of no moment to the scandalised feelings of the

Polish patriots. The Ukrainians, on the other hand, were outraged by the requisitionings conducted by the German and Austrian troops; so that they had no hesitation, when the time came, in proclaiming their own independence and setting up their own Government—whose fate it was indeed to see the Poles in *de facto* control of its country, while it legislated platonically for three years from offices in Vienna.

The Czechs, through Masaryk, had won the peculiar grace of President Wilson and had been recognised early in the year by the Entente as an allied State. The Southern Slavs were losing their last hesitations as to resolving finally on a free federation with Serbia. Slovaks and Rumanians were busy privately. Only Hungary and German-Austria remained.

In Hungary, the pacifist, separatist, anti-German feeling was growing fast. Much of the population remained loyal to the Crown; but only if it would support the integrity of Hungary, which meant denying the rights to the minorities. And the Crown was no longer able to do this. Poor Kaiser Karl made despairing efforts to straighten out the tangle. He hurried down to Hungary and at once committed perhaps the greatest *faux-pas* in his power by allowing the Austrian national anthem to be played in front of his house. He cast off his faithful servants and found no one to replace them. He appointed two prime ministers in one day without telling either about the other. Politicians dashed madly from Vienna to Budapest, tying ever fresh knots in an already hopeless tangle.

And in Austria almost every week brought a fresh strike. Social Democracy was growing ever stronger and it was clear that in the inevitable change of régime it would be the leading force. This was the only party whose principles allowed—nay compelled it—to foresee the complete collapse of the Monarchy and to lay its plans for that event. As early as January 1918 it had formulated its "national programme," recognising the rights of the Poles, Czechs and Southern Slavs to complete self-determination, and claiming for the Germans of Austria, as one nation, the same right to determine its future, which it envisaged as part of the democratic German corporation. In any case, it had done with the old Monarchy. Victor Adler said, "There are three kinds of rats; some are clever and leave the ship before it sinks; others are honourable and remain although she sinks; the third kind are stupid, notice nothing at all and go on board the ship. We are not going to be the third kind of rat."

On October 3rd, amid the growing disintegration, they repeated their demand thus: "We recognise the right of the Slav nations to form their own national States, but we protest sharply and for ever against a subjection of German districts to these States. We demand that all German districts of Austria be united in a German-Austrian State which shall regulate its relations to the other nations of Austria and to Germany as it itself requires."

In the autumn the end came with the military collapse.

On September 15th the Bulgarian front was broken. The troops retreated in disorder and marched on their own capital. On the 28th Bulgaria signed the agreement for an armistice, leaving the Balkan front open. On October 3rd Germany, Austria and Turkey addressed an appeal for an armistice to President Wilson.

The Austrian Government made a last effort to save the Monarchy. On October 1st the Prime Minister Hussarek

announced in Parliament that the State would be transformed into a federation of free nations. But the Slav
nations had tasted blood. They were no longer satisfied
with half measures. A fatal difficulty now arose with
Hungary. The Southern Slavs demanded an united State of
Serbs, Croats and Slovenes, and it was essential to pacify
them. But the Hungarians Tisza and Wekerle refused to
allow the "integrity" of Hungary to be touched. The confused negotiations went on. On October 12th the Kaiser
called together representatives of the nations to ask their
wills. These were clear, for by this time each had a local
Government of its own and was practically independent.
On the 7th the independent Polish State had been proclaimed in Warsaw. The Ruthenians announced the meeting of their National Council in Lemberg for the 19th.
The Czechs demonstrated in favour of the Republic on
the 14th and began to close their frontiers against the German provinces. On the same day they formed a Government under Masaryk at Paris. On the 16th the Kaiser
issued a manifesto, promising that every nation should
form a separate State. But the proclamation contained
the fatal clause that "the integrity of the provinces of the
holy Hungarian Crown is in no way affected." The Hungarian Minister, prehistoric in his mentality to the last,
had insisted on this clause, threatening to cut off the food
supplies unless it were inserted. These words completely
invalidated the whole attempt. But in any case, no one
took much notice of it, except to remark that it came anything from six months to fifty years too late.

The Germans of Austria now all saw that their destiny
was to be a separate State. They began to make their own
preparations. The Socialists took the lead. On October 3rd

they had demanded the recognition of the rights of the Slav States and the formation of a German-Austrian State. On the following day, the German Nationalists accepted "the general principles of the German Social Democrat Party as a basis for further negotiations." On the 9th the Christian Socialists gave their agreement although, loyal to the Kaiser, they still stipulated that the German-Austrian State should form one of a federation of nations into which the Monarchy was to be transformed.

Verbal negotiations began among the party leaders. The bourgeois parties desired the formation of a *bloc* of all German deputies in the Austrian Parliament. The Social Democrats insisted on the proclamation of a separate German-Austrian Assembly which should constitute itself the provisional Parliament of the new State, and appoint a Government for it.

The Kaiser's manifesto of the 16th legalised this suggestion and the other parties agreed to it. The answer of the Slavs showed that the manifesto would be fruitless. On October 21st the German deputies assembled under the presidency of the German Nationalist Walder. An unanimous resolution was passed: "The German people in Austria is resolved to determine for itself its future form of State, to form an independent German-Austrian State, and to regulate its relations to the other nations by a free agreement." The State was to include "all districts inhabited by Germans." "The German people in Austria will elect a constituent assembly...to determine the constitution of the German-Austrian State." For the time being the deputies carried on as the Government to represent the people in the negotiations for peace, and arrange for the transfer of the administrative machinery to the new national States and settle the future relations of German-Austria to them.

Victor Adler, in the name of the Social Democrats, demanded that the new State should be a democratic Republic. The bourgeois parties protested; their speakers affirmed their allegiance to the constitutional Monarchy. But matters were deciding themselves without the politicians. Even the Socialists were doing no more than ride forward on the wave of events. On the same day President Wilson's answer to the request for an armistice reached Vienna; it called attention to the Fourteen Points, and made the complete satisfaction of the wishes of the Slavs a condition of the armistice.

And the armistice was now a matter of life and death. A fresh offensive broke out on the Italian front. The situation was remarkable. Behind the line every province was forming a Government; half of them were declaring themselves friends of the Entente, not one of them but desired to be quit of the old order. At the front, the united forces of the Imperial and Royal armies shed their blood for a State which had ceased to exist. During the first days of the offensive the soldiers held out manfully. Then the front cracked.

The Hungarians began the collapse. Since Bulgaria had signed the armistice the path to Hungary lay open before the allied troops in the Balkans. The Hungarian troops in Italy began to mutiny. They clamoured to be conveyed back to Hungary to defend their own homes. The demand was echoed in Hungary.

News came that Croat troops had mutinied in Fiume on the 23rd and disarmed the local Hungarian forces. Regiment after regiment of Hungarians refused to fight and demanded to be sent home. Where the demand was not granted, they began to leave their posts and make their own way back. On the following days Rumanian and Slav troops mutinied. As the Italian offensive pressed forward, the entire burden of resistance was thrown on the German regiments.

On October 27th Andrássy, who had become Foreign Minister in this highly unpropitious hour, telegraphed to Wilson recognising the rights of the Czechs and the Yugo-Slavs, and begging again for an armistice. A new Government was formed in Vienna under Professor Lammasch, the one man who enjoyed the respect of the old authorities without having incurred the dislike of the Socialists and the Slavs. He was ordered to "carry through the transfer of a central administration to that of the National States in constant agreement with the National Governments." General Weber was empowered to ask the Italians for an immediate armistice.

But the negotiations hung fire. While the generals were debating, the Italians advanced continuously and the confusion along the front increased. For the first time German troops began to refuse obedience. The front collapsed completely. Some of the troops, who through a misunderstanding believed the armistice to be already concluded, took matters easily and were made prisoners of war. The rest went home. Not generally as units, unless their ways happened to lie together, but every man for himself, throwing aside or selling his rifle and equipment as he went.

And now the final dissolution came. On October 28th the civil authority in Prague passed definitely into the hands of the autonomists; on the 30th the military. In Yugo-

M   6

Slavia the fleet mutinied on the 28th, and handed itself over to the Croats. On the 29th the provincial Government in Agram declared itself sovereign, on the 31st that in Laibach, on November 1st the Habsburg authority ceased in Sarajevo. In Trieste, Cracow and Lemberg the nations proclaimed their independence. On October 30th a national Hungarian Government under Karolyi formed itself in Budapest and on the following day Tisza was assassinated.

In the last days of October the German-Austrian Provisional Government met again. Mass demonstrations of the workmen demanded a Republic and the release of Friedrich Adler[1].

The Socialists were supported by the German National-ists, who now shared their programme of the abolition of the old régime, as a first step towards final incorporation with Germany. The Provisional Parliament was not yet ready to proclaim a Republic; but it passed a resolution that the right of legislation belonged to itself, while the executive power lay in the hands of a National Council, to be elected immediately by Parliament.

On November 2nd the Kaiser gave the order to accept the conditions of armistice offered by the Italians. On the 9th the Republic was proclaimed in Germany. On the 11th the Kaiser issued his last proclamation: "Filled now as ever with unchangeable love for my people I will no longer set my person as a barrier to their free development. I recognise in advance the decision which German-Austria will take on its future form of State. The people has now taken over the government through its

---

[1] Adler's sentence of death had been commuted to imprisonment by the Kaiser Karl.

representatives. I renounce any participation in the business of the State. Simultaneously I relieve my Austrian Government of office."

That evening the Kaiser and his family left Vienna. On the following day the provisional Parliament proclaimed the constitution of the German-Austrian Republic and proceeded to the election of a new Government.

CHAPTER IV

THE REPUBLIC

SELDOM have pilgrims entered on a less delectable promised land than the political heirs of the Habsburgs. With its dying breath, the old régime concluded the armistice which stopped hostilities on the Italian front; but if the guns no longer thundered, the economic warfare of blockade continued, and in a far aggravated form. On all sides, the German-speaking districts, which were to form the Republic of Austria, found themselves surrounded by new and bitter enemies. Hungary snapped the last frail cord which still bound her to Vienna; the Slav provinces of the south proclaimed their adherence to the new Yugoslav State, stretching a frontier right across Styria and Carinthia; the Czechs declared their independence, and claimed for themselves the whole of Bohemia and Moravia. Further north, East Galicia had proclaimed itself a sovereign State, West Galicia had joined the other Polish districts as a new Republic; in Silesia, Poles, Czechs and Germans squabbled desperately for the all-important coalfields.

The old economic structure was torn violently asunder. Whatever remained was among the poorest of all parts of the Habsburg Monarchy, and withal the most highly organised and the most expensive to keep up. There were expensive industries, highly developed railways, a great administrative apparatus, the middle-class population of a vast Imperial city. A splendid structure, but one not built to stand alone. It had been built up as the central point of a great Empire, dependent for its very existence on the resources of that Empire. Now these resources were cut off. Behind new, bristling barriers lay the food, the coal, the raw materials without which it could not live.

Freedom from restriction, elbow-room, free intercourse with her neighbours were the urgent needs. Instead, the restrictions, the barriers, the frontiers multiplied. The Entente blockade was not lifted for many months, while the Peace negotiations were proceeding; and it was reinforced by the action of the new "Succession States." These were themselves in no comfortable condition. Not one but had its hands fully occupied with its own problems. All alike had suffered cruelly from the war, were harassed by the same difficulties as Austria herself, of depletion of supplies, disorganisation, shortage of man-power. All had, in addition, thorny political problems with which to grapple. There were constitutions to work out, new forms of administration to initiate, national armies to raise. The Czechs had to find a *modus vivendi* with the Germans, Slovaks, and Hungarians within their frontiers; the Serbs to settle their relations to the Croats and Slovenes; the Hungarians to decide whether "red" or "white" had the right to massacre the other side. With the best will in the world, none of them would have had time or money to spare for Austria.

But in addition, all were in the throes of a violent attack of chauvinism. National liberty is a heady tonic. The pent-up emotions of years of servitude, the hatred smouldering so long and liberally fanned by the Allies in the war, now burst into roaring flame. It was dangerous to speak German in the streets of Prague; it was forbidden to take Austrian newspapers over the Yugoslav frontier. The hatred against Austria was bitter and universal. Against it, the few far-sighted statesmen of the new Republics—President Masaryk and Beneš were almost the only such—could do nothing, if they would. For all alike were urgent to make the break as final and complete as possible; to eliminate from their territories every vestige of the old times. In those days, even common civility between two individuals of different States in Central Europe seemed black treason, calculated to bring the Habsburg bogy bounding back to crunch up the Governments, seven at a bite.

So Austria stood surrounded by enemies on almost every side. Only in the west her shortest frontier marched with a nervous neutral and a friend in a little better plight than herself. And both the German and Swiss frontiers were hallowed by time, guarded by the ghosts of old tariffs which had made of them real divisions. On the other sides, east, north and south, essential but inaccessible, lay the coal of Silesia and Bohemia, the oil of Galicia, the food supplies of Hungary, Moravia and Southern Styria, the port of Trieste. And in the centre, a great machine racing in the air.

The frontiers were closed, the supplies cut off in most cases even before the proclamation of the Republic; by Hungary, early in the war; by Czechoslovakia, during the first days of November 1918. But the full measure was attained only with the conclusion of the armistice, the disbandment of the army, and the stoppage of the war industry. Then the new rulers, taking stock of their situation, found themselves left with twenty-three per cent. of the population of the old Empire, thirty per cent. of the industrial workers, twenty per cent. of the heating surface of the steam-boilers. Against this, the home produce of coal was one half per cent., and that of poor quality. Practically all the coal needed both for household consumption, for industry and for the railways had to be imported. Most of the raw materials required for industry were in like case. The food situation was little better. Before the war, German-Austria had produced enough to cover one-fifth of her own needs. But the war, with its requisitionings and shortage of labour, machinery and fertilisers, had cut down by half the output of the grain-bearing areas. The Alpine districts were much worse off still. The cattle on which they depended had been so diminished that they could not support themselves, much less yield a surplus. Even by reducing rations to the bare minimum necessary for existence, and assuming that the farmers would give up for rations every ounce of surplus, Austria could only hope to feed herself for a few months in the year.

Meanwhile, out of some of the poorest resources in Europe, there was quite the most expensive machinery to keep up. Austrian Government services had always been run, owing mainly to the complex character of her national problems, with a super-abundance of man-power. If this system had been unsound in normal times, its economic consequences were disastrous now. In the Ministries, the post-offices, the railway terminuses, the overgrown staffs remained, while the work for them was gone. A bureaucracy disproportionately large for the needs of twenty-five millions of men now administered the affairs of six million, of whom they themselves formed no mean proportion. Big railway terminuses with great staffs of clerks opened on to stumps of lines thirty or fifty miles long. In one or two cases, the lines retained their original length; but precisely these lines ran through mountainous countries, and are among the most expensive in Europe to run. Much of the middle-class population of Vienna was in a very similar position; a head without a body. There were doctors enough to cure, professors to make wise half Central Europe, while inexorable Governments barricaded off from them the people who, God knows, needed both healing and wisdom sorely enough. Newspapers of Imperial standing circulated, at a loss, in one big city and a few provincial towns, and were driven by lack of matter to attacking each other, like Kilkenny cats. Over the frontiers, the German language was no longer *à la mode*. Banks and businesses with wide ramifications were hampered at every turn by the efforts of the Succession States to divert the centre of business and finance away from Vienna.

Such, in the very broadest outlines, were the main difficulties besetting the new Austrian Government. It has been fashionable to blame the Peace Treaties for them. In fact, the treaties did little, except in the prohibition of the "Anschluss" with Germany, beyond legalising a *de facto* state of things. Where, however, they bore exceedingly hard on the new State was in the uncertainty which they caused and prolonged for nearly a year, before the treaty was finally signed. During this time everything was perforce uncertain, provisional. The frontiers were not fixed for long. Until the treaty was signed, it was not known whether Italy's occupation of South Tirol would be final. The rest of the Southern frontiers fluctuated continuously. In Styria, the first line occupied by the Yugo-slavs was only a few miles in advance of that finally adopted. In Carinthia the differences were far more serious. Here the population was very mixed. There was a large Slovene minority, but this had little spiritual connection with the Slavs further East. Shortly after the armistice, however, Slovene troops advanced over the line of demarcation with the proclaimed intention of occupying Klagenfurt. The Allies restored peace, but in the spring the Yugoslavs advanced again. The population rose against them, and troops of the new Austrian army were sent down to its assistance. The fighting cost Austria 300 dead and 800 wounded before peace was restored and a commission established which finally decided the frontier on the basis of a plebiscite.

Far more important was the northern frontier. The large German minority in Bohemia forms a ring round the Czech centre of that province, so that some German districts march with Austria, some with Germany, others are entirely cut off. Nowhere has German Nationalist feeling ever been stronger than in precisely these districts, which have ever been at feud with their Czech neighbours, and all of which, at the break-up of the Monarchy, proclaimed their adherence to German-Austria. The protest was in every case useless. The northern districts were immediately occupied by Czech troops, and their provisional governments dissolved. The strip of land along the Austrian frontier was also occupied, the weak and undisciplined Austrian troops sent to defend it retiring in disorder. Resistance was impossible, since the Czechs represented the Entente, and also had in their hands the whole of Austria's coal supply. The uncertainty and wrangling lasted a whole winter, and ended in every case with Austria's discomfiture—in this case a very serious one for her. For the disputed districts are not only peculiarly rich, but also support the most intelligent and the most patriotic German population in all Central Europe.

Only on the Hungarian frontier did Austria meet her adversary on so far equal terms, that neither unfortunate had succeeded in becoming one of the Allied and Associated Powers. In fact, the Treaty envisaged the grant to Austria of a long strip of fertile territory, of mixed German, Hungarian and Croat population. Yet she did not enter into its possession until 1922, and then in a mutilated form and without the chief city of Oedenburg. There were long and acrimonious discussions, appeals and counter-appeals, ill-controlled plebiscites; everything, in fact, which could reduce the population of the country concerned to sheer desperation. Finally, the Hungarians armed semi-irregular bands and made trial of the matter *vi et armis*. The Austrian army found itself engaged in a campaign which it was in no condition to face and ended, here too, by getting considerably less than she had been entitled to hope for at first.

Not only was every frontier undefined, but the whole State was uncertain of its future form. For the Republic as it exists to-day is as little the product of the will of its inhabitants as was the old Monarchy. The Provisional Government of November 12th, which inaugurated its existence, actually proclaimed it to be a part of the new German Republic, and, in doing so, certainly voiced the wishes of the majority of its inhabitants. The German Nationalists had for years made this wish part of their programme. They were joined now by the Social Democrats, who looked for a reinforcement of their position from the German Socialists, and who saw in union with Germany the only certain means of finally laying the

Habsburg ghost. Everyone was tired of the dead weight which the old eastern, Slavonic orientation had imposed. This had dropped away now, but with it had vanished the advantage which the Germans had enjoyed as the leading nation of Central Europe. The North, East and South were iron bars, caging them in; only to the West the way was open. The few Austrian opponents were the small and discouraged group of Monarchists, and those financiers and business men who still saw that all Vienna's natural outlets, could they but be cleared of obstruction, lay towards the East. In 1919 those outlets were blocked; almost the whole nation longed ardently for union with Germany and in the excitement of the hour invested the idea with all the attributes of an universal panacea. Let them once join Germany, they thought, and all their troubles would be at an end; there would be a sound currency, an efficient administration, a regular supply of coal and raw materials, an unimpeded market for finished products.

The vetoes of the Entente prevented the fulfilment of these wishes; even forced the new State to change its name from "German-Austria" to "Austria." It is a curious comment on the real value of the "right of self-determination" to watch the fluctuations of the pro-German feeling in Austria. In 1919 no one who had sincerely based his decision on that right could have refused the union, so general was the feeling in favour of it. When it was refused to the country as a whole, some of the western provinces attempted to carry it through independently. In 1921, when things were at their worst, German agitators, liberally financed by Hugo Stinnes, carried through a plebiscite in the Tirol which declared by an overwhelming majority for union with Germany, and the same thing would have happened in Salzburg, and with the same result, had it not been forbidden. Yet Vorarlberg, certainly not less German than the Tirol, declared with equal decision against Germany and for Switzerland, the votes cast for the two countries being roughly in proportion to the value of their currencies. Shortly after, the north of Germany fell into disrepute as a hotbed of Protestantism and Communism; Bavaria coquetted with separation; and the same men who had been so enthusiastic for Great Germany would now hear of nothing but a Greater Bavaria. Finally, when the mark achieved a figure beside which that of the krone was a child's first attempt, the Ruhr was occupied and the Fatherland going to rack and ruin; while Austria, under a clerical leader and an adviser from the League of Nations, was enjoying peace and prosperity, the frontier poles erstwhile pulled down were hurriedly re-erected and none heard any more talk of union with Germany.

Yet the genuine strength of the feeling at first was sufficient proof of the universal distaste with which all Austrians regarded their new-born Republic, and of the frightful difficulties which must accompany any efforts to form of it a real and living State. Indeed, for the first year it hardly existed as an organism at all, and this year forms one of the most confused in history.

In one respect, indeed, things went remarkably easily. The Monarchy and the feudal system dropped away like over-ripe fruits from a tree. The army disbanded itself. A few units returned in order to Vienna; most broke up incontinently, and each man made his own shortest way home. The Emperor, after leaving Vienna on November 12th, remained quietly near by at Schloss Eckartsau until

March, when he left for Switzerland after the first regular Government had re-affirmed the Republic. In Hungary he could still count on sufficient loyalty to tempt him back on two several occasions, to try his fortunes. But in Austria his cause was lost. The widespread sentiment of regard for the Emperor's person, and of regret for lost Imperial glories, never looked like being translated into action, and five years after 1918 only one Monarchist deputy sat in Parliament, and the avowed Monarchist parties hardly numbered 10,000 organised members between them. A few laws of April 1919 decreed the expulsion from Austria and the expropriation of the Habsburg family, except those who renounced all rights; abolished the rank of nobility, and certain orders and titles; and did away with all ex-territorial status not founded on international law. This was all the political revolution which Austria saw. The administration remained the same, except for the Imperial lieutenants. The rest of the civil service worked on quietly under its new masters without break or alteration, a continuity which did much to save Austria from bloodshed and confusion. The police, fortunately, although widely decried by the populace as Monarchist and reactionary, offered its services to the Republic on the day of its proclamation, and served it faithfully.

But it was one thing to abolish the Monarchy; another to form the Republic, especially a Republic whose life was so uncertain. The shedding of the political trappings brought clear to sight the economic antagonism which had been growing in strength during the war. Stripped of its central, supreme authority, Austria was seen to consist of two separate *blocs* with no real economic, historical or national bond to join them in the face of the forces driving them apart. Except Lower Austria, which until 1920 still formed an administrative unit with Vienna, the remaining provinces had, theoretically, been no more closely connected with the capital of the Empire than Dalmatia or the Bukovina. Like those districts, they had been ruled by Imperial Governors, and the central Government had not hesitated to sacrifice their interests to those of Czechs or Poles if the general political situation demanded it. Economically, the Alpine provinces were far more independent of Vienna than were Bohemia or Moravia; and even from the national point of view, there was little community between the essentially parochial Germans of the Alpine valleys and the no less essentially "Weltbürger" of the capital. On the other side, there was the antagonism between the agricultural and industrial classes, which the privations of wartime had fanned into a lively hate; between the socialism of the factory hand and the obstinate individualism of the peasant proprietor; between the freethinking of the city and the clericalism of the province.

Far stronger than any loyalty to this new and strange Republic was the local patriotism which their distinct history, dialect and admixture of blood had engendered among the inhabitants of each province. When the unifying power of the Habsburgs was gone, every man felt himself a citizen of his province: a Styrian, a Carinthian, or a Viennese. Pending the passing of the new Constitution, the provinces were indeed practically and to a large extent legally independent of one another. A hurried provisional law transferred the powers of the old Imperial governors to provincial Diets, with democratic councils as executive organs and elected Presidents and Vice-Presidents at their heads. Even before this law was passed,

several provinces had already formed for themselves provisional Governments which had indeed often to act with
sovereign and summary powers: to preserve the food
supply of their constituents, to save their homes from the
plunderings of the returning army, in some cases even to
defend their frontiers against foreign aggression.

The war, with its drain on their man-power and resources,
had indeed made the peasants into Republicans as sincere
as, if less flamboyant, than the factory hands. But the
short-lived brotherhood between peasant and workman
soldiers born of common dangers and a common hateful
constraint expired abruptly as soon as the peasants returned to their homes. Their one interest now was to
restore their homesteads and to repair the losses caused
by war and requisitioning. But they found that, although
war had stopped, requisitioning was continuing unabated;
and now no longer to save their homes, or at the behoof
of those in whom they recognised their lawful masters,
but in order to feed the unemployed of a city which could
offer them nothing in return, at the command of a Government of Jews and Socialists.

It was hardly surprising that the provinces, which the
new laws had delivered over to the control of the peasants
and their traditional rulers, showed an energy and ingenuity
in turning their backs on Vienna from which the Czechs
themselves could learn little. Where their choice lay
clearly only between adherence to Vienna and submission
to a Slav or Magyar State, they showed indeed no hesitation in declaring for the former; and it speaks much for the
quality of the much-abused Imperial administration that in
the mixed districts, even when the economic chaos in Austria
was at its worst, no German and few of mixed blood

96   THE REPUBLIC

declared for any State but Austria. Even the South
Tiroleans, who seemed to have a promising alternative,
remained German in heart to a man. But where the choice
was one of German against German, they did not conceal
their eagerness to be quit of Austria. Vorarlberg held a
plebiscite and voted for union with Switzerland; the Tirol
with Germany. Both the Tirol and Styria were known to
have worked out plans in every detail for cutting loose
altogether from Austria if occasion arose; and this not
only in the first months; for in 1922, when the financial
chaos was at its worst, these plans were revived and
brought up to date.

Meanwhile, the provinces carried on as semi-indepen-
dent republics, teaching themselves democracy, and teaching the world how narrow a thing democracy can be unless
a far-sighted authority be at its head. Every province, even
every parish, enclosed itself in a watertight compartment
of restrictions, designed jealously to guard the all-important food supply. An Austrian needed a passport and
visa to travel from one province to another of his own
country. On the journey his pockets were searched ex-
haustively, not for cocaine or diamonds, but for flour and
potatoes. The writer remembers vividly sitting for fourteen hours in the railway station of Graz, waiting for the
so-called connection and unable to obtain permission to
go into the town. He remembers no less freshly the
examination through which he was put by a corporal of
the Styrian army; for every province, in not quite un-
grounded distrust of the new Republican army, had formed
a semi-secret army of its own, originally, in most cases,
for defence against foreign invasion, but actually more
often used as a threat against Socialism.

Thanks to these strict and natural, if not over-idealistic precautions, the provinces did in fact manage to weather the worst of the storm without much general suffering. Indeed, by boycotting the central requisitioning organs and selling only a little of their surplus under the rose at an excessive price, the peasants often succeeded in amassing considerable riches. Added to this was the fact that many of the provincial Governments were extremely competent. The restrictions and local independence were upheld in their entirety so long as a Socialist Government was in power in Vienna. After this Government had been replaced by a second coalition, in which bourgeois interests were much more strongly represented, the relations of the provinces were at last regulated, after much disagreement, on very wide federal lines. In the meanwhile, the supplies of the country were being gradually replenished. Little by little the food shortage vanished and the restrictions were removed. By 1921 Austria had assumed the appearance of a single State.

Meanwhile, in Vienna were reigning the most remarkable conditions which Europe, Russia perhaps excepted, had seen in modern times. Here was one of the most complicated organisms of human society which modern times have evolved, one which depended for its virtue and its very existence on not being obliged to produce its own primary necessities, suddenly cut off from all its outer supplies. A three-fold ring encircled it: the Entente blockade; the hostile Succession States; the hardly less hostile provinces. Within the ring the great city, its seats of art and learning, its Government offices, its shops and factories standing helpless, without food, heating or raw materials. A conquered city into the bargain, unable even

M 7

to decide its own future without continued reference to the will of its conquerors. Old things swept away, and with them the foundations on which the new should have been built.

The first few weeks were a time of hand-to-mouth measures. Probably no other city in the world would have weathered them without copious bloodshed. But the patience, even the apathy of the Viennese stood them in good stead. Much passed off more quietly than anyone had dared to hope. The Czech, Polish, and Magyar troops returning from the front, the Italian and Russian prisoners of war, were only in a hurry to get away. From some of the troop-trains shots were fired, and the Italian prisoners threatened for a day to advance on Vienna; but these dangers were soon averted. The foreign element drained away quickly from the desperate city. The native population, too, awaited its destiny quietly. The civil service and police continued at their posts, the Imperial family moved quietly away. It was quickly seen that any attempt at a restoration was quite hopeless. The power was in the hands of the Socialists alone. For their leaders, by far the gravest danger was an outbreak of mob violence which should overthrow all authorities of any sort.

For it was the hour of the people. The idol of the day was Friedrich Adler, who a week previously had been released from prison amid undescribable enthusiasm. Only leaders to whom no trace of the old régime adhered could hope to influence the mob of returned soldiers and idle workmen who paraded the streets shouting "All power to the Soldiers' and Workmen's Councils."

The hurriedly formed provisional Government was nominally a coalition of all the three parties, but actually the more advanced among the Socialists dictated. They worked feverishly at a double task: to secure the revolution which had borne them to power and to push it to the furthest limit beyond which anarchy would commence. For the supplies in the town consisted of little more than the army stocks. Some, left unguarded, were plundered by the populace; others were placed under a guard and rationed out. They could not last for long. When they were exhausted, Vienna would be dependent on outside help; and should a dictatorship on the Russian model be proclaimed, as many demanded, all such help would certainly be cut off and Vienna perish miserably.

In those first weeks, the Socialists steered between Scylla and Charybdis with a skill which their worst enemies cannot deny. One of the most urgent needs was an armed force to defend the country and keep order. There were many candidates for this duty; the old officers, who not unnaturally thought themselves most fitted for it; bands of students; middle-class would-be special constables; a determined group of Communists, who had established a Red Guard with which they hoped to set up a dictatorship. The successful candidate, who by his success ensured the supremacy of the Social Democrats, was a Socialist leader named Deutsch, who had spent the last months of the war, during which he was attached to the War Office, in preparing a secret organisation among the troops quartered in Vienna. This cadre was now hurriedly expanded into a new "people's army." It was an entirely fresh force, with no sort of connection with the old army whose methods it might indeed have been well advised to copy more closely than it did. There was only one strict condition of enlistment, which was Republican sentiment. A revo-

lutionary force is not always the most reliable guardian of
the peace, and, in fact, this force proved so undisciplined
that parts of it could not be trusted by its own masters;
while from the military point of view it was a tragic farce.
But at least it was raised and proclaimed the official army
of new Austria. It absorbed a number of the unemployed,
and by its great numerical superiority over any rival force
was able to overawe any thought of a counter-revolution
which must have led to disastrous civil war. The new
Socialist Government had force behind it, and sat firmly
in the saddle.

And little by little, the authority of the Socialist leaders
reasserted itself. For a while it had been somewhat nebu-
lous. The real power during the first days had indeed lain
with the " councils " of soldiers and workmen which formed
themselves everywhere to take often most unprofitable
charge of things in general, so far as they lay under their
noses; hunting out profiteers, commandeering empty
houses, intervening where employers or authorities crossed
their ideas of justice and liberty, and invading the countryside to requisition food from the scandalised peasants. The
power of these rudimentary councils declined as the first
intoxication of revolution vanished. The soldiers returned
to civilian life, or joined the new army; the factories took
up peace work again one by one and the hard everyday
struggle for existence once more absorbed the energies
of all.

The first elections, in February 1919, brought a certain
crystallisation of the situation. The Social Democrats won
an indisputable victory, being returned as the strongest
party with the votes of all the workmen and many of other
classes who, if discontented with the new conditions, at

least desired no return to the old régime. The peasant votes gave the Christian Socialists a strong minority which entitled them to form a coalition with the Social Democrats.

The new rulers were Austrian and Socialists at once; a difficult two-faced position which set very definite bounds on their ambitions. The general destinies of Austria were almost entirely taken out of their hands. A word from the Entente prevented their plan of uniting with Germany; the Entente controlled their military forces, their supplies, and to a large extent their finances. They were not strong enough, and they knew it, to defy their neighbours and their own countrymen by any display of truculence. As far as relations with the outside world were concerned, they were confined to attempting to secure such food and fuel as would keep Austria alive.

The most desperate efforts could secure them no more. Bauer, who was then Foreign Minister, writes that it took five separate diplomatic negotiations with the Czechs to secure the passage of a single train of coal. The Czechs and Poles held up the supplies; even if a train started for Vienna, it was not unlikely that trucks and their loads together would vanish on the way. The amount of coal received, from abroad or by home production, in 1919 was only twenty-seven per cent. of the estimated requirements. Factories had to work shorthanded, or close down altogether, for lack of fuel. The Alpine Montan works in Styria, the biggest industrial concern in Austria, was obliged to blow out six of the seven blast furnaces working before the war. The paper manufacturing trade was only able to work at twenty per cent. of its full capacity during 1920. The railway ran a miserable skeleton service with frequent interruptions; even the tram service in Vienna had to stop several times for lack of coal for the electricity works.

The food supply was rationed down to between one-third and one-quarter of normal peace-time amounts. Many articles, such as milk and butter, were unobtainable altogether. The small supplies available were reserved for hospitals, or bought up at horrific prices by conscienceless profiteers, and the managers of the great hotels frequented by the foreigners who came to study Austrian conditions at first hand.

Before long, the Inter-Allied Commissions took over the control of the fuel supply. Thanks to their efforts, a small driblet of supplies trickled through, enough to keep Vienna in a state of semi-suspended animation. The food supply was taken over by the American Relief action under Hoover, supplemented by the efforts of a great number of charitable societies, among which that of the Friends was the most prominent. "We were entirely in Hoover's hands," writes Bauer, in this gracious but laconic phrase summing up one of the greatest of the few manifestations of a world conscience which modern times have seen. Without this foreign help, probably a third of Vienna's population must have starved to death. Most of all, the coming generation must have been almost wiped out. Help for babies and nursing mothers in Austria was extended on the widest scale, and in addition, 40,000 children were sent abroad in 1919 and 90,000 in the first half of 1920. In spite of this, of 186,000 Viennese school-children who were examined, over one-half were found to be far under-nourished, less than four per cent. sufficiently nourished.

Certainly, no nation has ever lain more helpless at its conqueror's feet than did Austria, and this situation created a curious vacuum in which its first Government worked. As statesmen they could do nothing; as Socialists, only so much as would not call down a stoppage of supplies. The situation was difficult, the more so as it was not understood except by the leaders. The masses were continually discontented with the caution displayed by their leaders, with their non-fulfilment of earlier promises, above all with their action in forming a coalition with the peasants instead of establishing an immediate dictatorship over them. Especially in the spring of 1919 this discontent ran high. The emissaries of Russia were preaching revolution everywhere, and in fact, Bolshevik governments were set up, first in Hungary, then in Bavaria. The Austrian Communist Party, if smaller, was far more noisy than the Social Democrats. So long as Bela Kun remained in power, they never ceased to hope for victory. In the workmen's council in which they met the Socialists on common ground, and which embodied all the revolutionary sentiment and much of the executive power of the day, they moved again and again for Vienna to follow the example of Budapest. Once or twice, they were near success. Once they provoked a serious riot which ended in loss of life, the only such loss during the whole revolution in Vienna. With difficulty the Social Democrats maintained their hold over the masses, and after the fall of Bela Kun it was not again seriously threatened. Nor were the capitalist classes in 1919 in a state to assume the government. For a year the Socialists could make what experiments they liked within the strict limits set them by the international situation.

In many respects, they made good use of their time. They had never lacked thinkers and leaders with a profound knowledge of labour problems. In that year, they did much to improve the lot of the workman. The workmen of Austria suffered from the general conditions like all the rest of her inhabitants, but far less than they would have done under a non-Socialist Government. Wages and the unemployment dole were high—the latter unwarrantably so; unemployment itself was reduced by a radical measure which forced every business of over a very small size to take on one-fifth more hands than it had previously employed. The eight-hour day was introduced, industrial councils and workmen's chambers set up, collective contracts imposed, the trade unions expanded, and a great number of minor measures passed for the benefit of the workman and the strengthening of his position. Certain minor attempts at socialisation were made, but not carried far.

These measures, however, in so far as they increased Austria's general financial burden, were a luxury which she could ill justify, except as a health insurance for the next generation. They could be no argument for the soundness of Socialism, for they were paid for, ultimately, by the charitable associations relieving the wants of the middle classes. Only inflation of the currency could raise the generous quantity of money required to pay for them and for the enormous system of doles with which the Government burdened Austria. An extensive system of free passes increased the deficit at which railways were running; cheap bread, and rations issued under cost price, burdened the treasury with an ever-increasing debt, which was invariably met in the same way.

All this added to the necessary disproportion between the revenue and the expenses of the State, and combined with the effect of the Peace Treaty and the general disturbed state of Central Europe to produce that phenomenon in depreciation with which the Austrian currency of the time startled Europe. The krone began to sink immediately on the cessation of hostilities. In the following spring, when the Succession States cut their currency loose from the Austrian, it increased its pace. After that, there was no stopping it. The Government stood entirely helpless, watching the spectacle as though it had been an earthquake, and only occupied in bringing into temporary safety the belongings of its own supporters. The banks soon discovered that an even easier profit can be made out of a falling currency than a rising one, and began a series of speculations *à la baisse* which drove it lower still. The middle classes sold their belongings, and starved when these were gone.

The currency catastrophe had, however, one good result; it helped to restart industry. During this period all prices in Austria, even for articles which did not receive the State subsidy, were ridiculously low. Labour itself was dear only in proportion to other commodities and not, as has been often asserted, in comparison with pre-war or general world rates. In spite of difficulties with coal and raw materials, the factories were able to restart in the spring of 1919. The number of unemployed, which had reached its highest figure of 185,000 in May 1919, sank very rapidly to only 15,000 in the autumn of 1920, and as it sank so sank the desperation of the workmen and the probability of a Bolshevik revolution. By the time that the Peace Treaty was issued to Austria, she was already again a living, working organism, even if few believed that she could live for long.

The terms of the treaty were seen on publication to be much severer than the Austrians had hoped. They confirmed the loss of all the disputed frontier districts, and also imposed heavy financial burdens. After their ratification, the first Government resigned. It was replaced by a second coalition in which, however, the Christian Socialists, although still the weaker party, composed a more formidable opposition and one based less on the peasants and more on the middle classes. With the fall of the Bolshevik Governments in Munich and Budapest and the resumption of industry and consequent decrease of unemployment, the revolutionary forces in Vienna had spent their energies.

The forces for and against Socialism were now almost evenly balanced, so evenly indeed that the second coalition Government was almost powerless to effect progress in any direction. In the summer of the year 1920 it had to be dissolved and a provisional proportional Government entrusted with the tasks which everyone agreed were important: the framing of a capital levy, the settlement of the Constitution and of the new army which, under the provisions of the Peace Treaty, was to replace Deutsch's hurriedly raised force.

In the autumn of 1920 new elections were held, as a result of which the Social Democrat Party returned to the opposition, government being vested in the hands of a coalition of the bourgeois parties. This period, like the preceding one, was one of inactivity. The new Chancellor, Dr Mayr, a professor from Innsbruck, was universally recognised to be honest and well-meaning, but showed little constructive ability. Events took their course. A gradual return to more normal conditions began. The country districts had already gone far towards recovery. Deficiencies in livestock were made up, production revived, the barriers and restrictions were removed and intercourse between town and country revived. If the legislation of 1919 had favoured the workmen, that of subsequent Governments favoured the peasants, whose votes supported the Government and who were able in consequence to keep their taxation extraordinarily low. Even in Vienna, there was a difference. The city benefited from the improvement in the country and in Central Europe generally. The Reparations Commission had taken over the handling of the food and fuel question, and under its pressure, larger and more regular supplies were coming in. A few commercial agreements facilitated imports and exchange, and some passport officials grew human.

The falling exchange and the need for replenishing stocks depleted by the war kept industry and commerce busy. Unemployment was low, exports increasing, and within the country trade was brisk, since everyone was anxious to make his turnover as quick as possible, in order not to be left with the devaluating money. Trams no longer stopped running at half-past eight; no longer at eight o'clock did all electric light go out, leaving the town dependent till morning on candles and explosive acetylene lamps, while bread, tobacco or matches could be obtained in shops and not only by whispered bargainings with some villainous-looking intermediary in the darkest corner of a café.

Politically, people lost the feeling of sitting on rumbling volcanoes. The Communist Party lost way, and was finally

broken as an active danger in the spring of 1920. The
Socialist leaders reaffirmed their hold over the workmen,
and gradually transferred the authority back from the
workmen's and soldiers' councils to the party executive
and the trade unions.

Yet sometimes one felt that a little vigorous Bolshevism
would have been preferable to the complete inertia which
replaced it. The slight improvement in the conditions of
living could not make up for the hopeless, overwhelming
depression which Austria endured during these two years.
The terms of the Peace Treaty had been a genuine shock
to all Austrians, and seemed to crush out of them the
last drops of that courage which had established the
Republic and made an attempt at least to establish a new
order. The crushing financial terms gave a new impulse
to the downward course of the krone, which began to
gather ever more speed. The great difference between its
value and that of the Czech and German currencies, in
which most of the purchases for Austrian industry had to
be made, soon made its low value more of a hindrance than
a help to industry. Whoever was in charge of the State
finances seemed to have lost his head completely. Inflation
and rises in prices, rises in wages and inflation followed
each other in a dizzy round. None was interested enough
in the fortunes of Austria to attempt to stop it by courageously taking a part of the burden on his own class and per-
suading other classes to do likewise. The Socialists, while
still in power, worked out the plans for a great capital levy,
which they asserted would balance the budget. Their
partners in government watered it down, the capitalists
evaded it, and it produced in the end an amount grossly
inferior to the expectations and to needs. For this failure,

the Socialists rightly accused their opponents of being too frightened to tax the rich classes, and too incompetent to prevent evasions of taxation. Yet no taxes which Austria could raise would have met the deficit caused by the system of doles and subsidies, inaugurated and perpetuated by the Socialists themselves; nor the other great drain of the salaries of the public servants, of which everyone agreed there were far too many; but none were dismissed, because at the first threat the political party to which they belonged threatened such fire and thunder that the Government always ended by giving way. When the Social Democrats went out, the Christian Socialists came in; they were quick to condemn the iniquity of the dole system, but made the most half-hearted efforts to tax capital, and none at all to tax the peasants.

The universal remedy of making Austria a part of Germany was now replaced by that of credits from the Entente. On this one string the daily press, headed by the *Neue Freie Presse*, played unceasingly. Credit, credit, credit! But none remembered that there are two meanings of the word, and while they chorused their demands for an Entente credit, they let the credit of Austria drift from bad to worse by a display of helpless apathy relieved only by inter-party bickering.

As a matter of fact, money from the Entente alone had been keeping Austria precariously alive from the first. The Entente Governments themselves seemed not very interested in the fate of Austria so long as there was no Bolshevik revolution; but the Reparations Commission, under Sir William Goode, early transformed itself from a machine for getting money out of Austria into one for putting it in, and struggled gallantly between Austrian

helplessness and foreign indifference. The first food supplies were perforce granted on credit. In May 1919 a
further relief credit of thirty (later increased to forty-eight)
million dollars was granted by France, Great Britain and
Italy on the security of certain Austrian public assets.
After the Austrian Government had formally undertaken
to make the repayment of such loans a prior charge on all
its revenues, the sub-committee of the Organisations Committee of the Reparations Commission reported in favour
of further relief in kind to extend over six months, the
consolidation of the forty-eight million dollar loan, and
a further loan of a hundred million dollars pending a
definite scheme of reconstruction to be worked out by a
committee of bankers and financiers.

On this basis the Organisations Committee proposed to
consolidate all credits, past and future, and all securities
for them, under the control of the Austrian sub-committee,
against proper pledges from the Austrian Government,
and to prepare definite plans for putting Austria in a state
to pay reparations. The Austrian section of the Reparations
Commission came into being in June 1920. The International Relief Credits Committee, meanwhile, was called
into being, and assisted the Reparations Commission in
drawing up the conditions under which Austria might be
granted advances. The Reparations Commission was empowered to authorise the Austrian Government to issue
bearer bonds which should be a first charge on State assets,
with priority over any reparations claims whatever.

In November 1920 Sir William Goode submitted a
comprehensive scheme of a drastic character, involving a
loan of two hundred and fifty million dollars, to be spread
over a period of five years. The British Prime Minister,

Mr Lloyd George, promptly suggested that the salvation of Austria was a problem concerning her neighbours; and the French thereupon shelved the scheme and appointed a new committee which, after long delays, produced a totally ineffectual scheme of its own for an inadequate loan to be raised by the Powers, the Central European States and Austrian banks, to be administered by the Inter-Allied Commission.

The plan promptly followed its predecessor into some pigeon-hole—*omnes eodem cogimur*—and for nearly two years fresh schemes were broached, endless fresh committees of experts came and studied the situation on the spot, but no money was forthcoming except hurried temporary palliatives when Austria appeared to be going over the edge of complete disaster. One or the other of the many Governments owning a lien on Austrian assets invariably failed to consent to its suspension, so that during all this long and heartbreaking period no real progress at all was made.

So certain did Austria's final collapse appear to be that both her own inhabitants and her neighbours made quite open preparations for it, which destroyed the last remnant of credit which she still possessed. "She's no muckle to spier at the noo, but a doot she'll make a gran' corpse," as the Scotchman said of his wife. Austria occupies a delicate central position. From north to south, she lies across the line connecting the Slav states of the Little Entente; from east to south-west that joining Italy and Hungary; and in the north-west she abuts on Germany. Thus she has on her frontiers three *blocs*, each of which is interested, or at least suspects the other two of being interested, in increasing its territory by a slice of Austria.

A web of intrigue spun itself round the country. Hungary refused to give up the district destined to become the province of Burgenland. Bavaria intrigued with the Alpine provinces to join them in a Greater Bavaria reaching to the frontiers of Upper Austria. Germany suddenly revived her interest in Austria, started a mighty agitation and persuaded one province to hold a plebiscite for "Anschluss" and two others to make preparations for the same thing. So trouble and uncertainty in her foreign politics were added to Austria's internal difficulties of finance.

It is still not sufficiently realised how much the foreign situation complicated affairs as a whole, and how much credit is due to the first Chancellor who succeeded in winning general confidence and in raising Austria from the position of a prospective theatre of war to that of a real live State. This man was Dr Schober, the President of Police, who was elected Chancellor in June 1921, after the death of Dr Mayr. Schober was more of a competent official than a heaven-born statesman; but he had enough obvious honesty, combined with a first-class past record, to win the confidence of the Entente and enough common sense to realise that in spite of appearances, the Entente was still more powerful in the long run than the gang of Central European adventurers who defied it successively for a few months at a time each. Immediately after election, he was able to stop the spread of the pro-"Anschluss" plebiscites which had elicited from the Entente a threat to stop all foreign help, and even to cancel the promise of the Burgenland. He thus scored a success for which his countrymen ought to be eternally grateful to him. Yet his term of office was destined to be brief and troubled. In August and September when Austria should have entered

into possession of the Burgenland, the Hungarians opposed
the advance with semi-irregular bands, so that the simple
operation cost a small war, a host of negotiations, and
finally the loss of the chief town in the province, Oedenburg. In October, the ex-Kaiser made his second and last
attempt to recover his lost throne, landing near Oedenburg
by aeroplane. This ill-fated adventure provoked an universal atmosphere of mutual jealousy and suspicion which
brought Central Europe to the verge of a general catastrophe. The first step to put an end to this was taken by
President Schober, who in December 1921 concluded a
political and economic agreement with Czechoslovakia.
This Treaty of Lana, the first concluded by Austria with
any of her neighbours, bound the contracting parties to
respect the Treaties of Saint Germain and Trianon, to
guarantee each other's frontiers, to observe neutrality, in
case of the other being attacked, to support one another
against reaction, etc., etc.

President Schober's courage eventually cost him his
post, since the Pan-German Party, bitterly offended by the
treaty with Czechoslovakia, from now on turned against
the Chancellor; an attitude which led to his retirement in
May 1922. His period of office had been a distinct advance
in every way on those preceding it.

At the end of 1921 the Finance Minister had at last made
up his mind to abolish the system of State subsidies and
to introduce a more energetic system of taxation. In
finance, as well as in foreign policy, the close of 1921 really
marked the turning point. Yet the new measures were
far too feeble to affect at first the general situation. As
the hopes of an Allied credit were disappointed again and
again, as the deficit and the debt grew, the krone fell and

fell, until it seemed as though nothing could stop it. Prices were soaring dizzily. The index figure of the cost of living was calculated every fortnight, and even so, the rise in wages never kept pace with that of prices. The shops began to hoard their stocks, or to price them in dollars or Swiss francs. The country districts hesitated to send their products into the towns. The provinces revived their plans for separation, and the Social Democrats in Vienna began to consider how to act if their city were once more thrown on its own resources. A return to the conditions of 1919 seemed imminent.

Yet it was averted, for, after all, the general situation had changed greatly in the intervening years. Austria was no longer the scapegoat of Europe, both in the eyes of the Entente and of her neighbours. Much of the chauvinism of the years of war had died away and the Succession States had come to realise that Central Europe cannot be divided up into watertight compartments, each sufficient unto itself. None wanted to overthrow again the financial and commercial relations which had laboriously been re-established. Moreover, the poverty and shortage of capital of the Austrian concerns had led to an influx of foreign money which by this time had come to occupy a very important position in Austrian finance. Two great banks and many leading industrial concerns were now in foreign hands, many others dependent on foreign credits. The foreign capitalists had every interest now in supporting a stable and conservative régime in Austria and in preventing such a collapse as would lead to the return of the Social Democrats to power, with a campaign against foreign capital and probably a heavy capital levy.

Dr Schober's successor, the Christian Socialist Dr Seipel,

was faced with a situation teeming with difficulties, but relieved by great possibilities, were he able to turn them to account. It was Austria's good fortune that Dr Seipel was by far the most adroit statesman and the best brain (excepting possibly Dr Bauer) who had engaged in her politics since the war. A priest, a Jesuit, a man devoted to his religion and of an unimpeachable private life, he had a full share of the political cunning which his great Order condescends to employ on practical ends. Out of Austria's very weakness he built up her strength by the most ingenious adaptation of the old system of *divide et impera*. As none had seen before him, Czech, Italian and Hungarian could still be played off one against the other, even more effectually than while the old Empire still existed, since each preferred an Austria independent to an Austria under the sway of a hostile combination. Similarly, capital preferred a bourgeois Austria, even at the cost of a little more money, to a Socialist.

During anxious months of negotiations, Dr Seipel at last succeeded in convincing the world that Austria was worth saving. In August 1922, the Supreme Council once more referred the problem to the League of Nations, intimating that the Allied Governments, as such, were not in a position to grant further credits. The League of Nations for the second time referred the financial side to its own Financial Committee, following this up by creating a special Austrian Committee, on which Britain, France, Italy, Czechoslovakia and Austria were represented, to consider the political side.

The Financial Committee reported in favour of a new loan, which should include repayment of those previously granted, on condition that a strict financial control be imposed at the same time. By dint of strict reforms and the severest economy, the Austrian budget could be balanced and the loan secured.

On October 4th, 1922, a protocol was signed in Geneva which at last guaranteed the long-looked-for loan. Great Britain, France, Italy and Czechoslovakia pledged themselves to respect Austria's political independence, territorial integrity and sovereignty; to seek no special financial or economic advantage which would compromise that independence; and, if occasion arose, to refer the matter to the Council of the League and comply with its decisions. Austria entered into corresponding obligations. The loan of £30,000,000 was guaranteed by the four Governments above mentioned. A Commissioner General, appointed by the League, was to collaborate with the Austrian Government in its programme of reform and the execution thereof.

The Commissioner General, who was the representative, not of the guaranteeing Powers, but of the League, was given very wide powers. The Austrian Government surrendered all right to issue paper money and would not, except with special permission, negotiate or conclude loans. A new bank of issue, established under very stringent conditions, was to issue all further currency, being independent of the Government.

The loans were fully subscribed and, although the opposition in Austria raised a loud outcry against the "Slavery of Geneva," this was not serious, and in fact all parties in the country were agreed on the scheme. The legislation for the bank of issue was passed on November 14th. The inflatory issue of notes stopped four days later. The new bank opened on January 2nd, 1923. It is not our purpose to go into minute financial details as to the results of the new plan. For the time, it was wholly successful. The currency remained stable, as against the dollar, from the day that inflation ceased.

From the point of view of State finance, the Reconstruction Scheme has been an unqualified success. The budget was balanced even earlier than was expected, and it proved unnecessary even to call up the whole of the loan. After all, in a State as in a private budget, it is only necessary to see definitely what is the maximum income on which one can reckon, and to cut down one's expenditure within that limit. Unfortunately, the drastic reduction in expenditure necessary to attain that result has brought extremely severe trials to the Austrian population. Certain newspapers have compared the Reconstruction to the experiment which the gipsy made on his horse to teach it to live without food. He had got the animal down to a consumption of a straw a day when it died, so he never knew how his experiment would have worked out.

The first social effect of the Reconstruction was to shift the balance of advantage back from the workmen to the middle classes. The days of subsidies and doles were over, the Social Democrats were driven back within their last stronghold, the municipality of Vienna. The business and speculative classes at first did very well out of the new arrangements, and a great industrial boom lasted for about eighteen months. Afterwards, this collapsed, and the capitalists, like the workmen, began to feel the real effects of Austria's essential poverty. The most hardly hit of all were the numerous Government servants who fell victims to the "axe," and who joined the swelling numbers of the unemployed as the great stagnation began to paralyse trade and industry alike.

These questions will be discussed more fully in the final chapter of this book.

CHAPTER V

SOCIALISM AT THE CROSS-ROADS

THE position of the Austrian Social Democrat Party before the war was comparatively simple. Its strength was already great, and growing, among the workmen in the industrial districts near Vienna and in Bohemia and Moravia; but elsewhere it counted for little, and did not in fact command the votes of more than some fifteen per cent. of the total electorate. In the heterogeneous Parliament of those days, the ends towards which it worked were too frequently disregarded in the turmoil of national disputes, and its strength lay in the agility with which it could turn those disputes to its own advantage, thanks to the close organisation which Adler had given it, and which it had preserved for twenty-five years. Revolution, or the establishment of a Socialist State, could be no more than utopistic dreams in the face of such a strength as established authority could muster. There was no feasible alternative to the straightforward programme of social reform, as understood by the International of the day.

The war, whose aftermath was to bring the party such a mighty increase of power, shook its foundations, and endangered and for a while almost destroyed its unity. The leaders in 1914—most of them men no longer young, men with a long experience in Parliamentary work and an old habit of Austrian conditions behind them—gave their support to their country at war. The International disappeared; the Social Democrats, in their congress of 1915, declared it their duty to defend Western rights, culture and progress against the Imperialist greed of Czarism. In any case, Socialism was at a discount during the first half of the war. The factories were taken over for war-work and "militarised." The workmen kept on in them were under the strictest control, and at any sign of mutiny the authorities brought them to heel by the simple method of declaring them to be soldiers, thus by a word reducing their pay to the humorous pittance which conscript soldiers receive and making them subject to all the rigours of military discipline. The remainder were swallowed up in the armed forces of the Monarchy, so that practically all the rank and file were soon under the effectual control of persons who were anything rather than Socialist.

These years mark the nadir of Socialism in Austria. In 1916 the number of organised members in the whole Monarchy had sunk to 35,000, and in the following year had only increased by 5000. The forces on the other side were overwhelmingly strong, physically and morally.

The leaders acquiesced with a very fair grace. They sent no delegate to the Congress of Zimmerwald in 1915, and when Friedrich Adler submitted to them a programme based on the decisions of this congress, they rejected it almost unanimously. Their active work was reduced to helping as far as possible to alleviate the conditions of the poor, especially the munition workers.

Adler's murder of Stürgkh, and then the Russian Revolution, changed the situation. In the Party Congress of 1917 there was already a strong opposition composed of younger men whose imaginations had been fired by the events in Russia. This new "left" wing was not yet strong among the leaders but as time went on and the first prisoners of war began to return after the Peace of Brest

Litovsk, its adherents in the rank and file grew very numerous. These men had watched the reversal of all power and the establishment of a republic of workmen and peasants, had shared in the first intoxication of newly-won liberty; and returning to Austria, had found—war, starvation, a political system unchanged in many respects for centuries past, and at present, at least, definitely hostile to the workman. For them "Parliament" became a phrase almost synonymous with "reaction." They looked away from the impotent Deputies to the prison where sat Adler, a year before a solitary and stigmatised outcast, now elevated by the turn of history on to the throne of a popular idol.

Moreover, the old, detested political system was crumbling. The leader of the left wing, Otto Bauer, saw rightly who were the men of the future and threw in his lot with them; his nationalities programme had already brought him near them. In 1917 he laid before his party a declaration demanding autonomy for the nations of Austria. For the rest, the programme of his party was that of the Independent Socialists of Germany, pacifist, revolutionary, a long step forward beyond the old tenets of his party. It contained an express warning against any such insistence on reforms as should seem to countenance the existing state of affairs. Revolution was in the air.

In the last year of the war, events moved with bewildering rapidity. The right wing was left behind; the leadership fell naturally to the left, whose prophecies were all coming true; but even it had ado to keep up with history. The party found itself reimbued, one may feel a little tardily, with its pre-war enthusiasm for peace, in favour of which it demonstrated zealously; and peace was drawing near over the field of battle. It spoke for national autonomy; and in Paris, London and Washington the new nations were being arranged. It worked for a Republic, but far less effectively than did the Imperial houses of Habsburg and Hohenzollern.

In the slums and factories, under the direct, compelling pressure of hunger and war weariness, the masses left their leaders behind. The gap widened. To bridge it over, in January 1918, the first Workmen's Council was formed.

This Council, composed of the workmen themselves and unhampered by position, dignity or contact with official-dom, was the body which organised and carried through the great series of strikes in 1918 which, apart from Friedrich Adler's explosive "protest," were the only really revolutionary acts in all Austria's "revolution." It was still a part of the Social Democrat Party, acting under the orders of its leaders; for there was as yet no other Labour party in Austria, although a "left radical" group already existed. But it expressed the feelings of the rank and file much more simply and truly and therefore much more radically, than the "learned grave and reverend doctors" who were still hampered by having, before every move, to consider, firstly, how it looked in the light of the general situation, and secondly, what Karl Marx would have thought about it.

In 1918 the right wing was depleted by death, and further weakened, on the proclamation of the Republic, by its members being engaged in Ministerial duties. Yet even the left wing, in spite of Adler's enormous popularity, could command no unquestioning obedience. He, Deutsch, Bauer and other men who were recognised as revolutionary could still get a hearing and wield some authority; but for a while it was touch and go whether they would be able to keep their positions. The fact is that the tried, disciplined members of the party were in a minority; the ranks of Socialism were swollen suddenly, dangerously, by a rush of recruits from all classes of society. The long and unhappy war had made most Austrians Republicans. Those who remained loyal to their misguided and unfortunate Emperor were few in number. In the towns intellectuals, journalists, members of the free professions, even tradesmen and industrials—everyone of liberal ideas, everyone who was impatient of restraint and authority, desirous of change and hopeful for the future, threw in his lot with the party which most loudly and persistently had advocated change. The Republic came about almost of itself, but the Socialists could at least point to an old Republican programme. In the country, the peasants streaming back from the front were still half soldiers, weary of fighting, sick of being ordered about, united for a moment with the town labourers in a common hatred of war and of the officer's authority imposed from above; eager too to take into their own hands the conduct of affairs in the place of the old autocratic officialdom.

Thus republicans, liberals and revolutionaries of all kinds joined the Socialist ranks in numbers which surprised everybody; many of these new adherents cared nothing for scientific Socialism, had never heard the names of the Socialist leaders, or heard them only with dislike. And even the "old guard" was out of hand; its members had absorbed the lessons of Russia all too easily and superficially, had filled their heads with visions of millenniums which they firmly believed could be realised on the spot.

The leaders were thus faced with a situation full of singular complications. As the strongest group in the country, they had to take charge of its destinies, and that under the most difficult conditions conceivable. They had to take over much of the heritage of the Habsburgs, at least in the eyes of their victorious enemies; they had to carry out, if they could, a programme laid down under quite other conditions; and, when they could go no further, they had—perhaps the hardest task of all—to reconcile their own followers to their impotence.

Put in concrete form: they had to defend the Republic, which had dropped into their mouths like a very over-ripe pear, against enemies within and without; to rule over its population and provide it with food and warmth; to advance, by execution and preparation, towards socialisation in Austria and in Europe; and to secure the obedience of their own followers.

It was a very slender tight-rope along which they had to dance, very high in the air and very insecurely fixed. Even the question of whether to enter the Government of the new democratic Republic was a problem, since they were not strong enough to do so unless in a coalition with the non-Socialist parties, who were their bitterest opponents. To do so meant to recognise and support the capitalist State in a moment when many believed that without such support it could be overthrown; to refuse was to risk a reaction.

In effect, they compromised. They entered the Government and took over the most important posts in it. A new Ministry for Social Welfare and a Secretary of State for Socialisation were added to the Cabinet. While the Parliamentarians occupied themselves with the official Government, the remainder of the party danced a gavotte, advancing towards and retreating from the idea of a dictatorship of the proletariat.

International relationships were at the time exceedingly confused. The old International was gone. The Socialist parties which had previously composed it and which still survived were sundered by the years of war, by the awful question of national responsibility for it and by the hostility of their Governments towards a resumption of friendly relationships. In almost every country the Labour movement was split; there were some who really went no further than their pre-war programmes of social reform; many who, without desiring an immediate revolution, yet felt that matters could be pushed a long way further towards it than had seemed even remotely possible in 1913; others who believed that they could realise in their own countries the example of Russia.

Russia, and the Third International which she directed, was in many respects the strongest force in the world. It was very obscure what was going on there; but at least it was certain that a revolution had been accomplished, and no party whose professed aim was revolution could afford, or desired, to break off relations with her. Of the Austrian leaders only one had had personal experience of the new conditions in Russia and this man, Dr Otto Bauer, was probably also the only man who really understood the political situation in Austria, with its possibilities and its limitations for practical Socialism. He, as a matter of fact, opposed the idea of Austria's following Russia's example; in the long discussions which took place he consistently supported the order of democracy as against dictatorship. But he could not prevent many of his followers from playing with the idea of a revolutionary dictatorship of the proletariat, nor could he have dismissed, had he wished it, the "councils" movement which diversified the first year of the Republic.

These "councils" took two forms: the soldiers' and the workmen's[1]. The latter was the more prominent, and in the first spring of the Republic was expanded to give part of the form, and for a while much of the reality, of a dictatorship of the proletariat.

This useful institution cut two ways. If in the politics of the world the Western democracies prevailed, it provided—and this turned out to be its real function—a safety-valve through which the impatient could blow off steam; if Russia proved the ultimate victor, the germ of a Soviet Government was there ready for development.

In 1919 and 1920 the party which, under powerful foreign influence, demanded the immediate establishment of a Soviet Republic, was considerable. Russia was still, in theory at least, purely Bolshevik. In Hungary a Bolshevik Government was in power for some months and another for a shorter time in Munich. Both the Russians and the Hungarians, who kept up a legation in Vienna, spent a great deal of money and labour in propaganda, which at times came very near being successful.

In 1917 a small party calling itself the "left radicals" had constituted itself for the first time near Wiener Neustadt, an important industrial town near the Hungarian frontier and the centre of the munition-making district. On the collapse of the Monarchy this group joined a body of returned prisoners of war from Russia to form the

[1] The "works councils" (shop stewards) discussed in the next chapter are essentially different.

Austrian Communist Party. In the first year of its exist
ence this was a large if incoherent body. With the advantage of working without limits, it attracted all violent
elements which were repelled by the cautious, doctrinaire
character of Social Democracy. The dividing line between
Socialists and Communists was not clearly drawn. After
all, the difference lies only in methods and considerations
of expediency. In those days there were many Communists
prepared to make a revolution but quite uncertain of how
to do it; and many Socialists who toyed with the idea,
unable to make up their minds whether it was expedient
or not. Both sides, so long as the situation remained uncertain, were anxious to avoid a breach. They remained
in contact, if not in amity. While the Communists quickly
lost the more sentimental of their followers, they were more
than once reinforced by groups splitting off from the main
Socialist body, and for many months hoped, if vainly, to
win over Friedrich Adler, with the huge following his
prestige would bring.

This uncertainty continued for a long year. The more
conservative Socialists had no longer the pillar of the old
International to which to cling. Until this could be re-
founded, they were left in the air; and in any case, it was
a time for deciding on new lines to follow, rather than
returning to old. So the Labour movement in Austria
was very confused and incoherent. Some, who felt themselves rather as social reformers and could bring themselves
to meet non-Socialists, were acting in that capacity as the
new Austrian Government; some, the left wing, would
have liked to join the Third International, but were letting
"I dare not" wait upon "I would." Otherwise "the new
left" and the Communists were anxious to join it forth-

with. Finally, there was a small but energetic group of Tolstoyan anarchists, who agreed with nobody at all.

The field on which the resultant battles were fought out was the Workmen's Council.

This body had been in existence for nearly a year when the Republic was proclaimed, but had, of course, been obliged to work entirely underground. With the sudden apparition of liberty, however, Councils became all the vogue. The idea of government by Soviets or Councils has been more variously understood, more elastically applied, than perhaps any other political conception. Its very vagueness makes it the more invaluable as a catchword. One can hardly expect a mob to consider that there is nothing new under the sun, and that our own House of Lords, for instance, is, or was until recently, a very pure-blooded "Soviet of Landed Proprietors and Bishops" whose powers, in theory, came very near the universally dreaded and detested idea of syndicalism. This thought had probably not entered the mind of the population of Vienna when, in November 1918, it swarmed through the streets of that city shouting "All power to the Soldiers' and Workmen's Councils." The very phrasing of this cry is an example of that vagueness of which we speak. For the only theoretical reason for differentiating soldiers' from workmen's Councils would be the assumption that soldiers neither work nor are unemployed; a penetrating but cynical judgement which one hesitates to attribute to the good-natured Viennese crowd.

The Soldiers' Councils did indeed come rapidly into being, and take charge, not only of the new army, but of a large and varied number of duties into which military noses are not usually poked. The cry for workmen's

Councils was not immediately answered; for the Socialist leaders had seen clearly the impossibility of establishing a dictatorship in the face of the opposition of the peasants and the Entente Powers, and the rank and file were content to await the elections in the hope of a majority, which would give them complete control of Parliament.

The elections in February 1919, although returning the Social Democrats as the strongest party, proved a disappointment in that it was obvious that only a coalition Government with the Christian Socialists was possible. Almost immediately afterwards a Bolshevik Government was established at Budapest. It was now that the more extreme elements, encouraged by the example of Hungary and disappointed by their failure in Parliament, renewed their cry for the Councils.

In theory it would seem that a Government of a democratic Parliament and Soviets side by side is an impossibility, and pushed to its logical conclusion, it would be so. For the essence of a Soviet or Council Government, as understood by the Bolsheviks, is the denial of representation of rights to all classes except the proletariat and the peasants. Its supporters regard themselves as the representatives of the true democracy of the future State, where there will be not merely political but economic equality; rejecting a Parliament based on the capitalist system as representing class interests. Logically therefore it should have been all or nothing—Soviet or Parliament. In fact, however, Austria achieved the impossible compromise and managed to keep both bodies functioning at the same time, although the Council was never legally authorised. One wing of the leaders would probably have preferred to do without the Council altogether. But the demand was too strong. Local

Councils were springing up all over the country, and there was danger that if ignored they would go over to Bolshevism and attempt a violent and disastrous revolution. Accordingly, a meeting was held in March 1919 to organise a body which should represent all parties and opinions "which recognise in the establishment of the Socialist order of society the end, and in class warfare the means of emancipation of the proletariat." That is to say, all shades of Socialists, Communists and Anarchists could meet on this common ground, and a definite collapse of the unity of the Labour movement be avoided. A committee was formed under Friedrich Adler, and on the system evolved by him the first elections for the Councils were held shortly after.

Each staff of workmen, the unemployed, the free professions, and women engaged on household work elected delegates to a Local Council, which was supplemented by co-opted members from the army, the Social Democrats' political organisation, the trade unions and other bodies. The Local Councils of a district elected together a District Council, with further co-opted members; the districts again, the National Council, whose co-opted members were men of real ability and importance. The Executive Committee of the National Council was the highest authority in the system.

The exact powers and functions of the Council were never laid down or fixed by law, in conformity to the general desire. For none regarded the arrangement as final. To some it was too little, to others too much. The Communists proposed to utilise it as a means to establish the immediate dictatorship of the proletariat. Some of the Social Democrats wanted to make it a second chamber parallel to Parliament, especially for attention to labour

M   9

problems. Max Adler, the most careful and ingenious exponent of its theory, wished it to be at first parallel to Parliament, and later to supersede it. Until ready to take over the whole power, it was to deal with all matters of economics, communications and finance, with the right of bringing Bills before Parliament or vetoing the decrees of that body, which was only to be left with such political and cultural questions as did not touch on economics.

As matters turned out, the Council did none of these things. During its chequered career it performed a number of tasks, but never really touched on the competencies of Parliament. It was, however, a body of great power in its early stage. The Socialist Government found it convenient to entrust this body, in which it had much more confidence than in Parliament or in the police, with the administration of such parts of the law as Socialism especially desired to be enforced. Thus the Council took over the whole of the task of appropriating and allotting accommodation to relieve the housing shortage. It attempted to control the food supply, to punish hoarding, "Schleichhandel[1]" and profiteering, and to support magistrates in their duty. It watched over the army stocks of arms and munitions to see that they were not sold under the rose to reactionary States or formations.

Since at that time almost everybody was regularly evading the law in one way or another, and most people lived either by or on such evasion, such an assistance to authority was not superfluous. The remedy, however, was

[1] This quite untranslatable word was one of the most familiar in Austria during the hard times. It means the buying in secret and at the seller's price of articles which the law decreed must be given up for rations at the State's controlled price.

little better than the disease. The members of the Council
were not as a rule the most intelligent or public-spirited
among the population, but rather the most noisily dema-
gogic; and their activities, if accompanied with many
good results, were mixed with so many abuses as to fill
the middle classes and peasants with a deep dislike and
mistrust of Socialism, and to cause them to complain with
justification that they were subjected to an ignorant and
arbitrary red terror.

All this was however a side-issue. It disappeared when
conditions grew more settled; when the army stocks had
been disposed of, rationing abolished, the housing question
taken over by a regular office, and the remaining miscel-
laneous activities of the Councils in the workshops transferred to the trade unions. They were temporary ex-
pedients which could never be practised except where the
Government had been changed so suddenly as to leave
the new rulers distrustful of the regular civil service, police
and army.

The real importance of the Workmen's Council lay not
in its relation to the population as a whole but in the part
which it played in the Labour movement. To-day, hardly
its most enthusiastic advocates of 1919 would maintain that
it showed any fitness to supersede Parliament—even a
Central European Parliament—and to govern the country
extra wisely or well. On the other hand, for over a year it
performed most efficiently the function of a safety-valve
in constant, explosive use, or a ventilator turning continuously in a rushing wind. It was a common ground
where all shades of Marxist opinion met, where the violent
and the impatient could let off steam and satisfy themselves
with an appearance of doing something, where minorities

(as the Communists were) could make their voices heard, and were therefore not wholly driven back on to force. Its existence provided such a show of concession to revolution that many asked for nothing more.

The struggle between Communists and Socialists was fought out on this field, and fought out with a great and increasing bitterness. At first, and especially so long as Bela Kun ruled in Budapest, the Communists were sanguine of gaining the whole of the Council to their wishes and proclaiming a Soviet dictatorship in Vienna. At this time, they, no more than the Socialists, were anxious for a final split if it could be avoided, and they hoped to make their revolution through the Council. On several occasions they perfected all plans for a *coup d'état*. On one they tried to put them into action, only bringing about some utterly senseless street shooting and loss of life.

Slowly the Communists came to realise that it was useless to hope to win over the Social Democrats for revolution. When they, moreover, at last finally realised that the leaders of the Social Democrat Party were not going to join Communism, Moscow issued a violent letter denouncing the "social traitors" Bauer, Renner, Adler, etc. The split between Communism and Social Democracy had become a definite and irretrievable fact. With it, the chief use of the Council ceased for the Socialists. The system had, after the first few months of its existence, lost steadily in popularity. The incessant squabbles, the impossibility of ever reaching an agreement, were growing tedious. The political organisation and the trade unions were sufficient between them for all emergencies. As it was impossible, as well as contradictory to the very principle of the Councils' existence, to silence the Communists in them altogether, the Social Democrats, who formed the overwhelming majority, seceded and took to meeting by themselves under the title of "Social Democratic fraction of the Workmen's Council," all statutes, etc., being unaltered, only with the addition of the words "Social Democratic fraction." By this simple expedient, they broke off relations with the Communists, and with this move, the importance of the Council was over. If it still exists, it is but a wraith of its former self—a melancholy wraith, when one remembers what high hopes were formed of it, what volumes written about it by eager pens for its future historians to read.

From this time on, Communism and Social Democracy in Austria go different paths. The history of the Communist movement is a cheerless one. It has not recorded one real success, even if, when conditions have been particularly bad, its propaganda has been instrumental in increasing the general discontent. Generally, it has been in opposition to the Social Democrats, attacking them in its journal and speeches; but when the Social Democrat Party turns on it from time to time, it has no alternative but to retreat. When it has opened up negotiations for a reconciliation, they have been unsuccessful. The Socialist leaders are polite to Moscow, and not so opposed to it as to prevent them from doing business, through the socialised institutions, with Russia; but their own local Communists they either ignore blandly or blackguard savagely. The Communist Party has been continually torn by intrigue and faction, and weakened by corruption and incompetence. Its numbers are now well under five figures.

The history of the Soldiers' Councils is not altogether dissimilar from that of the Workmen's. The proletariat army was probably the most unpopular of all the Socialist experiments, and was such a fiasco from the military point of view that it is necessary to begin by pointing out that its avowed object was not to be an army at all. Whether it could ever have developed into one is an interesting question, but one to which the answer must remain largely a matter of opinion.

In the Austrian-Hungarian army the primary function of any army—the defence of its country in war—had for many years[1] been much less in evidence than its secondary object, that of maintaining internal law and order, which, under the circumstances, meant the unquestioning support of the Dynasty against nationalists, socialists or other heretics. It was not a people's army but an Imperial body-guard, just as the Empire itself was not a democracy, but a personal dominion of its ruler. Thus, although its fighting qualities were not neglected—it was far more up-to-date than Austrian trade, communications or education—it was taught before all things its duty towards its master. The type of officer which it developed was personally admirable; hardworking, capable and honourable; but identified with the ruling system, and as such hated by all the system's opponents.

The excessive strain of the years 1914–1918, while weakening the loyalty to the Dynasty, threw the odium for the miseries of war on the corps of officers. Above all, the makers of the Republic were haunted by the fear that the old army would lead a reaction unless wiped out of all existence. The fear was possibly justified at the time of the Kapp "putsch" in Germany, although even then the Entente and the Succession States would have intervened

[1] It had last taken the field in 1878.

to make such a reaction a very short one. Since then, it has most certainly been without any foundation. Yet in 1918 it was very present, and gave the Socialists a good excuse to secure for themselves the control, with its attendant political advantages, of the new Republican army. The idea of a people's army had been brought back by the returning prisoners of war, and the foundations for it laid by the Socialist leader Deutsch who, having spent the last months of the war as workmen's representative at the War Office, had employed his time in establishing a network of his own agents in the hinterland for the purpose of preventing the employment of the troops against strikers. When the breakdown came, and it was obviously necessary to raise a force to cope with the general chaos, the Provisional Government, composed of all political parties, was in charge of the task. But the Socialists, being the only people who had a plan ready, or indeed really knew what they wanted, were easily able to shoulder the other parties aside.

They were also the only people whose wishes stood any chance of being respected in Vienna. In fact, a provisional Soldiers' Council formed itself as early as October 1918 and in November a decree signed by all three presidents of the Provisional Council sanctioned the formation of Soldiers' Councils "to act as commissions for complaints and to remain in constant touch with the representatives of the people."

The Councils and Deutsch's agents, having established the necessity of abolishing all vestiges of the old army and recruiting an entirely new one, set to work in great haste. They were not without rivals. A very serious competitor was a Communist "red guard," which was bent on pro-

claiming the dictatorship of the proletariat on the spot.
There were middle-class special constables, bodies of
officers, and formations of the old army which had marched
back in good order to Vienna. Deutsch, however, whose
authority grew rapidly against that of the Councils, succeeded in establishing his monopoly. The provincial
organisations could not be stopped; the rest were suppressed[1], and the force raised by the Socialist leader became
the only legal one. Its numbers grew, at first slowly, later,
when unemployment increased, very rapidly, at one time
totalling 80,000. On November 1919 it was systematised.
Sufficient soldiers had been collected and approved as true
Republicans—no other test was asked of them. Officers
were appointed on probation for a month, after which the
Soldiers' Council was to decide whether they enjoyed the
confidence of their men. They were controlled by the
representatives of the soldiers.

The discipline of the force was to be not "militarist"
but "revolutionary" and "proletarian." It was secured by
an intricate system of Councils. The regular councillors
were elected "to safeguard the economical, political and
all other interests of the V.W., arising out of the soldier's
status."[2] In addition, there were disciplinary Councils,

[1] We say suppressed as a legal fiction. As a matter of fact, they
still flourish as local defence corps, often excellently armed, equipped
and drilled, and one or two of them have actually had to defend their
homes against foreign invaders, and have done so not worse than the
"army." The Socialists denounced them bitterly; but as soon as they
lost their own control in the army, they formed a private army, too; so
that everyone has got one now and people go on playing at soldiers
just as if our generation had had no opportunity to learn what an
awful and serious thing war is.

[2] "Die Währung der politischen und wirtschaftlichen, sowie aller
übrigen Interessen der Volkswehr-Männer, welche sich aus dem
Dienstverhältnisse derselben ergeben."

garrison Councils, whose functions were purely political and consisted in co-operating with the Workmen's Councils; and educational Councils, who lectured their comrades on such subjects as "the idea of class warfare" and "the teaching of Karl Marx." Without the authority of the Central Executive Committee, in which these Councils culminated, no orders were carried out, either of superior officers or of the Secretary of State for War himself.

If the makers of the new army had confined themselves to guarding against reactionary or over-militarist tendencies in a sensible and impartial way, little would have been said against the force. Unfortunately, they set to work instead to make it into a "party guard," and as recruits had been enlisted mostly on the sole recommendation of their "revolutionary sentiment," the force proved quite extraordinarily unruly and unpopular. There were bitter and well-grounded complaints of its conduct. Some fractions of it were indeed much "redder" than its masters at all desired, being purely Communist. These gave a great deal of trouble and nearly brought about a revolution under the leadership of Dr Frey, afterwards head of the Communist party. Naturally, the Social Democrat leaders did not desire either this or the individual acts of crime committed by the numerous bad characters who in the first hurry got smuggled into the ranks; but they must bear the responsibility for having deliberately turned away the more sober and respectable elements in their fear of reaction.

"Proletariat discipline" in time of peace is not likely to be successful when anything which does not appeal to the individual soldier is "bourgeois" or "capitalist," which it becomes his duty to resist. In the field it proved no less than a fiasco. When mobilised against Czechoslovakia, the new army had no more difficult orders than to retire quietly if the Czech opposition proved too strong. Yet the Czechs caught some units asleep in their beds, while others plundered to such an extent that the inhabitants, although Austrian, called in the help of the Czech troops. In February 1919 a battalion was despatched towards the Czech frontier to guard the railway. When the Councils heard against whom they were to be employed, they ordered the battalion to return to Vienna, which it did, so strong was the new discipline. In the fighting against Yugo-slavia, the commander of a battalion ordered all men to fall out whose principles did not urge them to go into action, which had the effect of reducing his unit to 140 men. Later, it was desired to raise a storm troop for actual fighting, and those who did not feel "morally and physi-cally up to the task" were again fallen out, which brought the grand total down to 80.

The Volkswehr was not exposed to further fighting, and was thus able to make the question of Council versus officer into a purely political one. It may be worth noting that the Hungarians, under Bela Kun, also had to raise a Bolshevik army against Rumanian invaders. The Hungarians are single-minded patriots, who mean business in such cases, and one of their own leaders writes: "The soldiers demanded that an iron discipline be established, since the experiences with the Soldiers' Councils in the first army had been very miserable."[1]

After a time, as the Socialist leaders got a better grip on

---

[1] "Die Soldaten forderten die Herstellung einer eisernen Disziplin, da man mit den Soldatenräten in der ersten Armee sehr schlechte und traurige Erfahrungen gemacht hatte."

the masses, the worst excesses began to vanish. Yet the system remained violently unpopular with the other parties, who wanted the whole force swept away and replaced by a really non-political army. When the first army was replaced, according to the terms of the Peace Treaty, by a new one in 1920, although the Councils were taken over, their power diminished, and has since then steadily been reduced in favour of that of the officers, and the new army has really become almost non-political. Or rather, the political forces in it are balanced; on the one side the officers, on the other the rank and file closely organised in a "red" trade union. As a mouthpiece of the real sentiments of the rank and file which no officer, however good, can understand, the Soldiers' Councils can well serve a useful purpose. And the red army can at least say that bloodshed was avoided and the Republic was not overthrown during its chequered career.

The red army was a bone of contention second to none between the Socialists and the other Austrian parties, and it was indeed largely on a quarrel over it that the former finally retired from the Government. If this difficult question could have been avoided—and with less suspicion and demagogy on both sides, one feels that it could have been—it is possible that the Socialist rule might have been more palatable to the rest of the country. For in 1919 the Social Democrat Party enjoyed a lot of sympathy, and the votes which brought it into power included many from among the peasants and the middle classes.

By the end of two years, however, these sympathies had been forfeited. The Austrian peasants had not indeed very much to gain from Socialism. The overwhelming majority of them were already proprietors—mostly, it is true,

heavily in debt owing to mortgages, but these debts were
wiped off through the fall in the currency. Legislation
could only meet their land-hunger in one respect, by
parcelling up the large districts which had been bought
up in recent years and turned into deer forests. A law to
this effect was actually passed, but its effects have remained
small, partly owing to the fact that the depleted Austrian
countryside cannot raise sufficient labour to take advantage
of it. It was far too little to counteract the embittered quarrel
between town and country which sprang up immediately
when the new Government, in order to feed Vienna, fixed
maximum prices at a rate which was usually grossly unfair
to the producer, and continued the hated requisitionings
which had been in force during the war. The coalition
between peasants and workmen soon became one of active
hatred, a hatred which was energetically fanned by the
all-powerful country priests, who did not hesitate to denounce Socialism from the pulpit as a work of Satan, and
especially to exploit beyond every limit the anti-Semitism
latent in the breast of all non-Jews where Jews are abun-
dant. Nor were the Socialists any more conciliatory. The
coalition was unpopular from the first among the more
extreme fraction of the rank and file. At the first Party
Congress after the war, the members for Wiener Neustadt
brought forward a resolution condemning it in no measured language[1], while the beautiful lady leader of the local
Communists, who later emigrated to Germany to upset
the minds and hearts of a larger circle of politicians, used
calmly to propose in the Workmen's Councils to invade
the Tirol with Communist battalions. Even the leaders
showed little understanding for the position of the peasant.

[1] The resolution was rejected by the Congress.

They organised the country labourers, thereby not only gaining votes for themselves, but also sensibly improving the lot of one of the most hardly-used classes of the whole population; but they found it necessary to do so on real factory lines, including a regular eight-hour day—a measure which annoyed the peasants as much as it bewildered them[1].

The alienation of the intellectuals and the middle classes was more gradual and infinitely more tragic. It is the record of a real opportunity of class reconciliation lost. As has been said, the intellectuals in general, in revolt against the old state of things, felt at first a very widespread sympathy for Socialism. But the Party was too inelastic to accommodate itself to them. It had existed for too long as a party of the town labourers, exactly organised and strictly disciplined. The intellectuals were lacking in discipline, and, instead of taking the word of the Socialist leaders, showed a habit of making up their own minds, which often resulted in violent difference of opinion. Sometimes they went too far to the left, sometimes to the right, of the oblique line along which the leaders were so painfully guiding their party. So that the latter deliberately preferred to reject them for the time, to wait until an opportunity should occur of organising them in trade unions, and then to receive them back into the fold. At first the brain-workers, their help rejected, went over pretty well *en masse* into the opposing camp. Later, however, the lower classes of them did begin to come back

[1] As Bauer writes: "When the whistle blew in the factory after eight hours, the farm labourer, too, laid down his tools." We can only judge by inference of the sentiments of the cows when the whistle blew just at milking-time and the logical labourers downed udders.

according to the Socialist programme. The bank clerks, the journalists, and such like are now organised in trade unions and are in very many cases faithful supporters of the Social Democrat Party. But the higher classes—the superior officials, the bank directors, most of the free professions, nearly all those whose work demands a real intelligence and initiative—are alienated, it seems, beyond recall. Nor are they likely to come back until the Socialists begin to amend their two great faults: their excessive materialism and their impatience of initiative among the rank and file.

For, in fact, the legislation of the Socialist Governments did little to conciliate the classes outside their old followers. Both financially and socially, it was directed almost exclusively towards improving the condition of the manual labourers.

This was especially the case with the financial legislation, over which the Socialists, although they did not supply the actual Ministers of Finance, had the last word. A starvation period was in any case inevitable; only foreign help could tide the country over that, and before its effects could be anything but temporary, such help would have to be on a very large scale indeed. There were three possible ways open: firstly, to increase revenue by wholesale and drastic measures; secondly, to reduce expenditure, both of the State and the standard of living, to the absolute minimum; or thirdly, to drift.

The difficulties in the way of the first were technical. Wealth was and always has been in Austria, but the classes owning it were either so numerous—as in the case of the peasants—or so influential—as with the Church—or so cunning—as with the financiers—that they could escape the necessity of disgorging it. All efforts to increase the burden of taxation on the peasants, or to induce the Church to part with her treasures, shipwrecked on the opposition of the country Deputies; the capital levy which was decreed and actually put through was very disappointing in its return. The Socialist leaders therefore chose the third method, and by the bland refusal which they opposed to the second, did much to bring about the fall of the currency and the economic chaos.

They invariably blame their successors for the collapse of the krone, but were themselves much to blame. Instead of reducing State expenditure, they increased it by a disproportionate unemployment dole, a high wage for the Socialist army, a system of free tickets on the railways and State subsidies for the necessaries of life, which were issued to the workmen at far below cost price. Later, they boasted that the depreciation which occurred under their rule was an actual service to the State by stimulating industry and decreasing unemployment. Yet this does not alter the fact that these praiseworthy results were attained at someone's expense; firstly, at the cost of the fixed-income class; secondly, at that of their own future State. Later, when a foreign credit had been granted and the middle-class Government was administering it, they were the first to complain of the rise in prices and hard conditions which it brought in its train; but failed to point out that if one lives on capital merrily for a while, and then stops, the resultant smaller income is not the fault of the present system, but the past.

The excuse for their policy lies in the fact that no one at all, at the time, understood the economics of a falling currency; the justification, perhaps, in its effects as a national health insurance for the future at a time when still further to lower the standard of life would have annihilated the health of the younger generation, already frightfully impaired by the years of the war. Its political effect at the time was to strengthen the trade unions, through whose help organised workmen could always force through a rise in wages to meet the rising prices; and thus to consolidate the position of the party among its own acknowledged followers while disregarding and alienating the rest of the nation.

Labour involving intellect and initiative was in fact very badly rewarded during these years. On this point a most heated controversy has been waged, provoked partly by a remarkable article in the *Arbeiterzeitung* comparing the work of an office charwoman with that of the office chief, to the disadvantage of the latter. These unlucky lines gave the opponents of Socialism an argument which was used copiously, and not always fairly. Yet it remains true that the Austrian Social Democrat Party understands best, and favours most, disciplined manual labour. Under its rule the gradations between intelligent work and drudgery were excessively reduced. Initiative was little encouraged; and after all, when the main argument against Socialism is its disregard of initiative, it is short-sighted folly not to do everything possible to disprove the truth of this argument.

So when the party retired again into opposition, it was back very nearly on its old lines. Among the manual labourers—its old class of followers—its power was greatly increased and it had been extended to include the farm-labourers and certain lower classes of the brain-worker; but it had not succeeded in attracting the mass of the population. In its general tone, too, it had recovered its balance.

The Councils had disappeared, or been reduced to impotence. The Communist Party, after a meteoric career, had dwindled away into a fitful spark. The masses had been finally convinced of the impossibility of establishing a Soviet Republic of Austria and their Bolshevik sympathies had been brought within amenable limits. The party was once more an unity, well in the hands of its oligarchy of leaders.

Its international relationships have developed along similar lines. Although these are of much greater importance than the career of the Councils, we do not need to treat them at the same length, since they are much better known. At the close of the war, the Internationals were completely disorganised. The old organisation seemed dead beyond recall, and the only unity which remained was in Russia. It was a long time before the Austrians finally admitted the impossibility of joining hands with Russia, and it was the desire not to close this door altogether which made them averse in the first years to forming common front with the Western parties. The urgent problem for Austrian Socialists was, however, to find a *modus vivendi* with their German colleagues. And precisely Germany, after the war, was in the state of direst confusion, with three separate Socialist parties at continual loggerheads with one another. Yet it was thought urgent to unite them, owing to the danger of a reaction in Germany.

The German Majority Socialists differed from the Austrian on important points; on the nationalities' programme of Renner and Bauer; on the attitude to the war; and on their policy towards Communists. For a while, the Austrians with the German Minority Socialists and the British Independent Labour Party formed the so-called

"two and a half International," in which they were really
the guiding spirits. The tenets of this International went
considerably beyond those of the years before the war,
and it still attempted to avoid an open breach with Russia.
But the desire for reconciliation, and the importance of
securing amity in Germany, combined with the complete
intransigeance of the Russian Bolsheviks, led them in 1923
to the Hamburg Conference. An agreement was reached
at last, the mediators being the British, where the Independent Labour Party belonged to the "two and a half
International," and the Labour Party to the second. The
two Internationals coalesced into one body, with its seat,
not in Vienna, but in London. This circumstance proved
of importance, for although Friedrich Adler, one of the
more extreme among the Austrian leaders, became the
party's secretary in London, yet the moderating influence
of the British Labour Party has been very noticeable in
the Austrian party since the fusion.

CHAPTER VI

SOCIALIST LEGISLATION

THE preceding chapter touched on the legislation passed by the Socialists only in so far as it affected the progress or the composition of the party. Such legislation was not very large in quantity, nor, as a rule, very successful. It is also unnecessary to dwell at any great length on the party's foreign policy. Austria's relations with her neighbours were in any case largely determined by the will of the Entente. Especially the movement for unification with Germany, which was taken up by the Socialists and made —indeed still remains—a cardinal point in their programme, was vetoed in summary fashion by the Allies. The remainder of the foreign policy has a certain interest from being based on unusual motives; that is, friendship or the reverse with any given State was grounded, not on considerations of mutual advantages to the two States, but on the position, prospects, etc., etc., of the Socialist parties in them. This fact has resulted in a very peculiar relationship between the Austrian Socialists and the Czechs. On the one hand, Czechoslovakia is a capitalist State, a military power, a *protégé* of the Entente and especially of France, and a member of the Little Entente whose function it is to counteract the influences of Germany and Hungary. From this point of view, the Socialists would always be against an alliance, or even a close co-operation, with their neighbours. On the other hand, many of the leading Czech statesmen are Socialists, and close personal bonds exist between the politicians of the two countries, dating from

10-2

the days when they squabbled together in one Parliament, sometimes in one party; so that there are very many cases where some point of policy, impossible for Austrians, has been got through by the friendly help of Czech ex-colleagues.

Besides Germany and Czechoslovakia, the only countries with which Dr Bauer, the first Austrian Foreign Minister, was at all immediately concerned were Hungary and Russia. In Hungary régimes changed rapidly. When the red Governments were in power, the Austrian Socialists showed no hesitation in letting arms be smuggled through to them and otherwise indulging in actions which went up to or over the verge of breaches of neutrality; as soon as the Hungarian reaction set in, opposition to that country by every means became the order of the day. As for Russia, the hostility to local Communists never extended to the more distant country, and the Austrian socialised industries actually existed to a large extent on Russian orders.

The aim of the leaders, when suddenly brought into power, was to socialise as far and as long as they could, without bringing about either revolution or reaction. Their original programme envisaged socialisation on a very large scale. The electoral appeal before the first elections—after proclaiming the necessity for a new army, separation of Church and State and Church and School and free education—went on to say: "We will give back to the people the property of the great factory owners, of the mineowners, the capital of the great banks and trading houses, the estates of the nobles, the Church and the capitalists....The State shall expropriate the great industrial and mining concerns, the great estates and banks...." The owners were to be recompensed out of a fund raised by a supertax, where at all, and the concerns run by committees of workmen. The large estates were to be run, where possible, on a socialised co-operative basis; where this proved impracticable, to be parcelled up among small peasant proprietors.

As a matter of fact, the socialisation actually carried through has been on a much more modest scale. The agricultural programme has hardly been realised at all, and practically no case of direct expropriation from private individuals has occurred anywhere. One undertaking was planned which would have been of the first magnitude; the socialisation of the great Alpine Montan Works, the largest industrial concern in Austria, which controls the greater part of the mining industry of Styria. This was frustrated by the sudden action of the Finance Minister, a non-Socialist, in placing this concern in Italian hands. The most important concerns taken over for experiments by the new Commission for Socialisation were the old State munition factories, water-power stations and other Government undertakings. One of the largest of these was the Arsenal of Vienna. Concerns in which foreign capital was engaged could not be touched.

Apart from these, a number of experiments were made on lines worked out by Dr Bauer and explained by him in *Der Weg zum Sozialismus*, to which pamphlet the reader is referred. They are the result of careful study based on the lessons, partly of English Guild Socialism, partly of the Russian Bolshevik experiments, adapted to local conditions. They are of two main types. The first is wholly socialised. The control is in the hands of a mixed body composed of the producers, the consumers and the State (for concerns on a limited or local scale, the State is replaced by the province or the municipality). In most cases the consumers are represented by the co-operative stores, with which these concerns work in close touch.

A second group is partly Socialist, partly private. A Bill was early passed allowing the public authorities the right of taking up to half the shares in any concern on its foundation, or of the new shares on a new issue. By these means, the State could get a foothold in industry without actual expropriation. The opportunities were exceptional in Austria just after the war, as during the shortage of capital and devaluation of currency, almost every concern in the country was obliged to resort again and again to fresh issues of shares. The shortage of capital, however, cut both ways, and prevented the State from making nearly as great use of its opportunities as it wished.

Between them, these socialised and semi-socialised concerns made up a fairly imposing total, although smaller than was expected, and confined to industry. The banks have not been touched, the State and Socialist Party confining itself to the Savings Banks and to an entirely new Workmen's Bank, which runs in connection with the co-operative stores, and undertakes no speculation—an unicorn among its colleagues. Among the newly founded businesses may be mentioned a large and excellent shoe factory, a no less excellent factory for supplying medicines and chemists' drugs, and a wood business.

The net profits on these works, after all dividends, mortgages, etc., etc., have been paid off, and the reserves set aside, are divided between the workmen and the founders. The workmen's share again is divided into two parts: one, for "beneficiary ends," is disposed of according as the Works Councillors decree; the other is put into the common funds.

It is very difficult to pass a judgement on these concerns, and practically impossible to say how they would have turned out under normal conditions. A German Commission has reported on them in many thick volumes, but the results of the report are not luminous. Certainly, they have afforded no proof of the impossibility of Socialism, but also none of the overwhelming necessity for it. They have been affected by great difficulties and great advantages, of which perhaps the former were less permanent or normal. They were founded at a time when money was short and the currency falling; at a time, however, when industry was passing through an era of prosperity, when, owing to the low cost of production, there was little unemployment in Austria, a market was easy to find, and everyone was spending up to the limit of his income, owing to the uselessness of saving. They had the great advantage of working in closely with the co-operative stores, which in Austria are far larger than any single private business, and later with the rich municipality of Vienna. Many of them were able to secure profitable contracts with Russia. They thus had a variety of consumers who were attracted to their goods by political as well as economic motives, and as these were themselves large concerns, were able to deal directly and cheaply, eliminating the long chain of intermediaries between consumer and producer which help to run prices up in Austria.

On the other hand, they have suffered very greatly from shortage of capital, accentuated by the hostility with which their capitalist rivals regard them. The same shortage has affected every Austrian concern very closely, but private firms of old standing have found financial backing much more readily. The bill which legalised the socialised con-

cerns did indeed give the Minister of Finance the right
to force banks to assist them; but so far no single Finance
Minister—indeed, none has been a Socialist—has made
use of this right. Thus they flourished as long as the trade
boom continued, but when a period of stagnation succeeded it, they were hit more heavily than the ordinary.
The management has often been capable, but in no case
very brilliant and often very imperfect. The quality of the
goods produced has, however, generally been admirable.

If we do not consider as socialisation the gradual conversion of middle-class incomes into doles for the labouring
classes, yet one side-issue of this process certainly deserves
the name. This is the particularly vexed housing question.
The rent restrictions act, established during the war,
has been upheld to this day (1925) with few relaxations.
The rent which the owner is allowed to collect to-day
amounts to about one-hundredth of its pre-war value in
gold—a fact which of course has brought about the result
that house property in Vienna is a drug on the market.
Moreover, the housing shortage is incredibly severe.
Before the war, the poorer classes in Vienna were probably
worse housed than anywhere in Europe, except Dublin.
Now a new law limits the number of rooms which any
family may inhabit; the poor have expanded into the vacant
rooms, and thereby enjoy a very sorely needed improvement. This, however, combines with the high cost of
labour and material, and the fact that, owing to the shortage
of money, capital deposited on interest in a bank can bring
in a far higher rate of interest than could be got from building and letting a new house, even though to such the rent
restrictions act does not apply, to bring about a complete
standstill in the building trade.

The Municipality of Vienna, to-day the stronghold of the Social Democrat Party and in many respects almost identical with it, has imposed on all rents a municipal tax. With this money it is building new houses under its own control. The justice of this arrangement to present house-owners is more than questionable, although local circumstances make the error human, since Viennese house-owners were among the most grasping and least conscientious in the world. But it makes a splendid political war-cry for elections, and the general election of 1923 was fought by the Social Democrat Party, not on theoretical or even broad issues, but simply and solely on the assertion that their opponents meant to abolish rent restrictions; and this disputed statement brought them in innumerable votes from those who like to live cheaply.

The actual social legislation of the period was in most cases a model of its kind. The Minister for Social Welfare was the late Ferdinand Hanusch, one of the most universally respected men in Austria. Beginning his career as a workman in one of the most miserably paid and situated industries in Europe—he was a weaver from the German districts of Bohemia, and to have some idea what a fate this was the reader may look to Gerhardt Hauptmann's *Die Weber*—he had a first-hand experience and understanding of the wants and hardships of the labouring classes. The measures passed under his auspices during a few months did more to better the condition of the masses than had previous decades of legislation from above. The list of them would be long. They include the introduction of insurance against accidents, the extension of that against sickness, State assistance for mothers and infants, a subsidy for children, the prohibition of night-work for women and juveniles, and of all work for children, the abolition of night-work for bakers, the laws legalising the eight-hour day and annual holidays for workmen, and a host of other measures for special cases. The sanitary measures, and the legislation for the protection of children, are particularly good and particularly necessary, considering the un-healthiness of Vienna under all circumstances and the fearful ravages caused by under-nourishment during the war and the years immediately succeeding it.

One or two of his measures had little more than a tem-porary justification, like the dole system which debased the currency. Such was a Bill passed in the spring of 1919 for the relief of unemployment, and compelling every employer of more than fourteen hands to increase his staff by twenty per cent. A whole network of complicated restrictions makes it very difficult for an employer to dis-charge a hand. Both in these measures and, one is reluctant to add, in the admirable eight-hour day, the Socialists have done much to justify the complaint of Austrian employers that "social burdens" make it impossible for them to com-pete on the world market. We will discuss in a later chapter how far they would in any case be able to compete; cer-tainly not far until antiquated methods are changed and overhead charges radically cut down. In the meanwhile, they do work at a heavy disadvantage as compared with Germany, and a levelling up will have to come from one side or the other if Austrian industry is to escape a swift and sure decline.

One of the most important institutions called into life in 1919 by the Socialising Commission—far more impor-tant, really, than the socialised concerns—is that of the

Works Councils[1], corresponding to our shop stewards. Although the idea was not new, it was now for the first time legalised and made compulsory. All staffs consisting regularly of at least twenty workers elected one or more councillors, according to their numbers. Analogous arrangements are made for the State services and for cases where the staff of one works is split up among several branches. Smaller works elect representatives, whose work is similar to that of the councillors on a reduced scale.

The duties of the Councils are laid down thus: "To attend to and prosecute the economic, social and cultural interests of the workmen and employees of a works." The law thus sets no definite limit to their activities, but calls special attention to a number of points, among them the following:

To co-operate with the trade unions, or to replace them where such are wanting, in seeing that collective wage agreements are adhered to, and where necessary, in improving and regulating them, and in fixing wages where no such agreements exist. To control the arrangement and duration of work, the books and payment of wages. To help in the administration of workmen's beneficent organisations, to watch over the observance of sanitary and other measures for the benefit of the workmen. To help preserve discipline among the staffs; and to prevent the members of a staff from being discharged on political grounds.

[1] By "Works" I translate the very general German word "Betrieb," defined by Adler as "any union, intended to last a long time, of forces of labour to attain definite results of labour. It includes therefore not only factories, but also public offices, museums, hotels, banks and businesses of all kinds."

The councillors have the right to examine trade balances, and to be represented, though without votes, on the boards of share companies.

All disputes with the employer are brought before a Court of Appeal, whose decision is final.

Wherever the work of the Councils brings them into contact with the trade unions, the latter override them.

Even if this institution has not borne all the fruits expected of it, it is yet probably the most important advance made by Austrian Socialism since the war. Its ultimate object is of course to fit the staffs to take over the work of their works in the Socialist State. Hitherto, the staffs have moved only a small way towards attaining this fitness. Except, for instance, in the case of some of the banks, the right to examine the books has proved of very platonic value. In the unsolid, get-rich-quick atmosphere prevalent since the war, the few subordinates intelligent enough to understand the books of their employers have usually preferred to turn their intelligence to their own uses in setting up businesses of their own. For the rest, the art of cooking balance sheets has been brought to such a high pitch in Austria that most employers can conceal what they want to conceal from their workmen. They have, after all, the experience of centuries to set off against that of four years. In the beginning, the abuses of the Councils' system were more obvious than its uses. The workmen, aggressive, new to their power and not yet conscious of its limitations, did a lot of harm both to themselves and their employers by meddling. The point on which most battles turned was the right of dismissal of a hand, and the Councils' system has heavily fortified the national character in causing that universal overstaffing which is one of the heaviest burdens on Austrian economic life[1]. These turbulent days are, however, passing, and many of the functions of the councillors are recognised as most helpful, not only to the staff, but also to the employers.

Politically, they are of the first importance. They secure for Socialism a foothold in the control of industry which, apart from its future value, should Socialism ever become general, is of the greatest present value to the Socialist Party. To this the councillors act as an intelligence service which is among the most efficient in Europe, supplying the party organisation with exact and detailed information, not only on the whole economic life of the country, but also on any vulnerable points which the individual capitalists may leave unguarded.

Another important gain for the workmen consists of the "Workmen's Chambers." This institution, which has not yet reached its full development, constitutes a legal representation of the interests of the workmen, able to meet on equal terms similar bodies representing the employers. The chambers have advisory, not executive, powers. Their objects are "to represent the economic interests of the working classes and to encourage efforts to better their economic and social situation," and to report, advise and mediate in social and economic-political questions, to keep relevant statistics and so on. The sections represent respectively industrial workmen, industrial salariat, and employees in the public services of communications. They are legally empowered to consult with the representatives of the

[1] Examples: (1) a newspaper office is not allowed to introduce modern mechanical type-setters, which save a very high percentage of labour; (2) the Viennese motor buses used to have a driver and two conductors each; to pay for their keep the fares were so high that the buses ran almost empty, and had to be taken off.

employers and chambers of commerce, and they are certainly among the most important of the too few links in Austria between employer and employee.

The work of these chambers, the statistical service, and the admirable library which is under their control, may one day make it possible to get an honest and impartial survey of labour conditions in Austria.

The above were the most important of the measures passed by the Social Democrat Party during its period of power, with the exception of the legislation on education, which aimed at making it more practical, less pedantic and free from Catholic influence. After just two years of participation in the Government it returned to opposition. "Without flattering ourselves," wrote one of the leaders, "we can say that of all proletarian groups we have achieved the greatest and the most practical gains from the revolution."

We have seen what these gains were. As a step towards the ultimate establishment of Socialism they were small. The institutions of the Works Councils and the Workmen's Chambers were probably the largest advances made in this direction; the actual experiments in socialisation are unimportant by comparison. They only extended their hold a little outside the classes of manual labour, leaving the other classes of society anything but reconciled to them. For the manual labourers they accomplished a very great deal along the lines of purely social legislation which was admirable of its kind.

The change from government to opposition did not really alter the party's position in many essentials. When in power, it was yet condemned to a large measure of impotence by the position of Austria as a vanquished State under Entente control, by the unruliness of its own members, and by the necessity of coalition with opponents little if at all less strong than itself. The Constitution of "the Federal State of Austria" is a very loose one, allowing wide local powers to the various provinces. This loose structure was imposed against the desire of the Socialists and at the will of their opponents, whose clerical instincts and local patriotism made the sway of Vienna abhorrent to them. Even during their governmental days, the Socialists fought an uphill battle outside Vienna, and their control only ran in the provinces to a very limited degree. But when they passed into opposition, this suddenly became an advantage for them. Vienna, separated from Lower Austria and raised to the dignity of a province, enjoyed the same autonomy which the country provinces had wrested for themselves, and since the municipality of Vienna was, and is likely to continue to be Socialist, the Social Democrat Party really found itself in possession of a practical power little diminished by its minority in Parliament. And even in the latter, it is so strong an opposition that any really important Government measure has to be bought with concessions, often perforce very liberal ones.

The municipality of Vienna is to-day probably the chief stronghold of Social Democracy in Europe. It is a curiously paradoxical fortress. Its finances are controlled by an extremely clever Jew, one of the finest financial brains in Austria, who went over to it from private banking. It made much of its reserves of capital by purely capitalist methods, and was in fact one of the heaviest buyers in Austria of foreign currencies at the time when all the banks were selling the krone and forcing it down. The remainder of its assets—what is raised by taxation—is drawn, after all, mostly from the profits of capitalist enterprises. This taxation is extremely, even crushingly, heavy. In any case, Vienna supplies nearly the whole of the taxation of Austria, since the peasants still pay very lightly on their small properties, and there are no other towns approaching the size or wealth of Vienna. It is the heart, the brain and the purse of Austria, and a very useful asset for Socialism to control.

This taxation is in no way applied for the benefit of the Social Democrat Party, but it is applied to objects which the party has at heart, and of which the principal contributors heartily disapprove. Whether they are right in doing so or not raises the question on which this work will express no opinion, as to whether Socialism is right and desirable or not. The best example of what I mean here is the building scheme mentioned above, which, if continued long enough, will gradually transfer the house property of the city into the hands of the municipality. It is in every way an admirably conducted concern, which not only carries out its duties most efficiently, but manages, while doing so, to pay its employees at a rate averaging some thirty-three per cent. higher than the groaning State of Austria can afford. It is a piquant situation, since the municipality is not, at any rate directly, liable for reparations or for the Entente loan, which makes its position particularly enviable when it is remembered that the Government of Austria is obliged to ask the permission of the financial controller of the League of Nations for any increase in its expenditure.

This fortunate circumstance has enabled the municipality to take over a number of matters which would perhaps ordinarily be under State control, and doubtless their list would be extended still farther were it not for the political opposition which refuses to see vantage-points pass into Socialist hands, even when they would themselves temporarily gain thereby.

As it is, the line between the powers of State and municipality (provinces) is very indistinctly drawn, and numerous conflicts arise, some of which are very comic. A good example of these is the famous crematorium question, which, after months or years, is still agitating Vienna.

The Catholic Church, on the strength of some passage in the Bible, objects to disposing of dead bodies other than by burial. A very obscure statute issued by, I believe, Josef II, is the latest thing in Austrian legislation concerning the disposal of corpses, and this is so worded as to leave it uncertain as to whether State or province has authority in this matter. If it is the State, so long as the Government is Christian Socialist it stands by Mother Church and burial under all circumstances. If it is the province, it is not so bound, and the mere fact that the Church dislikes something constitutes an irresistible temptation to Austrian Socialists to go and do it. The municipality of Vienna, accordingly, declared with a great flourish that a crematorium is an indispensable sign of culture, and built one. The Government quietly waited until it was all ready, and a suitable corpse in waiting, and then stepped in and forbade the cremation. The municipality, headed by the Burgomaster, damned the consequences and burned the corpse. The Government brought actions, firstly against the Burgomaster, secondly against the municipality. I forget how the matter ended, if it has yet ended at all. I believe the first Court declared that the

Socialists had transgressed in ignorance; once did not matter, but they must not do it again. But they burned someone else, and everybody appealed, and then, I believe, the last Court of Appeal of all gave judgement in favour of the municipality, so corpses are still being burned, but not in any great numbers, for the Viennese are not so cultivated as all that, and most of them, unless they are very keen politicians, really prefer to be buried.

At other times, the consequences of these differences are extremely tragic. An old statute allowed the Statthalter, or chiefs of provincial governments, to grant a dispensation permitting of re-marriage in cases where the Catholic Church forbade this. As, however, the Statthalter were always Catholics, this right was never exercised, so that no question was asked as to its validity. The first Social Democrat to hold the equivalent position at once made use of his authority, and numerous marriages were contracted on the strength of it. In some cases, however, the former husband or wife appealed, calling in question the legality of the later marriage. As the whole law is quite obscure, its interpretation depends largely on the personal views of the judge who happens to try the case; and it has been known that couples who have lived together for years, and founded families, have suddenly and without warning been declared adulterous and their children illegitimate.

But even apart from these disputed points, the municipality enjoys wide powers. It has always been accustomed to play a part in politics. In the Imperial days it was a stronghold of the Christian Socialists, whose famous leader, Lueger, made his name as burgomaster. In his era more attention was paid to public building, beautification and equipping the city with all the modern appliances now considered necessary. To-day the interest is far more directly concerned with the needs of the poor; their housing, schooling and especially their health. In their municipal, as in their State legislation, it is true that by far the best work accomplished by the Socialists has been that performed on behalf of the sick or the youthful.

It is behind this formidable bulwark that the Social Democrats to-day, driven from the Government, have been able to take up their stand. Outside Vienna they have little power; in the municipal governments of the few other large or middle-sized towns in Austria; in the mining and metal-working districts of Lower Austria and Styria along the lines of communications. Such as they are, they have constituted themselves to all intents and purposes a State within the State.

Thus with finance; they have not been able to get the Government taxation which they desired imposed on the peasants or the Church; but in Vienna, which provides seventy per cent. of Austria's total State income, they can impose municipal taxes to their hearts' content on the capitalists. The socialised institutions which they control are few, but in every business, every bank, every factory, they command the allegiance of the hands, and can reach into the innermost workings of the concern, to some small extent even determine its policy, through the Works Councillors.

Their power in the army has steadily declined. The Minister of War is now a Conservative, the authority of officers has replaced that of the Soldiers' Councillors. Yet they have an effective hold still. The bulk of the rank and file are Socialists, and organised in an obedient trade

11·2

union; the Parliamentary Commission, which controls the doings of the War Office, is headed by a Socialist; and, finally, there exists a hardly secret Socialist army, armed, drilled, uniformed, and two or three times as strong as the official force.

The railways, posts and telegraphs are owned and administered by the State. But although among some old servants of the Empire the former loyalty has not died away, the bulk of the employees are organised Socialists, members of trade unions and ready, as experience has shown, cheerfully to strike and paralyse the economic life of the country at a word from the leaders. When one remembers that Socialists also control the water and light of Vienna, it will be seen that, should matters come to a real emergency, the last word in policy rests with their leaders.

There are co-operative stores which, in spite of continuous financial difficulties, remain among the largest institutions of the world. There is a Workmen's Bank, and also the municipal savings banks. There are separate organisations for juveniles and children, educational institutions, bookshops and libraries, a party school, a "free-thinker's league," a teetotaller's league, a number of athletic and sporting clubs. It is a compact and well-organised State, settled firmly within the greater State, and hardly yielding to its power.

Finally, there is the same intimate touch with the trade unions which has always been so characteristic of the party, a legacy of the days before the franchise and the early work of Victor Adler, and to-day perhaps more conspicuous than ever.

It is not likely that the position of the Social Democrat

Party will change very greatly in the near future. The efforts of various groups to coax away the manual labourers from it have all failed, even under the most favourable conditions. Over these its hold is very strong, and rightly, since it has brought them a welcome and belated change in their conditions, and has not only raised them to be a political power, but has actually done a great deal to improve their material conditions. In more spiritual fields it has been less successful. The will is there, but still too little understanding. There is always the narrow and bigoted condemnation of the good contained in other systems of thought, or brought by other political parties, the same often unjudging approval of whatever those others preferred to condemn. The only two directions in which it might still achieve an expansion are among the lower grades of brain-workers who still remain hostile to them, and possibly among the poorer peasants.

But there is little chance that the Austrian Socialists will convert the remainder of the country to their point of view. The resistance to be overcome, headed as it is by the Church, would in any case be enormous. Even so, when their chance came, they could have made much more impression than they did had they been less narrow, less selfish and less materialistic. Their period of office did not give the impression that their ranks contained statesmen. There was one exception—Otto Bauer, an intellect of first order. But even Bauer, although he certainly had it in him to rise above party politics to statesmanship, in the main failed to do so. He, almost alone, showed that he understood the point of view of other classes in the nation, and their right to have a point of view. But, perhaps under the pressure of overwork, he failed to do much to meet it.

Nor can one honestly hope that the party, as it is at present, should advance its control much farther. The next step for it, now that its position is consolidated, would be to eliminate its faults. With all that it has achieved, it remains narrow, bigoted, doctrinaire and materialistic. And nominally fighting for democracy, it has never been above crushing its opponents by means honest or dishonest, forcing minorities to bow to its will, and imposing its ideas by methods which are the reverse of democratic.

CHAPTER VII

THE PEASANT

THE progress of the peasant has been so much less noisy than that of the industrial worker that we are very apt to neglect it, even to ignore its very existence. Looking back on a century of industrial development we find our attention fettered by the fate of those most immediately concerned in its processes and forget that the prime problem is not to secure tolerable conditions of living for the individual workman—for social legislation could regulate this—but to adjust the relations of his class as a whole to the rest of society. And society is based in the last end on the tiller of the soil.

Most laborious, most essential of mankind, his lot has yet seldom been a happy one. The workman in a hundred years has achieved an organisation and a fighting power which has enabled him to push his claim up to the extreme limit, or over it, which society can stand. The peasant has no weapon but that of passive resistance, and if it is strong it is blunt. His condition in Austria, at any rate, his social and economic position, has deteriorated rather than improved through long periods, and is probably little better to-day than it was six hundred years ago. If he has raised himself a small way from the earth, it is only to find priest and noble, capitalist and socialist, clamber on his broad back.

The first German settlers in the Eastern Alps were all peasants and warriors alike, free men serving only their own elected rulers. The Slavs whom they conquered and dispossessed were in many cases enslaved; yet the peasant class as a whole was a free one, and traces of its liberties lingered on for centuries in tradition and custom. As late as 1597 the Archduke of Austria, entering his dukedom of Carinthia, was received by a peasant and before he could " drive him from his seat" had to promise him to be a just judge, a patriotic ruler and a true Christian, and to make him presents.

But by that date such ceremonies were already no more than ritual. Mainly under the exigencies of incessant campaigns, a complicated feudal system had grown up, and a numerous lay and clerical nobility had established itself. The system of "Estates," which formed the basis of Austria's construction up to modern times, had been developed. These Estates were four in number: the Church, the nobility, the burghers, the peasants, and three of them were strong and one was weak. To him that has been given more shall be added. The monarchs had still no firm grasp over their unwieldy realms. The privileged classes found ever new means to extort fresh powers and prerogatives, while on the unfortunate peasants was heaped increasingly the whole burden of the State.

Taxes, duties, services multiplied. Besides the robot or forced labour on the lands of the master or for the State there were payments in money and kind, service of horse and cart, dues on hunting and fishing, tithes and a host of minor burdens. The unfree peasants were literally slaves; their masters could sell, exchange or pawn them at will.

The sixteenth century, the time of the great social and religious unrest, brought a series of desperate peasants' risings. In the Tirol alone, a district ever distinguished for its hardy and independent race, which has always retained a large measure of liberties, did these bring any advantage to their participants[1]. In most other parts of the Habsburg possessions, and especially in the non-German districts, they were crushed savagely. In Hungary the captured peasant "King" was seated on a throne of white-hot iron, a white-hot crown pressed on his head and a sceptre in his hand, and his starving followers forced to eat of his still living and roasting limbs. This in the year of our Lord 1516. After this war, the personal freedom of the peasant was abolished altogether in Hungary and Bohemia.

In the German districts matters did not go to such extremes, partly because the religious movement among the peasants had also spread widely among the burghers and nobles. The peasant never became technically a "chattel" in German-Austria. Yet, after the Jacqueries had failed, the shackles were fastened very firmly on his wrists. He was forbidden to practise any burgher's trade, or to emigrate to the greater liberty of the towns ("Town air makes free" ran the old edict), and might not buy land from burghers nor they from him. The Counter-Reformation crushed the Protestant movement none too gently, and drove the more independent spirits into exile; the remainder settled down under the strict surveillance of the Catholic Church.

In the eighteenth century matters changed at last. The feudal system was in its death throes. The long wars, especially the Thirty Years' War, had broken the power

---

[1] In this province the peasants were represented in the provincial Estates until they were abolished in 1848. Elsewhere, only nobles and clergy in person, and towns through a very small number of deputies, were represented.

of the privileged classes, and the monarchs were busy
erecting on the evacuated field a strong State, centralised
round the Crown and administered no longer by a feudal
aristocracy but by paid officials. A strong and flourishing
peasantry was a necessity to the "benevolent despots,"
both as a counterweight to the nobles and as a source for
the heavy taxes now demanded by the State's finances.
These taxes could not be paid so long as three-quarters
of the peasant's income was absorbed by dues and tithes
and his productive time shortened by robot, which was
growing more and more burdensome in consequence of
the rural depopulation and scarcity of tenants for the
bigger estates.

However genuine, therefore, the benevolence of Maria
Theresa and Josef II, yet "their heads certainly guided
their hands," as the palmistry books say. Their reforms
were strongly influenced by the "physiocrat" school of
thought, then popular, whose axiom it was that the land
is a source of all wealth and must be a first object of
solicitude of the State. The economic motive underlying
them appears very clearly in the fact that they stopped
short of the farm-labourers and assistants.

But for the peasants their benefits were great. Robot
was reduced to strict limits; on the Habsburg estates
abolished altogether. Dues were regulated and reduced;
and the peasants protected by tariffs and secured in their
possession by laws forbidding the overlord to take a
peasant's property for himself, or transfer it to another
person at will. He was allowed to marry freely, to change
his abode, to practise a trade, to sell or exchange his
property. Commissions were set up to protect him against
the overlord and he was even accorded free legal repre-

sentation in them. All dues in kind might be transmuted
in money or paid up in a lump sum. Personal servitude
was abolished.

These reforms still left much undone, but their effect
was to place the peasants of German-Austria in a condition which was not, perhaps, so bad as it appeared. If
the dues and taxes were numerous they were usually small.
By far the heaviest burden attendant on the state of serfdom,
or of the "nexus subditelae" introduced in its stead by
Josef II, was that of the robot. In countries such as Bohemia, Hungary or Galicia, where the great land-owning
nobles cultivated their own estates on a large scale, the
due of robot was ruthlessly exercised, often far beyond its
legal limitations. Its effect was paralysing for the peasant;
for the lord naturally called for the labour at harvest time
and other seasons when it was most urgently needed. The
peasant was therefore obliged to leave his land untilled just
at the moment when it was most necessary for him to work
on it. In the mountains, on the other hand, agriculture
on a large scale was not practised. The peasant was truly
in the position of a tenant farmer. The actual forced labour
exacted was small in quantity, the landlord being recompensed by payments in money or kind, which weighed
much less heavily on the peasant.

Furthermore, the institution of common land had been
preserved in the mountains to a much greater extent than
elsewhere, and played a much more important part.
Broadly speaking, only the land in the valleys—which are
usually very narrow—is suitable either for arable land or
for putting up for hay, and only such land was really the
private property of the peasant (under his lord). Every
commune possessed in addition a greater or lesser quantity

of common land, usually situated on the neighbouring hills, and surrounded by the forests. This was common land, and every villager had the right to graze his cattle there. As his cattle were and are the mainstay of the Austrian peasant's life, these common rights were of the greatest importance to him, and so long as he enjoyed them, he was not reduced to the last extremities. In addition, the peasants of a community enjoyed certain rights in the mountain forests, which in long-ago days had been no-man's land. In some cases they were allowed to graze their cattle there; always to gather wood for their own use, both as firewood and for domestic purposes, and often to take away fallen leaves and soil for manure.

These rights were continually contested by the overlord and in many—most—cases had been reduced far within their original limits. This was not, however, altogether a disadvantage, as experience was to prove. For forests are things which have to be treated delicately, and if the peasants had been allowed to cut down timber and cart away wood-loam at their own sweet will, they would soon have reduced the green Austrian mountains to the rocky desolation of the Herzegovinian or Carniolan steppes. As things were, the overlord guarded the peasants against themselves.

Similarly in the valleys, the peasant's land was only really his own so long as the crop was on it. He was obliged to sow and reap it simultaneously with his neighbours, and with similar crops. In the winter, when the mountains were snowed over, he was obliged to leave it free for the common grazing.

This state of semi-communism had as its result that the peasants clung together. If none were rich, few were destitute. This was, in fact, the aim of the legislation of the time. The distinction between dominical land, which only a noble could own, and urbarial land, which was reserved for peasants, and many other provisions against dividing up a farm, and against one peasant's owning more than one farm, were all directed towards maintaining a prosperous yeoman class. The peasant's tenure of land was in the main secure; it was common for it to be hereditary in a family, descending from father to elder son.

Yet another point about these days must not be forgotten. The peasants were the chief taxpayers of the community; but they were not the providers of its larder. The policy of the day was to encourage industry and to pay for imports of foodstuffs by exports of manufactured articles. It was, as many think, a radically false policy, and one of the chief reasons of Austria's lamentable financial situation. But the result for the peasant was that he had few dealings with money. Even his dues and payments were largely made in kind. His farm supplied the bulk of his own wants; and where he needed some articles which only a craftsman could manufacture, the raw material—the leather and what not—was frequently supplied from his own produce.

Semi-communism under strict restraint was in many ways a very healthy state for the ignorant peasant of the time. It was, however, accompanied by grave burdens. He was obliged to let the landlord graze his cattle over his stubble; to suffer without resistance depredations of game —and deer, where numerous, can work extraordinary havoc in a forest region; to pay dues and taxes; to supply the army with recruits from among his sons, and to receive the troops quartered on him. Furthermore, his own landlord was the magistrate who sat in judgement on him, and although an appeal to the Imperial Courts was allowed, its action was slow and its results little fruitful.

The growing discontent against the patrimonial courts —which was shared by the nobles themselves—and against the robot and dues, was one of the mainsprings of the revolution of 1848; although in that revolution it was the Bohemian, Galician and Hungarian peasants whose deeper grievances played a much more important part, the German-Austrian peasantry remaining comparatively passive.

The one great success of the revolution was the liberation of the peasant throughout all the Habsburg Monarchy. The patrimonial courts were abolished. Robot was done away with altogether. All dues based on the "nexus sub-ditelae" vanished without compensation, and the remaining dues were paid off at a cheap rate. It was calculated that the peasant himself had to pay in compensation not more than one-eighteenth of the value of his old obligations.

He now enjoyed complete freedom, the status of citizen, and equality before the law with all other citizens of Austria.

Time has brought him no further political changes, except two: the fall of the Monarchy, which has put into every peasant's hay-cart the baton of the President of the Republic (if the metaphor is allowable in connection with so essentially unmilitary an office); and the extension of the suffrage, which has ended by handing him a good half of the votes in the new Republic.

It is time to consider what manner of man this is, and what are the conditions under which he exercises the rights so painfully and belatedly attained.

Geographically, modern Austria falls into two distinct parts. The Alps, running the whole way from Switzerland to the old Hungarian frontier, occupy with their rugged configurations, their snowcapped summits, their forested flanks and narrow valleys practically the whole of Vorarlberg, Tirol, Salzburg, Carinthia, Styria, and the southern portions of Upper and Lower Austria. In all these provinces the only at all considerable plain is that round Graz in Styria. The northern portions of Upper and Lower Austria and the Burgenland are partly hilly, partly filled by the flat Danubian plain. The southern Burgenland stands apart, being still almost without communications with the rest of Austria, a gentle and pleasant land of undulating hills, of woods and orchards. Industry is concentrated round Vienna, in the plain between the capital and Wiener Neustadt and in the ore-bearing districts in the Styrian mountains. The rest of Austria is almost exclusively an agricultural land of peasant proprietors. The nobility, with few exceptions, is concentrated in Vienna and the middle classes are completely urban in their tastes. The one great land-owning family, the Habsburgs, was expropriated in 1919. The only large landowners to-day are the Church, whose rich convents own some of the most fertile country along the Danube, and the State, with large forests in the mountains.

The peasantry of the plains, with the advantages of comparatively fertile soils, proximity to market and better communications, is able to produce a surplus of meat,

corn, and especially milk for the towns. This class is, however, in a great minority compared with the small peasant
proprietors of the mountains[1].

His methods and characteristics may be taken as those
of the peasant as a whole; by his fate all Austria, outside
Vienna and a few other centres, stands and falls.

We have given in a few words his history. Rightly to
understand his character is more difficult. The sentimen-
talist, whose ideas are usually a rosy confusion of Andreas
Hofer and Vergil's *Eclogues*, is no less far and no farther
out than the superior city-bred man who dismisses the
peasant contemptuously as a mere clod, "hornless cattle."
The world of the peasant is a world apart into which few
strangers have ever really penetrated.

It is perfectly true to say of him, as his detractors
invariably do with their first breath, that he is absolutely,
obstinately, mulishly, incurably conservative. It is true,
moreover, to add that this conservatism is largely due to
both ignorance and stupidity, and that both are partly of
his own making. The reason is not far to seek. His life
is an incredibly hard one. From dawn to dusk he wrings
a scanty living in the sweat of his brow from stubborn and
ungrateful fields. In this harsh and precipitous land, on
these small and scattered properties, the work is far harder,
the hours far longer than on a large well-organised estate.
Each member of his small staff must be Jack of all trades,

[1] The figures of the *Österreichisches Jahrbuch* for 1922 (exclusive
of the Burgenland) reckon 4·5% of the total surface of Austria as
plain, 3·2% as hills, 92·3% as mountains. 89·1% of all properties
belong to the peasants, only 0·6% to large proprietors, and many of
the latter are let to small tenants (most of the Church lands). 10·3%
of the properties are less than $\frac{1}{2}$ hectare; 41·6% between $\frac{1}{2}$ and 5 hectares; only 2·7% over 50 hectares. The Burgenland still contains the
large estates of some noble Hungarian familes, notably the Esterhazy.

ready to attend to the horses and cattle, the sowing, ploughing and harvesting, the carting and marketing, the repairs and housework. The grown man has few hours of freedom, the woman and child none of those leisured years which we accord them as of right. The peasant woman is one of the most hardly-used creatures in the world. To an almost ceaseless drudgery on the farm she adds the toil of bearing and bringing up children, both of which processes she is consequently apt to perform hurriedly and carelessly, with disastrous results. As for the child, nominally his education up to the age of fourteen is compulsory. Actually, the peasant boycotts this law, and generally contrives to get the child to work at the farm by the time he is twelve years old. For him, theory and book-learning are things to be eschewed, even opposed actively. Manual labour of the narrowest kind, the nose to the plough, alone produces tangible results, and this alone does he hold useful. Thus, by his own action, he perpetuates the backwardness, spiritual and economic, of his class.

Outside of the routine of his farm, he has only two main interests, and both seem joined in an unholy alliance to keep him back: they are his religion and his drink.

The Catholic Church in Austria is intimately connected with the peasant's life in a way not easy for an Englishman to picture. Perhaps wisely, it has made no attempt to imitate the ideal of a "resident country gentleman in every parish." The local priest stands on a lower pedestal above his flock than the English parson. He is less immune from the common frailties of their flesh, but the nearer for that to their lives. Like his creed as a whole, he is warmer, more human, more tolerant of backsliding. He is most often himself a peasant's son, not differing greatly from his congregation in birth, education or even morals. But he is able to tap a natural supply of religious feeling, welling up alike in his soul and theirs, and, on the whole, he exerts the great influence which this gives him well according to his lights.

The peasant has little knowledge of the wide world, of his fellow-men, or even of the State, except as an oppressive force which takes the produce of his labour for taxes, or calls his son away from the plough to serve in the army. But he is continually face to face with God. God placed him where he is. God's bounty sent the harvest, God's act let down the hail and snow. The often incalculable moods of nature, on which his existence depends, are the decrees of God. Religion, his relation to God, colours all his life.

Indeed, his religion knows very little of abstruse theology, is very full of superstition, very nearly akin to nature-worship. The peasant's prayers do not differ greatly, except in the matter of proper names, from those which his dim forbears offered up to the tutelary deities of wood and stream, summer and winter. Old thoughts linger on and old customs. In the lighting of fires and the drawing of waters, the ploughing and harvesting, he follows with awe the customs of his pagan ancestors; and the only change is that his propitious and unpropitious days have put on new dresses and appear now as the Eve of St John, or the feast of the Conception.

This very blending with the earth and with old tradition makes his religion a very living thing. Not only the church in every little village bears witness to it, but the countless tiny shrines at the wayside, at the cross-roads, on the edge of the field. As he passes them, he crosses himself and

mutters a prayer; and on Sundays and his numerous holidays he leads down his family and household to worship
in the nearest church.

These reunions during and after Mass are not only the
spiritual occasions in his life but also almost the only
opportunities for social intercouse. Partly owing to the
selfishness and apathy of the richer classes, partly to the
conformation of the country, partly to the jealousy of the
priests, there is in Austria hardly any village life in the
English sense of clubs, reading-rooms, or working classes.
Outside the villages large enough to run a "Verein,"
musical, religious, or political, social life is confined to the
church or the village inn.

The absence of competition is a treasured advantage
of the Church. Only Socialism seriously challenges its
supremacy, and is therefore anathema to it. The mentality
of the peasant of the old style is peculiarly acceptable to
the Church. Submissiveness to authority, contentment
with one's lot, are virtues fragrant in God's nostrils, a
pleasant contrast to the stinking unrest, Socialism, atheism,
which the life of the great cities engenders. The ideal of
the Church is a healthy peasantry, decently prosperous,
but not necessarily endowed either with great riches or
with great brains. It is satisfied with the *status quo*, perhaps optimistically; but is logical in seeing nothing but
harm in all that we associate with the idea of progress.
The priest is not afraid to denounce Socialism from the
altar as a combination of Satan, to threaten its followers in
the confessional with the pains of hell-fire. And in her
anxiety to avoid the bad of modern times the Church has
narrowly rejected much of the good. She fought consistently
against the introduction of lay education, against the

lengthening of school years, even against modern ways of agriculture, and has made herself to no small degree responsible for the backwardness and much of the poverty of her adherents.

She has certainly succeeded in producing much that is to be liked and admired in the character of the peasant. But his moral code shows liberal gaps, often caused by the bouts of excess with which he recoups himself for the enforced austerity of his working hours. The percentage of illegitimacy among the children is startling: in Carinthia, if I remember rightly, something about forty per cent.[1]

He is hard and quarrelsome, and the holiday evenings often end in a general scrap. His vices spring to a large extent from the besetting sin of drunkenness, a great evil in Austria, which the Church as a whole has done scandalously little to combat, and has often even fostered in her character of large proprietor of vineyards, breweries and distilleries. Individual priests make brave efforts, but the Socialists, who have made temperance one point of their programme, have a right to claim great credit for it.

On Sundays and holidays, as soon as Mass is over, the congregation is wont to pass the rest of the day in the village inn, drinking, smoking, grumbling at the weather and talking politics. The strayed revellers who return home late at night are guided rather by God and long habit than by any clear perception of the road. These sessions often have disastrous sequels. For this is the time when romance most frequently alights on the peasant's horny breast, and

[1] This is largely due to the fact that the labourers, who cannot become independent farmers, are unable to marry. They were long legally forbidden to do so, and even to-day marriage is practically impossible for them.

these tipsy unions are largely responsible for the numerous cretins and idiots of the mountain parishes[1].

For the work of 1848 still left much undone. The purely political aspect of the task was quickly and easily performed; no less so the abolition of the robot and the dues, although their astounding complication took several years to unravel—in Moravia there were no less than 246 different kinds of obligation—but the further task of creating a peasantry equal to the demands of modern life proved too difficult for the legislators.

The legislation of the time was strongly influenced by the ideas of economic liberalism, controlled at the same time by the political absolutism and centralism with which the Emperor Franz Josef began his reign. The political administration of the country was completely reorganised, and political communes, under bureaucratic control, took the place of the old village community, with no good results.

It has already been pointed out how greatly the cattle-raising Alpine peasant was dependent on his share in the common land of the village community[2]. The rights which he enjoyed as a commoner were at least as important to him as his position as proprietor. While his farm and his field in the valley now became undisputedly his own, he

---

[1] The case of these idiots is pitiable to a degree. A case was recently reported where a Styrian peasant had kept his half-witted brother locked in a stable for twenty years. It is not uncommon for the parents of idiots to lock them in stables, pigsties or even underground and keep them there till they die, merely throwing them, from time to time, a little animal fodder on the end of a pitchfork, to salve their consciences of the charge of murder.

[2] Even after the process here detailed, it was estimated that fourteen per cent. of the whole taxable area of the old Austria, and thirty-one per cent. of the pasture-land, forests, etc., were in the hands of communities. The proportion was much higher in the mountainous districts, that is, in the Austria of to-day.

lost at the same time a great proportion of his rights as a commoner.

In the numerous cases where the peasants had enjoyed rights of pasturage and the like in the forests of the overlord, these rights were now reduced. In some cases, they were merely limited; in others the overlord bought the peasants out on a system which, as in the converse case, proved very advantageous to the paying party. In a third category of instances, specified tracts of land were handed over to individual peasants in lieu of their old rights over a wider area.

The common lands of the villages were also greatly reduced. Through a frequent confusion, commoner rights were identified with private property. In both these processes no regard was paid to rounding off individual properties, so that their scattered character was increased at the very time when a proper reform should have reduced it. In 1916, in the Tirol, eighty-three per cent. of the landed properties were thus split up, some of them over a very wide area. In Dalmatia, one hundred per cent. were split up.

The whole of the old communal life was thus thrown into confusion. In some cases the peasants lost their old rights altogether. In others, the rights remained, but the proper control over their exercise was gone. In others again, they were exchanged for the temporary advantage of private property.

The liberal legislation of the time, meanwhile, aimed at creating the greatest possible mobility of real property, acting on the idea that the automatic result of such mobility is that the land eventually comes to him who is best fitted to own it. The old safeguards against selling were removed —this in the case of the peasants only, since the entails of the great properties remained intact. The peasant was required to enter the lists with the financier and the great landlord as an equal competitor, neither artificially helped, nor artificially restrained.

At the same time, the transformation which modern life brings with it was beginning to change the face of Austria. Factories were springing up, roads and railways being built, organised industry killing the old home industry which had supplemented the peasant's income from time immemorial and occupied his winter evenings. The change was all in the favour of the few prosperous farmers of the valleys, where communications were good and the sale and utilisation of by-products feasible. These fortunate few were able to introduce modern methods, to profit by new conditions and to become real agricultural producers.

It was otherwise with the poor mountain peasants. They got all the disadvantages, few of the advantages of the change. On their small, scattered properties, their rocky mountain sides and forest steeps, modern methods of farming were inapplicable, even had the necessary capital been available. Unable to produce for sale, accustomed to supply their own wants and those of their families by the labour of their hands, while their few cheap necessaries were supplied by the profits of home industry and the occasional sale of a cow, they now found the need for ready money ever increasing—the more so as prices rose steadily—while the opportunities for acquiring it were stationary[1].

This process was not so apparent during the first years

---

[1] The story is world-wide and eternal. Cf. A. E. Zimmermann, *The Greek Commonwealth*, pp. 110–113; Damaschke, *Die Bodenreform*, tells the story as it happened among the Greeks, Romans and Hebrews.

after 1848, since the abolition of servitude did result in a great moral impulse and a remarkable improvement in production. But the defects of the new order soon became apparent. Economic liberalism gave free rein to the spoliation of the countryside, and especially of the forests, on which so much else depends. Even the large proprietors were felling their timber recklessly, to keep pace with the new demands. It was but natural that the peasants should follow suit. It was each man for himself. The common land was left uncared for, and devastated ruthlessly. The plots of woodland which the peasants had received in compensation for their old rights were laid bare. The deforestation brought about a general impoverishment of the country's natural resources, and very quickly of the individual peasants.

In a very short time the peasants were back in a new state of economic slavery. Their debts multiplied; they were obliged to mortgage their farms. Before the war no less than eighty per cent. of the peasant properties were mortgaged, often very heavily. The price of land is notoriously everywhere disproportionately high, as compared with the monetary value of its annual yield, and Austria was no exception. Especially when the effects of American competition began to be felt, the price paid by the travelling dealer for the peasant's produce was too low to be set off against the interests of the mortgages. Interest on debt became a heavier burden than rent had been. An increasing number of peasants sold their land and went to the towns in the hope of better things. *Nepioi.* They prospered little there; the men supplied generally the roughest forms of manual labour, the women the lower grades of household work. Other farmers were ruined through shortage of labour, since the farm-hands began to desert the land for the higher pay and shorter hours of the factory. Rural depopulation became a very serious problem, especially in the upper mountains. Large tracts were bought up by rich men who turned them into forests or sporting estates. The peasants who remained on the edge of these estates suffered in their turn from the depredations of game, the increase of weeds, and the hostility of the foresters.

Peter Rosegger, the Hesiod of Styria, has drawn a moving picture of the gradual disappearance of one such mountain parish in his novel *Jakob der Letzte*. A rich man wants to make a sporting estate and buys out the local peasants. The richest peasant of the district, tempted by a heavy price, goes early, and the others, now an arch without its keystone, follow one by one. The forest creeps up, the shades overhang the fields and the deer destroy the crops of the few who remain. The forester uses every trick to bully them into yielding, and at last all give way save one. He sticks doggedly to his ancestors' home, but under increasingly difficult conditions. After many years he enjoys the sour satisfaction of seeing his one-time neighbours return, broken by the hard competition of the outside world. The single survivor is driven to killing the deer, is caught and imprisoned. At last, in despair, he shoots the forester and commits suicide. An old friend puts up his rough tombstone—"Jakob Steinreuther, the last peasant of Altenmoos."

Although this history is not quite as usual as logrollers have made out, it is not very rare, nor painted untruly. The relations between forester and peasant are often most unhappy. As recently as 1923 a remarkable case occurred in the Burgenland. A certain forester was said to prevent the peasants from exercising their rights of grazing and gathering fuel, to molest them and to get them imprisoned on false charges. He was lynched by the infuriated villagers, and some thirty-five persons, including women and young boys, were committed to trial for his murder.

Much contributed to this unfortunate state of things. The structure of the Dual Monarchy, contrary to the general belief in England, was singularly unfavourable to economic advance. The problem of keeping a majority of the conflicting nationalities politically satisfied took up the time and energies of the Government.

The economic advantage of the reforms was therefore very incomplete, and was not greatly increased in the latter half of the century. The inner political history of Austria was a tragic record of unfruitful bargainings and exchanges. The Ministry of Agriculture changed hands twenty-seven times between 1868 and 1916. One Minister ruled for over fifteen years; the other twenty-six averaged under two years each. Relations with Hungary had to be settled anew every few years, and the basis of the adjustment was actually differently defined in the German and the Hungarian versions of the same "legislation." In the family, as it were, things were no better. If the Czechs needed a special grant for improvements, the Germans demonstrated against the favouritism of granting it, and by the time they were quieted the Ruthenes or the Dalmatians or someone else had chipped in. Politics degenerated into what has been called "an undignified system of tips," under which either a necessary improvement had to be given up because so many mouths wanted a bite at it that it became impossibly expensive; or else it was given, not to him who needed it most, but to him whose good temper was best worth buying by the Ministry of the moment. The comparison drawn by Strakosch[1] between Austrian and German conditions is illuminating as to the results of these methods. Austrian railways were much fewer than German and much more expensive, both in construction and in upkeep. Freights on them were higher by some ten per cent.; the price of agricultural implements and machinery averaged from twenty to thirty per cent. higher, and every difficulty which could attend the producer was heightened in much the same proportion.

Nor must one forget an overwhelmingly important and little-considered factor; the political influence of the great landed aristocracy, and especially that of Hungary and Galicia, in Austrian politics. Up to the turn of the century this class was quite frankly favoured out of all proportion to its numbers by the system of electoral colleges on which Austrian representation was based. The peasants had little direct voice in affairs at all; their only representation was through the " colleges " of country communes in the Diets. To this must be added the great personal influence of the aristocracy on Franz Josef. In large matters and small —in hunting rights in Lower Austria or in tariff wars with Serbia—it was the interests of the great proprietors which were consulted. Occasionally they coincided with those of the small peasants; often they ran directly counter to them.

Once the work of liberation had been accomplished, shamefully little legislation was passed in the direct interests of the peasants until the end of the century. The franchise had then been extended, the agitation of the Christian-Socialists swept the country, and the villagers began to combine in their own interest. For the first time,

[1] *Grundlagen der Agrarwirtschaft in Oesterreich.* Vienna, 1916.

an attempt was then made to get the vexed question of the grazing and pasturage rights put on a proper footing. Such legislation was, however, local, and very various.

At the same time, the Christian Socialist Party started an economic movement, parallel with its political organisation. A co-operative movement was set on foot, on strongly clerical lines. Farm produce was stored in bulk and sold direct to the consumer, and the machinery bought with the proceeds was hired out to the members for a fee proportionate to the size of the estate and the time of use required.

This organisation did a good deal of benefit, especially among the more prosperous yeoman farmers who alone could make full use of it. This richer peasant class attached itself firmly to the Christian Socialist Party and began to form a solid class of small capitalists. Nevertheless, progress was slow. Its ideas were unsympathetic to the individualist peasants who preferred their own ways, even where these were less profitable to themselves. Furthermore, the movement, being anti-Semitic, had to dispense with the help of the strongest and most intelligent force in Austria—the Jews. It was therefore at first so inefficiently and expensively run as to yield really only a very small improvement. It was only after a very long time that it took root, and such is the nature of the country, so scattered the farms, that it can never hope to become so widespread as the corresponding movements in more favoured countries.

It took a world war to change the mentality and conditions of life of the Austrian peasant. Three-fifths of the army were recruited from the admirable fighting stock of the peasants and the first calling up notices were enough to create a disastrous shortage of labour, whose swift aggravation could not be remedied by all the anxious measures of the Government: by releasing them for harvest labour or employing prisoners of war. Many of the peasants' horses were State property, and these too were called in, so that in the first year of the war the animal labour in the country was reduced by half. The harvest of 1916 already showed the consequences in a diminished crop and fields gone to ruin. In that year the State began to requisition cattle—a measure attended by the most fatal results, both moral and economic. Production was reduced to the point when it barely nourished the farmer's household at the most meagre rates, yet the requisitions continued and crystallised the political ideas of the peasant into a sullen hate against the townspeople as so many idle mouths, the Government as a band of instruments of oppression. Indeed, the military requisitioning apparatus, and to a lesser degree the State monopoly, often worked on clumsy, wasteful and stupid lines. Hay rotted on the fields before it was taken away, cattle stood for days on the railway without food or water, perishing miserably under the eyes of their late owners.

When the food shortage in the towns began, the peasants learnt for the first time all about the value of money. It was their unique chance of profiteering, and they used it. Evading or baffling the State officials, they enriched themselves remorselessly at the expense of the hungry townsmen. Soon they learned to distrust paper money and to insist on payment in gold or *objets d'art et de valeur*. Then would be seen the strange spectacle of a Countess bowed under the weight of a "rücksack" of potatoes, eggs and butter, while the peasant's lady bore off in exchange an opera-glass and three pairs of silken stockings.

When the Monarchy fell, most of the peasants, for all their deep-rooted dynastic sympathies, welcomed its fall. It brought them peace, it allowed their sons and farm-hands to come home—and the Austrian revolution was essentially a hurried journey home. It delivered into their hands a great deal of administrative power which hitherto had lain with the Imperial officials. Real men from the peasants' midst now ordered the parish affairs and represented the district in both Provincial and Central Parliaments. Many were enthusiastic enough for their new liberties to discard the influence of the clergy, which were compromised in their eyes by their association with Monarchy, and actually helped the Socialists with their votes to a majority in the first Parliament.

But these liberal heresies were shortlived. The unfortunate Socialist Government inherited all the bitters and none of the sweets of the Monarchy. It was forced to continue the requisitions, and they were now more and not less oppressive than in wartime. The Imperial and Royal officers had at least thrown their master's money about like gentlemen. The Socialists made unpleasant Jewish calculations and fixed maximum prices which rose more slowly than the currency fell, till they became a fraction of what could be obtained in "Schleichhandel." Moreover, they neither liked nor understood the peasant, and he knew it. He withdrew into his shell. Parish cut itself off from parish, and all shut themselves away impassibly from Vienna. Local patriotism became intense, Austrian patriotism sank something below zero, and the exasperation between town and country grew into hatred.

We nearly always hear the side of the townsmen, but indeed the time brought very little material advantage to the peasant. The falling currency did one thing for him. It enabled him to pay off his mortgages for a song and face the world again a free man. But the legislation of the period was very one-sided in its devotion to the interests of the industrial workmen. Only one important law was passed which should have brought the peasants a real improvement—that which provided for the resettlement of all districts which in recent years had been taken over for big forests and sporting estates; but the process of rural depopulation is too far advanced, and this well-meant act has proved of little practical use.

On the other hand, a falling currency bears particularly hard on the peasant with his slow turnover. He cannot arrange for a weekly rising income to meet the rising prices. He can only fix his prices as near the gold standard as the consumer can pay, and even so, every sale in a rapidly falling currency, however extortionate the price, is a sale at a loss.

And even this liberal profiteering did not benefit him much. Much ridicule has been poured on the accumulations of pianos, Zeiss glasses and Old Masters which to-day startle the eye in a cottage parlour. It is partly no doubt owing to stupidity that the peasants did not buy implements and machinery which would have been of real use to them; but not entirely, for some of these things were not to be had at any price, and none were readily offered. After all a hungry professor does not say to his wife: "My dear, we need cash, take our steam plough to the country and get some eggs with it"; he sells what he has.

Any benefits which the peasants gained from Socialism were fully counteracted by the new claims of the "village proletariat," the class of farm assistants and hired labourers.

This class had been perhaps the least regarded in the world. Early rulers ignored it completely or, if they opened their mouths on the subject, it was not to bless. "We observe," wrote the vigorous Maria Theresa, "not without displeasure what great torment, vexation and damage the peasant has to endure from his serving-folk, and how the insolence of these people has already grown so great that they lay down the law to the master of the house, leave their service at their good pleasure, and are not abashed to indulge their lewd desires, so far that much scandal arises therefrom, Almighty God is sorely offended and the good discipline on which Christian life is chiefly based is almost wholly broken down." But the lewd desires of the country labourers have never been exactly pampered. Their work was always as laborious as that of the peasant, their leisure small, their wages a pittance only, their accommodation often interchangeable with advantage against that of the cows. Before the Social Democrats came into power no one in Austria had really occupied himself with their condition. The Socialists organised them in a trade union, forced through a rise of wages for them, and even succeeded in including them in the universal application of the eight-hour day.

This last measure effectually frightened the better-to-do peasants away from Socialism. They drew together, and joined forces with the middle classes, with whom their community of interests, at least as regards opposition to Socialism, is strong, the conflicts slight. For Austria continues to import most of her food supply and the peasant producer is therefore only to a small degree opposed to the middle-class consumer.

And this force of the united peasantry, over which the

Church is gradually regaining much of her lost hold, is a very strong one. The extension of the suffrage has made the peasant a political power, at least equal to that of the industrial workman. The coalition which has ruled Austria since 1920 really rests on peasants' votes, and these are a majority hardly likely to decrease in the near future. If one asks what use has been made of this power, it is not easy to answer. After his temporary fit of prosperity, the peasant has returned to his customary state of poverty and, apparently, of political indifference. He remains a very passive factor in the State. His view is limited to the boundary of his own fields, his policy still simple and short-sighted. To strengthen the province against the central power, the country against the town; to keep the prices of his produce up and of labour down, is all his care, and protection is his most complicated ambition. He shows little interest or understanding for creating a prosperous market for his produce, or for improving communications and general conditions in the interest of the State as a whole, himself included. Nor is he likely to change, so long as the mutual dislike between the Church and the towns continues unabated. In return, the Government, even under the Christian Socialists, has occupied itself little with the country. It has been chiefly concerned with settling the urgent relations of industry, finance and labour in the towns.

Among agricultural labourers Social Democracy has made much progress, both among the workers on the farms and, especially, in the forests, where the application of Socialism is more logical. This strong movement has caused the peasant proprietor to retort by reducing hired labour to a minimum, even at the cost of production. But some sympathy for Socialism has spread beyond this class to that of the poorest peasant proprietors. There is a fairly numerous class of cottagers who are unable to afford for themselves the more expensive implements or farm animals, and are forced to borrow them from their richer neighbours in return for work on the latter's property, a forced renewal of the system of robot. To this class capitalism is no unmixed blessing.

The relations between agriculture and Socialism are extraordinarily interesting, and have so far proved one of the points on which the theories of reformers have most consistently broken down. So long as there is a class of tenant farmers or farm-labourers working for a landlord, it is possible to draw a parallel between the two sets of "blood suckers," but as soon as a reform or revolution is attempted, the parallel breaks down hopelessly. The workmen want to take over their factory as a whole and work it as before, only keeping the profits for themselves; the peasants, on the other hand, have only one ambition; which is to become absolute owners of some small *angulus terrarum* for themselves. It is as if workmen wanted to scrap all factories and go back to one-man businesses. It has been pretty conclusively proved that farming on a large scale is more profitable than on a small, but this fact has not yet penetrated the brain of the farmer, who has still little to do with capital. In the last few years there have been revolutions throughout most of Central and Eastern Europe in the course of which the workmen of the towns, who formed the really revolutionary element, have availed themselves of the help of the peasants to overthrow the ruling caste of capitalists and landlords. Only by promising the great landed estates could the workmen secure this aid, and such has been done in Russia, Czechoslovakia, Rumania, Yugoslavia and, to a less extent, in Austria. But in every case, once the rent abolished and the landlord expelled, the revolutionary enthusiasm has waned. Indeed, his point once attained—once he becomes a proprietor himself—the peasant is the world's most unshakeable capitalist. The Socialists have therefore only exchanged a handful of enemies for a host. Like Frankenstein, they have raised up most intractable and formidable monsters; for a political dictatorship of peasants—who, after all, are uneducated and short-sighted all over the world—is narrower, more tyrannous, one-sided, unfair and grasping than any middle-class Government in the world. The rule of Stambulivsky in Bulgaria, a country of small peasant proprietors, is a sufficient example. His press used to talk about "sound basis," "guardians against Bolshevism" and so on; what it came down to was a systematic driving up of the prices of food with the most ruthless disregard of the town populations which it is possible to imagine.

Furthermore, the estates which have passed from the hands of educated landlords and trained bailiffs into those of peasants just freed from centuries of serfdom have gone to rack and ruin. They are tilled on prehistoric methods, have already deteriorated rapidly in value, and yield much less for the world than they did before the war.

And finally, there is no means of coercing the peasant against his will. Now that we have one man, one vote, his is generally the strongest party in the State. Even when he is outvoted, he cannot be compelled by physical force to work and produce a surplus, or to sell it at a low fixed price; I myself once saw a peasant in Bucharest stopped by a policeman from selling his melons at a price which the customer was willing to give, but was higher than the law allowed. Thereupon, the man jumped on them, and went on dancing till they were pulp.

The Russians have tried to solve their problem by juggling with the suffrage. One workman's vote counts the same as five peasants'. But while this is good enough for a moujik, who probably does not know what a vote is, it is not to be thought of in a country like Austria where the peasantry were accustomed to proprietorship and have political training and leaders; nor has any responsible leader been found to suggest any such measure.

The Austrian and German Socialists circle round the peasant problem wearily. Few of them have attempted to face it at all, and those who have, have mostly been in two minds about it. If the formula "all property is theft" had to be watered down by concessions in favour of personal property, these were yet theoretically justifiable. Yet to tamper with the "ownership by the community of means of production," to say that private ownership is all right as long as it is on a small scale: this is to admit a complete defeat for Socialism, to degrade it into a mere campaign against wealth. And yet, so tenacious is the peasant of his acres, that several even of the chief theoreticians of Socialism have been compelled to this admission.

Those who were too bigoted or too mentally honest for this, chief amongst them Kautsky and Bauer, have tried to work on other lines. Kautsky—whose work incidentally shows a quite sublime ignorance of real country life—endeavours to prove that the advantage gained by the abolition of rent or mortgages will outweigh all other considerations in the peasant's mind and convert him to Socialist ideas. Large estates will be provided with the most modern machinery and worked on a co-operative basis, everything will go beautifully, production will be increased so greatly that producers and consumers will live idyllically together. Each peasant would be allowed to keep his own cottage and garden; only the arable area would be worked in common. Kautsky justifies his argument by the perfectly true historical fact that until recently a great deal of practical communism did exist in agriculture, especially among the Slav nations.

Bauer evolved his scheme with less optimism but more practical knowledge. His ideal—the only one possible consistent with socialising agriculture at all—was to work the large fertile areas on a large scale by co-operative methods, and to exchange the produce with that of the workmen's co-operative stores in the towns, a mixed board of town and country workers adjusting the prices and relations of the exchange. One can, however, safely say that relations between town and country would have to change very radically, at any rate in Austria, before this board would have any chance to do anything but quarrel.

It is, moreover, a fact that agricultural co-operative societies have always broken down in the past unless they were based on complete private ownership. Dr Hainisch, who remarks on this, therefore advocates instead a revival of the State monopoly which controlled production and prices during the war. Perhaps because it was a war measure, this monopoly has made itself very unpopular, and the President's proposals awoke a good deal of surprise and little sympathy.

In any case, mountainous little Austria is not a country where farming on a big scale is practicable at all. If the world arrangements are ever really so adjusted that farming is done on the most economic lines, and the produce distributed internationally, only a part of Austria's present country population will be able to produce for the market at all. The small farms of the outlying mountain districts will remain outside the scheme of things, and their present occupiers, who, as far as they can exist at all, must do so mostly by supplying their own requirements, will remain a class outside organised society, neither capitalists nor exploited, an Absolute Value. To a large extent they are already in this position, and the question arises whether their existence, already threatened by its hardships and economic difficulties, with the consequent rural depopulation, be worth preserving. The question is less economic than spiritual; in the old days, military. Socialism, on the whole, answers no. The Church emphatically yes. And weighing in the balances much good and much evil, one is bound also to answer yes. The stock of the mountains is, after all, hardy and virile, capable of producing great things, given more wisdom and more consideration to those who are in authority over it. Even as an untouched reserve of strength, or a reservoir to reinforce and purify the adulterated blood of towns and factories, it is a factor which no State can lightly dare to do without. A State which has lost its independent peasantry is perilously near the verge of degeneration.

CHAPTER VIII

THE MIDDLE CLASSES

"Wo sind die Zeiten?"—"Where are the days of old?"—asks a Viennese writer in a book of charming, wistful little essays extending over the significant decade which began with 1909. And he goes on:

Never has a great city, a whole breed of human beings changed so utterly in so short a time—changed to remain at heart immutable and incorrigible...we are all, so to speak, our own grandchildren, and if we look into the unpleasant mirror of self-criticism, we are bound to admit: God knows, the race is not improved, the family has gone sadly downhill.

Many to-day repeat the author's question, and in a new world, where the successful seem utterly grabbing and selfish, the failures tired and embittered, look back across a barrier of years and see the old life—so short is human memory—already enveloped in a golden glamour. Those years seem to have purged away the copious injustice, the selfishness, the frivolity, the stupidity, the exploitation of many races and classes for the benefit of a fortunate minority. It is easier and more pleasant to dwell on the pomp, the grace and refinement of those days.

Many in their time have poured out their ink in efforts to capture the peculiar spirit of Vienna. Vienna, and that Austria which it represented, have been the theme of countless essays and epigrams. Most of the latter, rather surprisingly to the foreigner, were bitter; variations on the sardonic remark of Metternich that Asia begins on the Rennweg—the highway leading out of Vienna towards

Budapest, where incidentally the speaker had his own villa. Thus for the outside observer the native Viennese has two great nouns to express the condition of his home. If he is out of humour with it, he abuses its "Schlamperei"— its slipshodness. If the reverse, he extolls its "Gemüt-lichkeit"—a word which defies translation into English.

We usually render the adjective as "good-humoured" or "easy-going" and looking more closely we find it in fact very nearly akin to the noun of opprobrium. The two qualities are indeed only the two sides of the same coat in which tailors have dressed up the Viennese for so many years. Both have by now become so truly part of his being that it seems hardly likely that he will ever get rid of them.

For Vienna was essentially the creation of its rulers, and its character, for good and for ill, was imposed on it. The other towns in Austria, with their local industries, doctors and priests, are provincial centres not particularly different from the rest of their kind all the world over. But Vienna was an Imperial city through and through, the central point of a great Empire where all the nations of Central Europe met, the seat of the Dynasty, Church, army, bureaucracy and police which ruled that Empire. Even the large native industry and commerce which had sprung up naturally owing to the geographical position was not able to develop on its own lines. It was clipped and trained, fitted in with the whole, subordinated to Imperial interest. In later years, indeed, it suffered more than it gained from being Viennese and was really getting into the background, suppressed and hampered in favour of the Empire as a whole, so that among the many national movements under the Habsburgs not the least violent, certainly not the least important, was the German.

But the native German population could not before 1919 become so prominent as to spoil the whole effect. All nations and races met and mingled to form a population which is Viennese, and that alone. An Imperial population, whether directly engaged in administering the affairs of the Empire, as in the case of the formidable host of officials; or merely owing its existence thereto, as with the great mass of intellectual, professional or idle upper and middle classes.

Nor was the distinction between the officials and the laity so great as we might suppose. Only an actual or nominal Republic can produce the real type of absolute bureaucrat. In Austria, which has alternated for centuries between absolutism and a narrow oligarchy, according to the intellectual capacities of the Habsburg of the day, the most powerful bureaucrat had his vulnerable heel. He was the servant of his Emperor, who did not hesitate, did he displease him, did he even grow too powerful, to humble or break him with no more ado. In the shadow of the Dynasty all else took on to some extent the aspect of children playing under the walls of some immemorial fortress. And conversely, a reflected glory from the castle walls fell on the meanest subject of the city. Each had some share in his Monarch's destiny, were it the privilege of seeing him out on his morning drive, were it the fact that, thanks to his existence, the streets, the newspapers, the shops were contrived on the grand scale.

This halfway position, like that of a domestic animal, determined the character of the Viennese. They might have every privilege and advantage. Hardly any Habsburg ever reigned who was not genuinely concerned with the welfare of his people. They might hope to gratify any ambition

—save one: they must not "think themselves even such a one" as their Emperor. The proudest aristocrat, if he were privileged to write a letter to the Emperor, must sign himself "he who lies in the dust of your throne." Rebellion, and that alone, was the unforgivable sin in the eyes of the Dynasty as of the Church, whose opinions on this point were singularly at one with the Crown's, so that each might say with Caesar:

> Let me have men about me that are fat,
> Sleek-headed men, and such as sleep of nights.
> Yon Cassius has a lean and hungry look;
> He thinks too much; such men are dangerous.

And because in this imperfect world there must be always many who are lean and hungry, and given to thought, care was taken that at least a solid buffer should stand between them and the throne of fat and sleek-headed men to whose interests those of the proletariat and the peasant were long sacrificed. This was not out of malice, but because there was not enough to go round, so that the best arrangement appeared to be to make one class so weak, the other so contented, that neither could or would give trouble.

For the privileged classes, they might live as well as they could, so long as they kept quiet. Indeed, the more enjoyment they could get out of life, the quieter they were likely to be. These were gilded chains, and most of the Viennese wore them with grace, expending their really great talents on painting layer on layer of gilt on the chains. Under this system Vienna became one of the most pleasant and most beautiful cities of Europe. Few could display so much talent in every walk of life; such ingenious jour-. nalists, such learned doctors, or such lovely museums, galleries and gardens. In few places were the arts and amenities so sedulously cultivated, did there reign such a pomp combined with such a grace.

It is the Vienna of Arthur Schnitzler, that man of genius who saw and preserved it with the added clearness of vision and perhaps deeper sense of guardianship made possible by the little, hardly perceptible, unmistakable difference between Jew and Gentile. A keyboard on which the graver notes simply are not there; the struggles and developments of the ill-paid, ill-lodged working classes; the incessant labour of the peasant; the fanatical hatreds of Slav and Magyar. But on those few, dainty upper notes, what subtle variations, what delicate and delightful melodies! An enchanted world through which his Anatol drifts so gracefully, idle, humorous, vain, self-critical, correct, renewing his liaisons in the perfect manner, serious without exaggeration; or where his Viennese dance their round in couples, exactly alike through all their differences, since the same stamp is on them all.

It was the charm of Viennese life which most impressed the foreigner, yet all those who came to live for long in the charming city, like the natives themselves, seemed fated to end with a sense of cloyed satiety. In the end, one became conscious of a great void behind, one began to understand Metternich's epigram and that other one which declared that Austria lacked a soul. There were not wanting clear-headed men who protested that these sweets were after all a little undignified to be pressed continuously on grown men. "No one need be afraid of our indulging in dangerous or seditious talk," said one, bitterly, "Strauss or Lanner" (he is speaking of 1846, but the words fit 1913 very well) "or whoever happens to be in charge of public order on that particular day, taps on his fiddle, and before anyone can say or think anything about it that is not suitable for a good subject, the answer is waiting for him: tralala, bimbim, bum-bum, tralala, tralala bim bim bim." And Hermann Bahr wrote: "The Viennese is a man very unhappy in himself, who hates the Viennese, but can't live without the Viennese, who despises himself, but is moved by himself, who is always finding faults but wants incessant praise, who feels wretched, and enjoys it, who is always complaining, always threatening, but puts up with everything. Except being helped, there he draws the line."

For only the Anatols and the tourists could really find a full satisfaction in this existence. The chains weighed heavily on the productive classes, pushing them under a load of taxation, incompetent financial administration, frequent crises and a perpetual looming threat of State bankruptcy. Nor were they much lighter for the few who preserved their intellectual energy and independence. They must bitterly resent that eternal restraint which ordered them this, forbade them that, as though they were children. Truly to lack complete liberty is to lack a soul. And thus many, not strong enough to revolt, gave up the best of themselves, and became that most pathetic of types, the Viennese dilettante of the theatre and the café. Hardly anywhere in the world could one find so much talent as in the Viennese cafés; nor so much wasted on trivialities and the eternal second-rate.

Here and there, there were men who were really great —more perhaps than any one knew. But they sickened of the general atmosphere and shut themselves up to work alone. Or sometimes, not rarely, they caught the breath of the soul which Austria still possessed, the Imperialism of culture. After all, Vienna had a traditional mission which she had always fulfilled nobly. With all her own touch of Asia, she was a bulwark of Europe, and a civilising and teaching force of the highest order. The engineers, the doctors and the professors felt something of this mission and their work in fulfilment of it made Austria's chief justification.

Nor were the nations which profited by it yet in a state to carry on such work for themselves. Eastern and South-eastern Europe is still emerging painfully out of barbarism, and the schools and universities are still as much political pawns as centres of learning. It is still only in Vienna that there is an old enough tradition and a broad enough culture for men to work there truly for the sake of learning and teaching.

There were not a few in this Viennese society who welcomed the fall of the Monarchy. The really privileged classes were after all small in numbers; a clique centering round the court, the officers of the General Staff, and the upper clergy. The bourgeoisie of Austria rather prided themselves on their liberalism. They had led the revolution of 1848 and ever since that date they, far more than the Socialists, because their position was stronger, had worked for modern conditions. Especially the German Nationalist Party was avowedly Republican, seeing in the Monarchy only a re-actionary institution which sacrificed their interests to those of Polish or Magyar magnates. But it is one of the great mistakes of the Austrian Socialists that, obsessed by the idea of class warfare, eager to claim a desert for themselves and to gain a popular war-cry, they denounced as reactionary everyone who did not show an unlimited enthusiasm for the doctrines of Karl Marx, and turned against themselves a mass of feeling which would have helped them well to put in order the new Republic. The actual Monarchist parties have been ludicrously small in the number of their adherents. Their committees consist almost entirely of the immediate entourage of the old court, their rank and file of romantic ladies. The unhappy Karl's two escapades to Hungary woke almost no response in Austria, and the news of his death was received with an almost cynical indifference.

The opposition to the Republic and to its leaders was almost wholly economic, and did in fact become a matter of class. The conflict expressed itself, if one may say so, in terms of falling currency.

The relations between currency and class and currency and culture form one of the most interesting phenomena of modern times. A small volume might be written on the revolutionary effects of inflation, or inflation compared with war as an engine of destruction. The parallel is very exact, and leads us to the conclusion that we are wiser than our fathers, for all the hurly-burly of class struggles of earlier centuries, the peasants' risings, the Thirty Years' War, the bloodshed and the burning and the ravaging, never effected half such a speedy or radical social revolution as was accomplished in Vienna in two years by the inordinate printing of paper-money.

A characteristic of civilisation resting on the stable and gradual accumulation of wealth is that it enables a certain class to set the spiritual end before the material, the remote before the immediate. If it is true that it softens the struggle for existence, arrests the law of the survival of the fittest, creates a large parasitic class, and tends to bring about racial degeneration; yet it also arrests and preserves for us almost everything which makes life really valuable.

To it we owe not only orchestral music and dainty ladies' dresses, but also the development of all the altruistic virtues outside maternal love, and that state of things which enables a scholar or an engineer to perform that work which alone brings about a real progress even in material things. In this respect, capitalism with a stable currency is the successor of slave labour, the ultimate advantages of which to the human race are as great as its undesirability for the slaves.

Further, when money can be acquired with ease in small quantities, but only with difficulty in large, it attains its highest state of semi-invisibility. A servant and not a master, it promotes urbane manners and the humanities.

A falling currency reverses all these things. It is a more potent weapon than Yellow Cross gas, with which it shares its few virtues of temporarily stimulating industry, promoting the will to live and being deadly to parasites.

It affects different classes of society in very different ways, some even to their profit. In the following list of callings which I have made out, those named first profit by it, those in the middle can save themselves, while the last are its chosen victims. My list runs: dishonest financiers, bankers and honest financiers, manufacturers, tradesmen, peasants, organised labourers, civil servants, brain-workers, persons of fixed income.

My list is only a rough one and subject, of course, to great variations. The speculators and bankers are the only classes who really score heavily, assuming that they know their job. The manufacturer's profit depends on the foreign markets. If he is able to sell his wares abroad in good currency, he makes a profit on the cheapness of labour, since prices in a country of falling currency never rise quite so quickly as the foreign quotations, and wages, even with the index system, are always a little behind prices. He is therefore sure of a profit, and can even afford to sell his goods at a price below the normal, thus ensuring his market. The advantage is of course only clear where his raw material and power come from his own country. If he has to buy abroad he loses part of the advantage. This was in fact the case with most Austrian industries, and the chief handicap to their recovery after the war.

The tradesman loses on the depreciation during the time of his turnover, for which he can only compensate himself by raising his price to the limit which the consumer can bear. In this he generally acquires a mental agility which must be worth a lot in itself. The peasant is in a like case. His turnover is slow, his loss proportionately large; but he suffers less than any other class in his capacity as consumer. The organised workman forces up his wages to meet the rising prices, and did so in Austria with some success, although not to anything like the extent asserted by his political opponents. But he can never draw any permanent benefit from the conditions, as his wages never rise so fast as prices, and his savings are too small to allow him to speculate. Civil servants, even where organised, are handicapped by the slow method of the State as an employer, and by their own comparatively highly developed sense of duty, which makes them unwilling to assert their claims to the utmost, and which is so taken for granted by all other members of the community that if they do so assert themselves, they are always regarded and decried by the horrified press and business men as hardened criminals. Organised brain-workers are handicapped by their small numbers, but still come off better than members of the free professions, whose fate is very like that of the *rentiers*, who lose all the time.

Numerous variations occur, and nearly all could be traced, were the labour not too complicated, to the application of one or another law of economics, such as supply and demand, ultimate utility, or a manifestation in terms of morals and intellect of Gresham's law that the more debased currency always supplants the more valuable. Thus the different sub-categories of the intellectual middle classes themselves fared very variously in Vienna after the war. Doctors, for instance, could always maintain a claim to be considered indispensable, since they practise on other peoples' bodies, which remain of interest to their possessors even when the latter have lost almost all they have possessed in the way of minds or souls. Although obliged to work in great poverty, owing to the poverty of their clientèle, the doctors have had in Austria probably more to do than ever before, owing to the increase of diseases resulting from the war and the blockade, among which may be mentioned: complaints arising from under-nourishment, nervous ailments, and venereal diseases. Their compensations were, however, less great than those of the lawyers, who often profited exceedingly by the all too complicated dealings of the new generation of bankers and business men with one another, or with the public prosecutor; nor should one quite forget the libel actions between political parties, and especially those brought by Monarchist leaders against one another. Clergymen, on the other hand, do not appear to be considered "ultimately useful" by any one in hard times. In this their fate is on a par with that of such artists, authors and musicians as are neither conspicuously great nor noticeably incompetent. Of all this class, the worst sufferers were the sculptors, and after them, with cheaper raw materials, the artists. These two classes were hit by an interesting side influence, the competition of the past, caused by previously well-to-do families selling their old pictures and glutting the market. A perishable currency is discouraging to all that is not equally perishable, and this brought the architects in Vienna near destitution—by which is not meant that the architects are imperishable, but their materials are. Similarly with writers. A falling currency is fatal to the production of books, and especially of valuable works which call for long study in the writing, and must be sold·at a high price. Newspapers, on the other hand, have to struggle with the increased cost of machinery, paper, wages, etc., but being ephemeral and low in price sell readily at any time, and the more sensational, scurrilous and unworthy of existence the wider the circulation; the purest example of Gresham's law. In all the arts, the showy, the popular, and the vulgar can continue to exist by its universality of appeal, after the disappearance of a real cultured class of consumers has doomed better work to extinction. Bad artists are therefore not so hard hit by the falling currency as good. The most fortunate are those able to make an immediate appeal to the instinct of the newly rich to spend their money quickly and riotously; as the musical artists and dancers, and the composers of popular cabaret and operette songs. The number of bars, cabarets and night-clubs increased in inverted proportion to the value of the krone, and stopped increasing when the money was stabilised. On the other hand, artists of the very highest rank are saved by their ability to appeal, partly to the international market, partly to the ambitions of the *nouveaux riches*. Thus, fortunately, the individual members of the Viennese opera were able to support themselves by foreign tours, although at the expense of the *ensemble*, or at the worst they could go to the operette, while a special effort of the population preserved the Philharmonic Orchestra, probably the most valuable contribution made by Austria to modern civilisation.

Even among the *rentiers* there are variations, which as usual penalise the better for the benefit of the worse. The most striking and most dreadful example of this was the fate of the Austrian war loan, which was reduced in time to less than the value of the coupons as waste paper. A better example of the survival of the non-fittest could hardly be found than the complete ruin of such Austrians who were hasty enough to be patriots during the war, nor a better warning against the repetition of such folly, since successive Governments have left the holders of Government shares strictly to their fate with a cynical indifference. The same fate, slightly mitigated, overtook pensioners of the Government. Holders of industrial shares did better, as the shares rose at one period very rapidly; but they were still highly unprofitable as a source of income, since the dividends paid, even when they looked enormous, were rarely in any proportion to the original gold value of the shares. Indeed, Austrian finance since the war seems almost to have forgotten dividends, and to have interested itself solely in the mercurial rise and fall of shares on the market, while to produce the desired movement every sort of rumour, misrepresentation and lie was spread abroad or inserted in the venal newspapers corrupted or owned by large speculators.

For a year or so, a sort of paralysis seemed to descend

on those unfortunate classes whom the devaluated currency robbed of their all. In the difficulty and confusion of this time they were the prey of a boundless misery. It is painful to dwell on the details of their sufferings, and hardly necessary, since their dramatic character woke the sympathy of all the world. They could hardly be magnified in themselves but they have been dwelt on with some lack of proportion to the whole. The appeals of public and private charities drew universal attention to this class rather to the exclusion of others, and gave on the whole a false impression of the real course of events. For the bulk of the sufferings were an episode, if a gruesome one. Families affected by them lived on charity or on selling their possessions. Some, the oldest and feeblest, died of their privations. Others, most of the artists or professors of established reputation, managed somehow to struggle through until the arrival of better days. The rest little by little fitted themselves into other professions.

It is a curious fact that hardly any Austrian artist was able to draw inspiration from the confused horror of these times. Perhaps it was killed by the overwhelming pressure of economic realities, which occupied the mind to the exclusion of everything else. For there were materials there for a great and majestic drama. The tragic decay and the end of the House of Habsburg, and of many other families of hardly less renown or antiquity, were subjects eminently to awake the tragic emotions of pity and horror. Against the fall of the old, there was the rise of the new, the groping towards the light of vast masses, their first sight of freedom, their first basking in the sun of power. Perhaps this great movement insisted too severely on the materialistic basis of history; at all events, it failed to carry

the poets with it. In Austria as in England the war produced the usual literature of repulsion, part invective, part
satire. A real and pure emotion lies in lines of some of
these war poets, but hidden, even with the best of them,
under masses of very turbid verbosity. It is eminently
unfortunate that most of the Viennese young poets felt
that freedom called for the use of free verse, for no one
knows how bad free verse can be until he has read bad
German free verse. The German tongue is essentially
weighty and sedate. The poets who discarded the natural
limitations of their language only managed to yell and
shriek, to pile adjective on adverb, to contort themselves
into inextricable knots, and then to cut them with a string
of dots and exclamation marks highly bewildering to the
reader. Hardly one succeeded in reducing overflowing
emotions to ultimate simplicity expressed in a telling way,
as Sassoon could for us, or Barbusse or Henri Jacques for
France.

The same poets sang the revolution, the "red" cause.
For a while nearly all were seeing red, but even here they
fitted in ill with the new times, for they were attracted
mostly by the blood red of Moscow. The dry, practical
arrangements of Social Democracy repelled them, no less
than the vanishing market for verse. The revolution was
soon left without singers. Some were dumb, others,
whether poets or artists, abandoned themselves to a yearn-
ing regret for the old, happier days. For them, the present
was now only a bitter contrast to the remembered glamour
of the past. The artists went on painting their country
landscapes, their village spires and their lilac bushes; the
poets fluted their old love-notes. When later years look
for a picture of this time, they must leave the famous names

aside in their search. They will find what they want most truly in the jokes of the comic papers, the lampoons of the cabarets and perhaps in the *feuilletons* of a single journalist of great talent who constituted himself a sort of modern Petronius, won immense popularity and was finally murdered in consequence of it.

Most people had their attention too fully taken up with the more urgent problem of existence to think much of the fine arts, or to care about the mirror which they held up to it. Indeed, the saddest thing of all those years was not so much the fate of individual unfortunates as the way in which the whole attention of a class of civilised men was concentrated on the topics of eating, prices and the exchange. One might walk the streets of Vienna for whole evenings, and listen to the conversation of the passing crowd, without hearing a word unconnected with these topics. I tried the experience once for a measured hour, and the only remark I heard which differed from the others was a medical observation of blood-curdling impropriety which a Madonna-eyed flapper called across me, quite unabashed, to a friend. It is true, of course, that the better people avoided public places altogether. Yet it is hard to think that a nation of more virility would have let its moral and aesthetic tone collapse so completely.

In spite of the alleged overwhelming prosperity of the manual labourers, not many of the broken middle classes went to swell their ranks. In part, the prosperity was less than it was made out to be; in part, no doubt, the old rigid caste spirit of Austria survived on both sides and made such a move difficult. Nor did they turn peasant. The Socialist "back to the land" movement is no more than a scheme of allotment gardens for the spare time of the factory hands, and the peasants themselves have been the first to oppose any expansion of it, fearing its influence on their hired labour. One would have expected a large flow of emigration, but neither was this the case; partly because the more appetising countries had closed their frontiers to Austrian immigrants, partly owing to the innately home-keeping character of Austrian wits. As the shortage of capital and the difficulty of the European situation made it impossible to found new productive businesses, except in isolated cases, most of the refugees from the lower classes of our list—the *rentiers*, the members of free professions, the "axed" civil servants—skipped all intervening stages and entered direct into the topmost categories of speculative business, banking and speculation pure and simple.

Some day a book will be written on how those people made money during those years. Hundreds of thousands appeared to live in some mysterious way by "doing" one another, and perhaps this really was the case, since the Government was for ever issuing new money, while in the cafés ingenious people scrambled for their share of it. I once watched a man in the particular café where the jewellers and watch-makers meet make quite a tidy sum in one afternoon out of a bad watch, which he sold three times, each time buying it back at a reduction and betting with a friend that he would sell it again. Others smuggled rifles under the noses of the Inter-allied Commission, acted as house agents at high fees, evading the Housing Commission, or dealt in the currency in ways which varied from honest exchanging, through speculating *à la baisse*, to simple smuggling—there was a time, for instance, when the same notes were worth exactly twice as much in Prague as in

Vienna, and a brisk but dangerous trade was done in transporting them.

Even apart from these purely illicit deals and from the "black Bourse" of ringletted Jews which established itself in the cafés round the official Stock Exchange, and was periodically raided by the police whose headquarters, very conveniently, were situated exactly opposite—besides this, there really was for two or three years profitable occupation for an enormous number of bankers. The old-established banks opened new branches, and a countless number of new rivals appeared on the scene. Most of these, according to our ideas, could not be called banks at all. Legitimate business formed a very small fraction of their activities. Indeed, some of the most successful practitioners knew nothing of real banking at all. Immigrants, many of them of fortunately uncertain origin, seized occasion by the forelock, opened small offices on a capital consisting mostly of their inborn talent for fishing in troubled waters, and amassed rapid fortunes through speculations on the exchange and moneylending at exorbitant rates of interest. A gain of under thirty, forty or fifty per cent. on a speculation was no gain at all; it was get-rich-quick or nothing. The process was not so difficult as it might seem, since a fever of speculation had attacked the whole population. The housemaid, when she got her few shillings of wages, ran to have a flutter with it in Polish marks, or levas, or something of the sort. Everyone was buying, selling, shifting his money about, and brokerage and demurrage alone on these transactions made up a very fair source of income. But, further, helped by the confusion of the times and the ignorance of their clients, the less reputable of the banks were able to carry on a most lucrative practice. They bought packets of shares, and those which went up were booked for their private accounts, those which went down for their clients'. It was almost impossible to control such operations. Some bankers lost their clients' money, and some lost their own. There was a steady flow away of bankruptcies and defalcations, but for all that the number of banks and financial businesses continued to grow. When the currency was stabilised, its place, for purposes of speculation, was taken by the issues of industrial shares, which all the firms made in large numbers to avoid borrowing at the high current rates of interest. As Austrian banks—a very few conservative concerns of established reputation always excepted—did not confine their investments by considerations of safety, things went on just as merrily on these shares as they had on the exchange. Industry itself, including the most reputable, had become speculative. It passed largely into the hands of the banks, its shares were bandied about and used for the most improbable purposes, but ended in enriching the speculator at the expense of industry.

Consider this operation: a man X secures the majority of shares—51 %—in a firm which manufactures, let us say, toothpicks. He forms a second nominal company, consisting really of himself alone, in, say, France. With this he makes a contract at a price involving a large profit to 100 % x in France, as against a loss to 51 % x in Austria. After a while he breaks the contract, sues himself for breach, pays 51 % of the damages and pockets 100 %. Meanwhile, the price of toothpicks has gone up. And the Austrian company finds itself in difficulties to fulfil another contract with a company in Italy. The company insists on delivery. As a matter of fact, it consists solely of X, but no one knows that. So 51 % x (Austria) buys back the toothpicks it had sold shortly before to 100 % x (France) at a strangely generous price, after which it lets 100 % x (Italy) have them cheap.

This is how fortunes can be made if you know the ropes. It is not suggested that the ex-professors, poets, counts, colonels and civil servants of Austria made such fortunes. They did not. A high percentage of the winners by such processes were not Austrians at all, but immigrants from various theatres of war. Yet numbers of the Austrian middle classes found employment under or in connection with such speculators—as their bank clerks, their secretaries, or, more remotely, the managers of the night-clubs in which they spent their earnings royally. And many more, during the prolonged period of inflation of shares, were able to keep their heads above water through investments which, for a year or two at least, proved highly profitable.

So the financial collapse had corrupted morals and culture, and their decay again corrupted Austrian business and financial life. There were concerns, both financial and industrial, which preserved their good name and their solid basis. Yet even they came into difficulties, often through no fault of their own; and in any case, they no longer constituted anything like such a high proportion of the whole as they had before the war.

One of the effects of the Socialist legislation of the period —one certainly not intended by its authors—was to encourage dishonest business. Taxation was high; so high that it really became a severe drag on business. A further drag was the difficulty of getting rid of an employee, and the over-staffing for which Hanusch's law of 1919 (see Chapter VI) was largely responsible. There was every inducement to conceal gains and falsify books, and the necessity for this under the noses of a watchful flock of Staff Councillors developed a double agility in the practitioners of such methods. Although a special branch of the police was established to deal with these matters, yet experience has shown that the methods of the law are in nine cases out of ten too clumsy to lay hold of an alert man bent on making rapid gains. Prosecutions have been comparatively few; the end of most such businesses has been reached simply by their owner's over-reaching himself, or being devoured by a larger specimen of his own kind. In ordinary, honest business the Socialist control is now so strong that it is difficult to see how it can be increased much farther. The problem whether private or communal control of the means of production is superior depends on the calculation whether fairer distribution and elimination of the owner's profit counter-balances the loss of initiative. In Austria to-day the owner's profit has been reduced so greatly that it would be of very little use to anyone, were it taken from him. But the consequence has been, not that the community benefits by the "plus value," but that those who are bent on making money merely do it in other ways which are not even productive.

For only a small part of the busy activity of Vienna after the war was productive. The rest was merely a dizzy juggling with figures, a rapid shifting round, from one pocket to another, of a wealth which was not growing greater. After a time, a crash came. The pin which pricked the bubble was the French franc, when in the spring of 1924 it first fell rapidly, then recovered with a swing which proved the ruin of many who had been buying for advance delivery. To meet their obligations, they were obliged to put their shares on the market, out of which the bottom promptly dropped. The over-subscribed, over-quoted industrial shares, of which a quite insufficient proportion was paid up, the rest being held by speculators waiting for a rise, went down and down. The smaller and less secure banks began to go bankrupt, others called in the credits which they had given to industries, and these followed suit. The disaster spread until it affected the shares of the most stable concerns, and the pockets of people who had hardly even heard of the French franc.

Thus the Austrian middle classes followed up their crisis of 1919 by a second in 1924, but on different lines. The order of losers was now reversed: the *rentiers* and the State officials came off best, the business men and the bankers worst. But in essence the two crises were the same, for a pane of glass was broken and a hard northern wind of reality shrivelled an over-luxuriant growth. In each case, the weaker and more sickly plants perished incontinently, but each may end by setting the survivors, diminished in numbers, on a firmer and healthier basis.

In 1924 people began to realise again what they had said in 1919 and since forgotten, that Vienna was a head without a body to nourish it. There had been too many leisured middle classes, journalists and civil servants; so there were too many banks and too many changers and agencies. Both had to vanish, but one is bound to admit that the former class left the more savoury memory behind it.

Meanwhile, already the intellectual middle class which Austria can still afford—and that thanks to the country's central position and old traditions, is still a larger one than a Balkan State or a Russian province could possibly maintain—is returning to a more reasonable position. The pay of the upper civil servants has been raised considerably, it again costs something to consult a good doctor, and one can no longer buy pictures in the "Sezession" for a few shillings. Things are by no means where they were before the war, nor are they likely to be so long as a farm labourer's or a tram conductor's vote counts as much as a professor's. In Austria, as everywhere else, the intellectual middle class is nobody's child. But one may think that not much harm has been done by reducing its numbers and concentrating on quantity rather than quality.

The same process seems likely to occur now in the ranks of business, industry and finance. Just as in Austria before the war there was a fearful plethora of doctors of law (this being the degree necessary to enter the public service), but a scarcity of really first-rate ability, so even to-day, and even although bankruptcies run into thirty and forty a week, there are still an immense number of small banks and businesses where one big one, properly conducted, would suffice, and each of these, as a rule, works wastefully, with cumbersome methods and a superfluity of labour. There are often too many artisans, there are nearly always a whole lot of quite otiose gentlemen at the top who call themselves "Direktor," "Generaldirektor," "Direktorstellvertreter," "Verwalter," "Verwaltungsrat" and so on, whose presence increases overhead costs enormously without giving any noticeable return. The future trend of Austrian business, if it is to survive, will certainly be towards economy, simplification and concentration into fewer hands. The firms which work on these lines will be able to inspire confidence, to get credits on reasonable terms from abroad, and to enjoy a real and not merely apparent prosperity.

There still remains the problem of the superfluous man, and it is one to which, frankly, one can find no answer. After the crash of 1924 something of the tragic atmosphere of 1919 returned. There has since been a fearful increase in suicides, sometimes among unsuccessful speculators, sometimes among discharged clerks or bankrupt business men. Possibly a falling birth-rate will in the end bring an automatic solution of this difficulty; it is hard to see any other.

CHAPTER IX

JEWS, GERMANS AND GERMAN JEWS

THE Jews occupied an unique position in the Habsburg
Monarchy. In many respects the most important race
in it, they took no part in the fevered national struggles
which engaged all the other races. These struggles were
connected with territory, and the geographical arrangements of the Treaty of St Germain were thus able to give
an answer to them, even if not a final one. The Jewish
problem, however, which is spiritual rather than territorial, slipped through the fingers of the makers of maps.
Its development is on other lines and within other limits,
and its solution is still far away. It may indeed sometimes
appear farther away to-day than ever before, for in modern
times the problem has taken an entirely new aspect. To-
day we have this question: is there a Jewish problem at all
or is the difference of race on which this phrase is based a
purely imaginary one? In affirming the identity of his
race, the orthodox Jew to-day is in agreement with his
enemies, the Aryan nationalists; but the remainder of his
own people make the claim, novel in history, to be regarded
as part and parcel of the population amongst which they
live.

No doubts perplexed the inhabitants of Central Europe
in the Middle Ages, when first the Jews came from the
East to settle in considerable numbers in Poland, Hungary,
and other parts of what was to be Austria-Hungary. The
mediaeval rulers took their cue from the Church, whose
attitude, either by direct ordinance, or by her spiritual

and intellectual influence, determined the fate and position of the Jews. For her they were a nation apart, an accursed people, the deniers and murderers of the Saviour. It is interesting, however, to notice that this accusation was in no way racial, but purely religious. If a Jew recanted and received baptism he ceased to be a Jew, and this point of view was upheld through all the fury of the Crusades and the Inquisition itself. The stigma only clung to him so long as he remained true to his religion.

This identification of race with religion sounds oddly to us, but is still common among the Jews themselves, especially those who are baptised. Nor is it confined to Jews; most of the so-called Turks of the Balkans are pure-blooded Slavs whose ancestors saved their property by confessing Mahomet and have since been regarded by themselves and everybody else as Turks.

A quantity of edicts issued by the Church and observed by the princes separated the Jew from his neighbours. He wore a distinctive dress, he was confined to the ghetto. He was cut off from all the common social life of the surrounding population. Most important of all, he was forced into a distinct economic position. In all countries subject to canonical law, members of the Catholic Church were forbidden to take interest for money. This occupation was assigned to the Jews, and was almost the only one open to them; they were forbidden to own land or to enter the guilds which controlled industry and commerce; only a few special trades, mostly in jewels or precious metals, being reserved for them.

These restrictions took a new aspect as soon as land ceased to be the chief source of wealth and the gallant but improvident nobles began to suffer under a chronic shortage of money, which was aggravated by the gradual replacement of universal by mercenary armies. The cities in which the guilds were concentrated, as they grew in wealth grew also in strength, and it was rarely possible to impose heavy contributions on them against their wills. The Jews were few in number and unpopular. They were easily forced into granting loans, and when all else failed they could be and were expelled and their entire property seized.

Thus they came to fill the position of bankers to the ruling princes and dukes, and as such stood in a special relation to them. While not a few rulers encouraged and treated them well, all were careful to keep them well in hand. In Austria their legal status was one of "personal serfdom" to the rulers, who had the right to dispose of them "according to free pleasure." In return they often enjoyed special protection. Some were raised to the position of "Court Jews" with extraordinary immunities and privileges.

But it was an uncertain and temporary favour, like that of the goose which lays the golden eggs. The Church never relented towards them. If a prince got a fit of religion he expelled or slaughtered his Jews as an earnest of good faith, and the population, who did not share its ruler's profit, regarded them with a hatred born of religion and superstition.

Such feelings could not fail to spring up under the prevailing conditions. The curses of the Church volleyed down the ages against the devil's brood. An early Christian writer debated: "whether and how far the Devil is the father of the Jews" ("how far" is good), and this terrifying paternity was widely ascribed to them. Their dark and tortuous abodes, their outlandish speech and dress, their

swarthy foreign mien, lent colour to all sort of dark sur-
mises, no less than their financial prosperity, for which the
Devil was really far less responsible than the Pope. Many
sinister and inexplicable circumstances helped in this belief
in Satan's hand. When plague and pestilence swept over
Europe it was seen that the inhabitants of the ghetto were
often spared from the ravages which decimated the Catholic
population, and even quite correctly observed that the
poison was often contained in the Host itself. It was far
more natural to suppose Satanic devices than to realise
that the little fungus which causes the plague grows on
the Host, on the flesh of swine, and on polluted fat, and
that what saved the Jews were the ordinances of Moses,
probably based on old experience of these very diseases.

The story of the mediaeval pogroms is a gruesome one.
And as each century repeated its tale of blood, the gulf
between Jew and Christian grew ever wider, the mutual
hatred and contempt struck deeper roots. It was not really
till the eighteenth century that matters changed. The
growing development of Europe made the provisions of
canonical law more and more burdensome for the Christian
population. The Pope was petitioned to relax his embargo
on interest on money and at last he did so, although to this
day he has not removed it altogether. Hungary, whose
population was largely Calvinist, revolted against the
authority of the Church and abolished the ghetto. Here,
as elsewhere, it was coming to be realised that the part
played by the Jews in the general and economic life was
important and even useful.

In Austria proper the restrictions were kept up longer.
Maria Theresa, that devout and determined lady, confined the Jews to Vienna, and there they might only settle

with her written permission, and only in order to engage in industry. "They are to be kept away from here and avoided as much as possible," she wrote; and again, "I know no worse plague than this nation with its swindling, moneymaking and usury." But this vigorous point of view was no longer universal. It had been abandoned in Hungary and in Bohemia; the local authorities found the Jews profitable economically, and intervened to prevent their expulsion.

That unorthodox monarch Josef II, one of the few Habsburgs to make a stand against the Catholic Church (which to this day has not forgiven his memory for it), was the first Austrian ruler to afford a real measure of freedom to the Jews. At the time of his accession, in 1781, the Church had grown too powerful politically for the Monarch's taste. Among the steps which he took to strengthen his own position was the famous Patent of Toleration which, while retaining Catholicism as the State religion, allowed other confessions to erect their own places of worship and enjoy the right of citizenship.

Among the beneficiaries of the patent were the Jews, who, while not yet admitted to a full equality, were emancipated from "servitude" and allowed to rent land, to practise industry, wholesale trade and the free professions, and even to own land so long as they cultivated it themselves.

A few years later came the French Revolution with its liberty, equality and fraternity, which forced the French people to admit their Jews to full rights. The French principles found an echo over half Europe, and were paralleled in the liberal movement in Germany, where for the first time the Jews themselves began to change their attitude.

The great Jew Mendelssohn, an intimate friend of the philosophic and literary circles of the time (Lessing, his close friend, took him as model for his figure of "Nathan the Wise"), urged on his compatriots to come out of the ghetto in spirit as in body, to abandon their isolation, which was leading them to an increasing narrowness of view, to identify themselves with modern culture in its widest sense. His ideas produced a great effect. Many leading German Jews, including Mendelssohn's own daughter, were baptised, Germans and Jews struck a bond together, and many hoped and believed that Lessing's parable would be realised, and the three rings melted together again into one great ring of universal culture and wisdom.

The time of the Austrian Jews came later—everything comes later in Austria. They did not attain full legal equality till after the revolution of 1848, in which they took a prominent part; and even then, this equality was again temporarily restricted under the reaction which followed. But it was restored and their flowering time began. The ghetto was abandoned, the Jews spread over the country. Fifty or sixty years ago they were in fact more widely distributed than to-day. Every market, even in the Alpine districts, had its Jewish "Krämer," or general shopkeeper, who, sitting in his characteristic little booth, sold the peasant the oil, the pots and the implements which he needed in exchange for his farm products. A second class, the "Pinkeljuden," or pedlars, traversed the country roads, often on foot, their packs on their backs, making their round of the lonely mountain districts to return weekly for the celebration of the Sabbath. There was much that was picturesque in this rustic Jewish life, which still continues in the outlying parts of the old Monarchy, and friction between Jews and Christians as a rule only appeared when the former were in large numbers.

But with the improvement of communications, and especially of railways, the country markets lost their importance, and the Jews flowed back to their real element, the large towns, where they had quickly won an extraordinary position. They were supreme in commerce and finance and banking—in the latter almost without rivals, except for one or two deliberately oppositional and usually badly conducted concerns, and for the State Bank. In the free professions they supplied a high percentage of the doctors, of the professors hardly less, of the journalists (including the staffs of anti-Semite papers) an overwhelming proportion. In law, for which calling their training and habit of mind have especially fitted them, they enjoyed almost a monopoly. In industry they were less strong and they neither owned as a rule, nor cultivated land, but this apart, there was soon hardly a branch of the life of the country where they had not the controlling, although usually not the most prominent, position.

Perhaps an exception should be made in favour of the Church, although there are malicious whispers; hardly for the aristocracy, whose members married freely with baptised Jews, while its lower ranks were in recent years recruited by a great number of money peerages; so that it has been said, if not with entire justice, that in Austria the title of baron was a characteristic racial mark of the Hebrew.

We have said "controlling, but not most prominent." How universally this is true the Liberal Party is only just beginning to teach England. It is difficult or impossible

to say, whether this secrecy, this atmosphere of the
"hidden hand," the "man behind the throne," really comes
from the Jew or the Christian; from the justified caution
of the persecuted race who had learnt too well the sequence
of ὕβρις and ἄτη, or from the shame of the proud ruler
stealing secretly and by night for help to the despised
"servitors." However this may be, almost the normal
relation before the war was that of a Christian on the
throne and a Jew behind it to whisper in his ear. The
institution of the "Hausjude" had become proverbial. If
the bank president was an Aryan, his Jewish directors and
clerks kept his books and thought out his speculations. In
the public offices the Christian Minister received the depu-
tations and made the speeches, and his young aristocratic
subordinates yawned and lounged and flitted down to the
Prater to ride or off to the country to shoot; while in a grimy
back room an earnest young Hebrew, consumed with
ambition and industry, bowed himself over the accumulated dossiers with a religious zeal. The feudal nobility,
whose lives were spent in shooting and flirting, left their
estates and affairs in charge of canny Jewish underlings.
The relationship was even augustly reproduced between
the Emperor himself and the head of the House of Roth-
schild. Even Parliament had its proverbial representative,
a fantastic little old man, who trotted to and fro, indifferent
to speeches and causes, cajoling this and that leader till
he had coaxed together a majority for the Government.

Thus, although the Court, diplomacy, the upper ranks
of the army, the navy almost entirely, the regular pro-
fessorial appointments of the universities, the Austrian-
Hungarian Bank, even the companies of the State theatres,

admitted few or no Jews, in reality they were the most important race in the Monarchy; the more so that they were not confined to one part of it, but distributed over its whole surface.

Both the character and the treatment of the Jews naturally varied very widely in different provinces. In the agricultural Slav provinces of the south, the Jewish question has never been acute. The sporadic settlers there belonged to the nobler type of Sephardim or Spanish Jews. A small colony of this race is settled in Vienna, where it follows the, to us, un-Hebraic calling of dealing in onions. In the rest of the Monarchy the Jews are often the Ashkenazim, or German-Polish branch, which again with the passing of time had taken on widely different characteristics according to whether its abode had been in Poland, Hungary or the western provinces.

The Polish or Galician Jew is generally accounted the lowest specimen of his race. The fate of this branch since its reception by King Casimir[1] has been singularly unfortunate. The national Polish temperament has been adverse to assimilation and in practice if not in law the ghetto and the talar subsist to-day. The swarming Jewish population of Galicia exists for the most part in a filth and poverty shared by the other inhabitants of that backward land. The Polish and Ruthenian peasants are both quarrelsome and stupid, and the pogroms of this quarter of Europe are classic. The Jews, themselves usually abjectly poor, have developed into a truly repulsive race—sly, extortionate,

---

[1] King Casimir of Poland received great quantities of Jews on their expulsion from Germany. His case is a singularly exact parallel to that of Ahasuerus; for his kindness to the race was due to his devotion to his Jewish mistress named Esther.

dishonest and cringing—which has reaped a well-grounded and universal dislike and distrust[1].

Hungary, on the other hand, was for long very liberal to the Jews, who in return allied themselves with the ruling Magyars against the subject nationalities in the country. The Liberal Party, for long the strongest in Hungary, and before it the '48 Party of Kossuth, allowed the Jews to gain such an ascendancy that at last the Magyars themselves turned against them. Certainly, the product of their treatment had been repellent in the extreme—to the writer's mind the arrogant and brutal Hungarian Jew is even more antipathetic than his humbler cousin of Galicia; but this is a subject which can be, and is, argued for hours at a time. The Jews had constituted themselves spokesmen of the extreme Magyar chauvinism, which is unbearable where it is not even native. At the turn of the century the reaction began with a disgraceful revival of the old tale of ritual murder. Although it was proved that the raiser of the cry had suborned the accused man's idiot son to bear false witness against him, the spark had been set to accumulated passions, and a reign of anti-Semitism set in. The climax of Jewish influence in Hungary came, however, after the war, when the Bolshevik government was in power for some months. Most of the leaders, including Bela Kun himself and the bloodthirsty terrorist Szamuely, were Jews, and their rule was disgraced by many atrocities. Their fall was succeeded by a violent anti-Semite régime, which vied with the Bolshevists in deeds of blood and did not spend its fury for long years.

[1] A recent action in the Viennese law courts turned on the question whether the words "we are not in Galicia here" constituted a libel on the person to whom they were addressed. "Tarnopoler Moral," from Tarnopol in East Galicia, is a current Viennese expression for swindling.

Both the Jews and the anti-Semites in Vienna are happily
of a more friendly type. The Jewish population of this
city assimilated itself very rapidly when the restrictions
were removed. Many or most of the older families enjoy
general esteem, take a highly useful place in the life of the
country, and are hardly to be distinguished unless by name
from the rest of the population[1].

Indeed, these families themselves found the annual influx
of new blood from Galicia so undesirable that at one time
they wanted to make Vienna, Lower Austria and Bohemia
"a closed area" for Jewish immigration.

At the same time, the rapid hold which they took on the
country was disagreeable to many, and above all to the
clerical party. An anti-Semite movement made a small
beginning under the lead of Prince Alois Lichtenstein, and
assumed large proportions after the financial crash of 1873
and the extension of the franchise to the "five-gulden
men" (see Chapter 1). That inspired demagogue, Dr Karl
Lueger, afterwards Mayor of Vienna, was driven out of
the Liberal Party of the day by the jealousies of its leaders.
Going over to the Christian Socialists he soon made of
them a big party, especially in the municipal government
of Vienna, almost solely on the cry of anti-Semitism—the
protection of the small traders against the more modern
Jewish methods, of the workmen against the domination
of Jewish capital. Thanks to Lueger's personality, almost

[1] Jews were compelled by Maria Theresa to take German names,
and these were generally confined to certain classes of words; names of
natural objects, moral qualities, etc. They were made to pay for regis-
tration; the higher the fee the prettier the name, which is therefore
sometimes charmingly poetical: Rosenstock, Morgenstern, or Grüss-
gott, sometimes ridiculous or obscene, as Wieselthier, Blaubauch,
Blasbalg.

the strongest Austrian party was one based on anti-Semitism, and essentially reactionary. Lueger was, however, neither malicious nor stupid. His constructive anti-Semitism was the more than justifiable effort to raise the Christians to the level of the Jews where they fell short of it; his destructive expressed itself much more in laughing at the Jews than in injuring them, and he had himself many friends among them. He was strongly supported by the Church, and Austrian anti-Semitism until after 1900 was still largely, if not essentially, religious.

Meanwhile, among the Jews themselves a new movement had begun. The idea of Zionism originated in the middle of the century in Russia, where the repressive measures were extraordinarily severe. But here it met with little response, and was dying out when it was revived suddenly in Vienna by a remarkable man, Dr Theodor Herzl. Herzl was a Budapest Jew by birth, but had made his career in Vienna, as literary editor of the *Neue Freie Presse*, the leading exponent of the assimilationist idea. He himself was led away from this idea by the taunts of some children who mocked him for Jew on account of his long black beard. This trivial circumstance led him to deep consideration of the problem of his race. At that time, most Jews in Vienna were in a state of semi-assimilation. Many of them had been baptised, had intermarried with Christians, had forsaken their religion, and with it lost the characteristic Jewish virtues without managing to adopt those of the Aryan, his physical aspect, or his way of wearing his clothes. They remained a sort of unsatisfactory half-breed. By the orthodox Jews they were despised as renegades, by the Christians disliked and derided for intruders.

Herzl's ideas passed through many phases. He began by advocating complete assimilation, as a first step towards which he proposed that he himself, with all the leading Jews from Vienna, should proceed to the cathedral and there receive baptism. Convinced at last of the impossibility of this scheme, he veered round to the idea of a Zionist State.

His idea roused the widest interest. Various methods of putting it into practice were propounded. Some were for colonising Palestine, buying Turkey's consent and support; others for founding an entirely new State—the British Government proposed the east coast of Africa. Herzl was able to interest most of Europe's rulers in his scheme; yet the "Sick Man" was still tenaciously alive and there seemed no immediate likelihood of founding a Palestinian State, or of fulfilling the real dream of the Jews of the Diaspora, never forgotten in their prayers—the rebuilding of the Temple. Yet the thought of Zionism was not unfruitful. It did much to re-awaken national and self-respect among the Jews. The young Zionists, instead of denying their race, gloried in it.

They began a movement for the revival of Jewish culture and the protection of Jewish interests. The students of the university formed a Jewish national organisation to compare and compete with that of the Germans or Czechs. Most interesting because most unexpected was the sporting movement, which contrary to all expectation achieved a blaze of glory in 1923 and roused Viennese Jews to a frenzy of enthusiasm by meeting and beating West Ham United, that year's finalists of the English Association Cup.

This movement formed a very exact parallel to the Sokols of the Slav nations of the Monarchy, and like them had its roots in the national feeling whose growth has been such a characteristic of our era. The popular cry of nationality has to-day in all walks of life largely usurped the place of religion. It is therefore not surprising that the latest anti-Semite movement is no longer religious but national. The history of the Austrian Christian Socialist Party is indeed one of the most curious on record. The dismemberment of the Monarchy cut much of the ground from under the feet of the German Nationalists. On the other hand, the Social Democrats rose suddenly to great power. The Christian Socialists found themselves grow more and more to be the anti-Socialist party, in which capacity they protected the interests of Jewish bankers, merchants and industrialists not less than those of priests and peasants. In fact, the Jewish middle classes began to support the party with both votes and money, so that its anti-Semitism dwindled down to a very half-hearted campaign against the Jewish Socialist leaders. The electioneering posters in Vienna are a remarkable sight. The one side presents caricatures of fat Jews sitting on money bags, the other side cartoons of lean Jews misleading workmen, and both sets are designed by the same artist and executed by the same firm. A genuine anti-Semite must be sorely perplexed.

Such persons—and they are not wanting—have had to take refuge with the National Socialist movement, which opposes the Jews on racial grounds. The question here is no longer religious. This party claims to represent the original German culture, and it even succeeded in discovering specimens of this improbable bird. This culture sprang from the land and is inherent in its true inhabitants. It supplies all the virtues which any one needs—honesty, good-fellowship, staunchness, courage, patriotism, a hard head. If the Jews have other virtues, they are qualities which the Germans can do without; let them go and practise them elsewhere. In Germany and Austria the Jews are a subtle poison, sapping away all true Teutonicity. Out with them. In this point of view extremes meet, and the German Nationalist finds himself in unexpected agreement with the Zionist.

This party venerates General Ludendorff as its leader, and has far more hold among the uncouth North Germans than in the kindlier climate of Vienna. The population of that city is, moreover, one of the most mixed in the world. Even setting aside the Jewish strain, it is an inextricable blend of German, Celt, Magyar, Italian and assorted Slav, and naturally cannot take very kindly to the ideals of the German Nationalists, who are wholehoggers. Rejecting even Christianity as a Jewish invention, the latter look forward to Valhalla and march out on midsummer mornings to worship the rising sun—an imposing sight. Their principal supporters in Vienna have been among the unripe students, who have often disgraced themselves by rowdy excesses foreign to the Viennese character.

The strongest outburst of anti-Semitism seen in Vienna in recent years was, by way of exception, due to purely economic causes, and had its roots in the abnormal conditions after the war. The Russian invasion of Poland had driven great multitudes of Galician Jews to seek refuge in Vienna. In 1919 these immigrants were reinforced by a second exodus from Hungary, following on the fall of Bela Kun. Most of these immigrants, especially the Galicians, were utterly destitute, and their swarming presence frightfully increased the food difficulties and the housing shortage. Deprived of all regular means of existence, they

mostly lived on speculation, for which the abnormal conditions, the rationing and restrictions, and, later, the falling
currency, offered them unique opportunities. If not the
founders, they were the most adept organisers of Schleichhandel, and largely controlled the secret food market,
which grew far more important than the official rations.
Such were the restrictions and the shortage, that almost
the only practical way to get a square meal or a roof over
one's head was to obtain them at an extortionate price
from an immigrant Jew seated in a dirty café. In the
money market, the immigrants came out even stronger.
Probably no one really understood the confused economics
of the falling currency; but the Jews quickly learnt how
to turn them to their own use. They manipulated with the
exchange, speculated in foreign currencies, smuggled and
played *à la baisse*. Sometimes they stuck to honest if ruthless finance; more often they evaded or broke the regulations. A wave of speculation swept over Austria. Jews and
Gentiles speculated alike; but the Gentile lost and the Jew
won. On the one side the big Jewish banks, working in
conspicuous security, amassed huge fortunes which they
adroitly concealed in, or not in, their complicated books.
On the other, next to the great red-brick Börse, a "black
Bourse" was set up in the dirty adjacent cafés, where
greasy immigrants fought for papers with the latest quotations, where the waiters were half detectives and half
chuckers-out, and the spoons were either chained to the
table or printed with the simple epitaph "Stolen from
Café so and so."

Almost the whole of Austrian business and finance had
become what Germans well call "unsolid," a state from
which it has not recovered to-day. The profits to be made

by honest trade were nothing in comparison with those of clever speculation and sharp practice—could indeed hardly be realised without them. Into the pockets of the Jews, more agile-minded, more calculating and often less scrupulous than their neighbours, flowed the profits of the industrialists, the incomes of the professional men, the savings of waiters and maid-servants.

During this period anti-Jewish feeling ran very high. A second Lueger could have made untold capital out of the almost universal disgust with which the Jews were regarded. But no Lueger arose, and the manifestations remained aimless and without programme, a sort of disheartened rowdyism which led nowhere. It was directed mainly against the poor Jews and small speculators, the destitute immigrants who had themselves lost almost everything through the war; most especially it was embittered by the housing shortage. Later on, the immigrants began to return home, and the feeling abated. It is not lacking against the big financiers and bankers; but it glances harmlessly off their hides.

The immigrants were episodic. But the war and the revolution have permanently altered the position of the Jew in Austria. To some extent they have strengthened it. The Jewish banks amassed great fortunes, brought industry almost wholly under their control, achieved an extraordinary position of importance in the State. But the real increase of power was accompanied by a much greater apparent increase. If the conservative parties still cling to the institution of the Hausjude, the Socialists and Communists do without it. Their leaders are largely of Jewish race, and do not trouble to conceal the fact. Jewish writers have often pointed out the absurdity of accusing the Jews in one breath of leading world capitalism and world socialism. Nevertheless, the charge is perfectly true, and not to be altered by the fact that Ford, Stinnes or Lenin were non-Jews. Nor is it really absurd. We, by our own action, have concentrated the Jewish mind on finance, and have systematically denied him any real community in the life of the country. Only by riches could he attain to power, and we gave him no inducement to share those riches with the country which treated him as an alien. On the other hand, all restrictions, all oppression weighed doubly heavily on the Jew. He felt them more acutely, and his mind, trained to activity, and lacking in the dumb acquiescence of the Slav peasant, or the feeling of national kinship with his own oppressors or superiors, was naturally led to schemes of revolution. This acquisition of wealth or this revolutionary energy was in either case carried through with the peculiar tenacious fanaticism which seems to be almost the only abiding characteristic of Jewish mentality.

When we look back over the history of Jews and their enemies from Biblical to modern times, one very peculiar circumstance strikes us; the Jews have always been hated, and always for different reasons. The qualities which awoke continuous enmity have themselves varied. To-day, they are reproached with Bolshevism, with disregard of the country in which they live, with materialism and money-grabbing. They are represented as cowardly usurers, who contrive to snatch a personal and financial advantage out of the misfortunes of the country where they live. But the Jews of the Bible are quite different. It is not lack of courage, but rather bloodthirsty cruelty, combined with a devotion to the arts and a passionate patriotism, which distinguished them. They were in fact apparently very like Scottish chieftains of the seventeenth century. And as regards the charge of usury, this is not brought against them one single time in all the writings of the early Christian Fathers. Yet the ancient Jews were clearly as heartily and generally disliked as their modern descendants, and pogroms are as old as the Pharaohs. One feels that something very deep and fundamental must lie behind this, something which cannot and ought not to be ignored in dealing with the Jewish problem.

For this problem to-day is twofold. Firstly, can the Jews be so completely absorbed in their surroundings as to cease to form an alien body? Secondly, if not, are the Jewish qualities and characteristics, whether blended with the Aryan in the individual by intermarriage or in the nation by settlement, beneficial to the community or not?

This is a question which a nation has the right to ask and a right to act logically on the answer. One cannot doubt, from the experience of countries with small Jewish populations, that where Jews abandon their religion, intermarry and live like their neighbours, they very soon become quite indistinguishable. On the other hand, where they form a very large minority, as in Galicia or in Hungary, or in Vienna, their qualities must obviously affect the product of a fusion. For although the contrary has been proved ethnographically and historically, the fact remains that they are a race with pronounced racial qualities of their own. The Jew of pure descent is physically, morally and mentally different from the Teuton and in many respects greatly his superior. In industry, abstemiousness, feeling for his children and his fellows and generosity he leaves him far behind. It is impossible not to admire the Jews and yet

M   16

difficult to feel a full sympathy for them. A liberal-thinking man who is yet conscious in his own mind of this ineradicable antipathy must search very deeply for its causes, rejecting a hundred ratiocinations in his search.

It appears to come down to a primitive difference in composition. Blind emotion and reasoning intellect have both their share in our souls, in greater or lesser quantities. In the Jew, the latter usually rules the former; in the Nordic and Slav races it is the reverse. Among the Latins the balance is better held, and in fact the Latin races have assimilated their Jewish population with comparative ease. One often finds Gentiles cleverer than Jews and Jews deeper in feeling than Gentiles. But Teutons and Slavs do not live by their intellect and where they use it, it is in the service of their emotions. The whole melancholy history of Germany is one of generally misdirected and entirely unhumorous[1] emotions and enthusiasm. They are right to worship Wotan to-day, for they have never outgrown him. With their beer and their Kameradschaft, their Kultur and their Shining Armour, they are still to-day the pugnacious, visionary hard drinkers, hard eaters and hard fighters of Tacitus' time.

Not so the Jew. His whole being is logical. Jehovah, Moses and the author of the Talmud alike work out life on a careful system of *quid pro quo*. Religion, for us a vague, swooning emotion, playing on the most sensitive

---

[1] One of the most striking differences between Gentile and Jew in Austria is the monopoly of humour, or at any rate wit, enjoyed by the latter. Practically all Viennese jokes are either by or about Jews, generally both. Perhaps humour is a direct result of emotion controlled by logic. Or perhaps Thomas Hardy's parish clerk hit the nail on the head when he said "entering the Church is the ruin of a man's wit, for wit's nothing without a faint shadow of sin."

portions of our heart, is for them a logical system for the attainment of every sort of well-being. Moses was not a religious preacher in our sense of the word. He was a sanitary lawgiver, and the practical virtues (among which may be mentioned cleanliness and abstinence) were the ones he cared about. Jehovah, too, was an extremely practical person. His objection to other gods was not based on any monotheistic idealism, but on jealousy and the probable shortage of the fat of bulls and calves. He looked after his people, they looked after him. If, as some philosophers assert, all virtues are merely expediency, Jehovah and Moses knew that long ago. Where such expediency might seem doubtful to the individual, extra pressure was put on, as in the fifth commandment, which always sticks in the gullets of idealists.

The religion of the Old Testament has no place in it for asceticism for its own sake. It insists the more on such a wise and sober way of living as is likely to bring every personal advantage to those who practise it. The Talmud goes a step further, but in the same direction. With its endless quibbles, refinements and hair-splittings, it is only carrying out the Scriptures to a logical conclusion. As a matter of fact, the Christian scholastic philosophy indulged in convolutions quite as complicated as those of the Talmud; but they were not suited to our natures, and we rejected them in favour of broader, less exact ideas.

But in the world to-day our eating, wiving, amusements, friendships—the real intimate, inner life of each of us—are based on the emotions. But our money-making, which is our means to the end of living, is most naturally and easily conducted by the intellect. And the man who is to scoop off the cream of the emotional life is not he in whom the desire to do so is strongest, but he who has cultivated the intellect and put money in his purse. This could easily be remedied if we imitated the industry of the Jew, for he is not naturally more intelligent than ourselves, only we seldom do so.

But there is a still deeper contradiction behind. We accepted the teaching of Christ, whom the Jews rejected as not fulfilling the Scriptures. But Christ being a Jew forced us to accept the Jewish Scriptures. And these contain a religion fundamentally unsuited to us. Hence arises the difference between Jewish and Christian religious fanatics; the latter must always be half insincere—must always keep one eye closed to the real facts of his nominal religion. One cannot imagine the Jewish race being satisfied with a Bible of which half has to be expurgated, as it is for the Catholics.

Seen in the light of this deep psychological difference, the Jewish problem is religious and racial at once. If we cannot absorb the Jews, it appears that we have to take our ideas from them permanently. But if we are not willing to do this, then it must seem that anti-Semitism as a principle (not murder, bullying or stupid riots) is justified.

I would be the last to put this forward as the final solution of the Jewish mystery. Anyone who has been a week in Central Europe must begin to cudgel his brains over this strange race, so universally despised and hated, yet so much more powerful and prosperous than its persecutors. I have talked on the matter with many Christian and many Jewish friends, and can confirm from experience what is often said in jest, that the worst anti-Semites are themselves Jews. Most of my Jewish friends began the discussion by admitting an inferiority. One, a prominent Zionist and orthodox believer, said: "I must despise the Jews, because they rejected Christ." I do not think that this is due to a cowardly feeling that he who shouts most loudly for persecution will escape it himself; in the case of this speaker certainly not, for he wore Jewish dress and lived in every respect according to the laws of his religion. It is certainly true that few people have really hated the Jews whole-heartedly who had not themselves at least a strain of the Jew in them. In the case of the Catholic Church, the strain is in the faith, instead of the blood. In my own mind I am convinced of an inferiority of the Jewish spirit, and it is for this very reason that I would condemn pogroms and violence, for I think it degrading that we should not be able to prove ourselves the Jews' betters by honourable means. A pure-blooded Aryan can take his feelings on the subject coolly; but a man of mixed blood, who feels an inferiority of the Jewish strain in him and resents it, is much more embittered; and more still the pure Jew. Otto Weininger, the young philosopher, who wrote one of the most brilliant, if most controversial, books of recent years[1] and then committed suicide, was a Jew; and in the chapter which he devoted to his countrymen says some of the most bitter things imaginable. For him there is a Jewish spirit, which is found generally but not exclusively in the Jewish race; some of this race are without it and others, of different blood, possess it. To it he attributes every degree of inferiority. He quite rightly points out that the Jew, for all his talent, has hardly attained the greatest heights. In modern times the most distinguished Jews have been a Spinoza, a Heine, a Mendelssohn, a Josef Israels, great

---

[1] *Geschlecht und Charakter.*

men, but Christians can show far greater; even in the
matter of money-making, the greatest fortunes have been
made by Christians. For him the Jew has no personality,
no individuality; from this follows his disbelief in immor-
tality, his lack of faith and the steadiness and simplicity
which faith brings. He is incapable of greatness until he
shall have rejected the Jew in him; and this is the greatness
of Christ; to have overcome and rejected the Jewish spirit
absolutely, so that he had no longer the slightest thing in
common with it. It is indubitable that the Jew lacks simplicity and faith in himself. He replaces it by a mental
agility, a slyness which is always quick to seize the momentary advantage and usually ends, for that very reason, in
defeating its own aims. These are qualities which can help
him to a leading position among the backward or un-
intelligent races, but which end by pervading the whole
life of such races with a fatal unsoundness. This is at the
back of the acute present-day Jewish problem in Central
Europe, which is practical and economical. The Jews have
been placed in the position of the financiers and middle
classes of a large part of Europe. Where the Christians
have long been able to meet them on their own ground,
as in Scotland, there is no problem of excessive Jewish
influence. Where they are quickly learning to do so, as
in Germany, it is vanishing. Recent years, in spite of the
confusion caused by the war, have seen on the whole a
diminution of Jewish power and numbers in Germany and
a large emigration of Jews to Palestine and the United
States of America, where the naïve illusion of the inhabitants, that they are born business men, must prove singularly tempting to the more sophisticated Hebrew. In
Austria matters are not so far advanced. The population

is indolent, easy-going, artistic rather than intellectual. Here we get Jewish control and anti-Semitism.

It is not easy to say how far the Jews are an influence for good or evil in Austria. The experience of Spain shows that they are a great intellectual and economic advantage to a semi-developed State. On the other hand, they form beyond doubt an uncomfortably large alien element. A State which has reached the level of England, France or Germany no longer needs its Jews. A State which is less advanced, and which has let them acquire a greater domination, is in a different position. Probably the truth was about hit off a couple of years ago by a witty writer who since the war has attained an immense popularity in certain circles, and who perhaps better than any other writer has caught the less pleasing aspects of the hectic and nervous years which have succeeded the war. His sketch *The City without Jews* pictures Vienna after the war, in all its confusion of falling currency, housing and food shortage, rising prices and general economic and social chaos. The Prime Minister of the day, a stalwart German, introduces a Bill to expel from Austria all Jews, baptised Jews and children of mixed marriages. The Bill is passed, the Jews removed. At first a great deal of difficulty is caused by the unexpected number of mixed marriages. It is found that the law affects most of the best brains in the land, and many relatives of the aristocracy and even the clergy. But it goes through; anti-Semite organisations abroad carry through the financial liquidation of Jewish property, and after the last Jew has gone, the Minister addresses a monster meeting at the Town Hall, amidst enormous enthusiasm, in a fiery speech beginning: "My dear Christians!"

At first there is jubilation. There are plenty of flats to be had, plenty of seats in the opera, and prices fall. But matters soon change. The krone continues to sink. The new men who have taken over the great Jewish banks and business houses are incapable of running them. The wealthy portion of the population is gone, and the luxury industry of Vienna is at a standstill. Cafés and restaurants close down; theatres play the classics to empty houses; newspapers become too dull to read. Bankruptcies are now common, unemployment increases. The State is burdened with vast unemployment doles, inflation continues, the krone falls and falls. Vienna becomes a great village, where everyone wears country costumes, and Prague and Budapest, who have kept their Jews, succeed to her position as a financial and commercial centre.

At last a single Jew comes back, disguised and travelling on a false passport. He opens a campaign for the return of his race, and a political party is founded with this for its aim. New elections are held, but the majority in favour of repeal is too small by one vote. But the motion is brought in, and the Jew manages to decoy away a single Deputy, to make him blind drunk and to leave him sleeping off his potations in a motor car outside the lunatic asylum near Vienna, while the fateful motion is passed by a bare majority.

Now the Jew's presence becomes known (he is believed to have motored down from the Czech frontier the moment the Act was passed). A monster meeting is held outside the Town Hall. The Jew is carried to it on the shoulders of the population, and amidst enormous enthusiasm, the Mayor of Vienna addresses the meeting in a fiery speech beginning: "My dear Jew!"

CHAPTER X

AUSTRIA AND CENTRAL EUROPE

ANY attempt to discuss the position which Austria now holds, and is likely in the future to hold in Central Europe, is a delicate and difficult task, involving almost inevitably some criticism of the Peace Treaty which created her. For in fact, until November 1918, Austria did not exist; what we loosely called by this name being defined in the country itself much more circumstantially as "the kingdoms and provinces represented in the Imperial Council." The new Austria came to light sorely against her own will; of her inhabitants, some wanted her back in her old position, others, who welcomed the separation of the German race from the Slavs and Hungarians, took as an absolute condition of this its immediate union with its brothers in Germany.

Whoever, during the first year or two, attempted to say a word for the arrangements made by the Treaties was treated more or less as a criminal lunatic. Officially and privately, it was taken as axiomatic that the new State could not exist. But it was forced to exist, and helped to do so, while Germany, stronger and therefore more intractable, involved herself more and more deeply with her enemies. The pendulum swung far in the opposite direction, and a boundless optimism reigned, which at the time of writing is giving way to renewed misgivings.

The problem, round which has centred much confused and inaccurate thinking, has been complicated by so many side issues that it is really difficult to disentangle its real nature.

At the time of the signing of the Treaty, the self-determination of nations happened to be the popular cry, and it was according to this principle—more or less—that the map of Central Europe was redrawn. The Slav nations of the old Monarchy (except the Ukrainians of East Galicia[1]) received the treatment which they demanded; so did the Italians and Rumanians. The Austrians came off entirely empty-handed, and this in two separate respects. Firstly, as a whole nation, they voted for unity with Germany, and this was denied them; secondly, the boundaries of their new State were so drawn as to leave outside it very important and undeniably German districts. The province of South Tirol, assigned to Italy, is purely German down to a line south of Bozen; there are small German minorities in Hungary and Yugoslavia; and finally, by far the most important, there are over three million Germans in Czechoslovakia, many of them inhabiting districts lying directly along the new frontier and all of them constituting a population which in wealth, industry and intelligence is among the first in Central Europe, and in true German racial character and patriotism far excels the indolent, cosmopolitan Viennese.

So here is Austria; a most unexpected and certainly a misshapen creature whom nobody really wanted. She is no natural birth, gradually and inevitably formed, as a State ought to be; rather the product, partly of influences of the present which have little direct concern with her— the rivalry between France and Germany, natural sym-

[1] It is now commonly asserted that the Croats and Slovenes of Yugoslavia, and the Slovaks, were forced into their respective States against their wills. This is not the case; they worked and voted for the States which they got, even if their position in them is less happy than they had expected.

pathy between Professor Wilson and Professor Masaryk; partly of conditions in the past which were themselves artificial.

For certainly there was no inevitability about the frontiers or the constitution of the Habsburg Dominions. Those who to-day so readily repeat the catchword that these dominions formed an "economic unity" overlook the fact that there has hardly passed a generation for centuries when they have remained the same. It is only a few years since Bosnia and Herzegovina were under Turkish rule, only yesterday in history—and much of it within the memory of a certain old man who died in 1916—that Cracow, Salzburg and Dalmatia were brought under Habsburg rule, and Lombardy, with Venice, shook loose from it; and only sixty years since the Monarchy finally renounced her ambition to be the leading German State, and turned her eyes towards the East.

Viewed in this light, the epigram that "if Austria did not exist, we should have to invent her" takes on a different air.

Yet they, too, would be wrong who denied the Dual Monarchy any *raison d'être* whatever. Three or four hundred years ago, the Habsburgs had probably more justification for exercising the strong arm than any rulers in Europe. It is hard for us to realise to-day what a weight of terror for centuries the menace of Turkish invasion spread over Central Europe. What the Turks touched, they destroyed. They wiped out the culture of the Balkans, annihilated hardly less completely that of Hungary, threatened all the Mediterranean. Twice they pressed up to the walls of Vienna. On the second of these occasions, in 1683, there was every likelihood that their siege would be successful.

The defenders were almost at the end of their forces when the relieving army under Pan Sobieski arrived, and before the final battle were addressed by their leader:

We fight for our own country, and under the walls of Vienna we are defending those of Warsaw and Cracow. We have to save to-day, not a single city, but the whole of Christendom, of which that city of Vienna is the bulwark [1].

If Vienna had fallen then, civilisation would have been set back for centuries over a patch of land the extent of which it is not possible to guess; possibly as far west as the Rhine.

In those days, religious, military and dynastic considerations not only weighed more in men's minds than economic ones, but largely determined them. Prosperity depended not so much on cheapness of labour and proximity of market as on personal safety. The nations which gathered round the Habsburgs, which placed themselves voluntarily under their protection, did so for their own good.

For long centuries the Habsburg Monarchy was, in fact and in theory, "the bulwark of Europe." Its justification and its character alike were clerical and military. Indeed, a great strip of land running right across the new Turkish marches of the Balkans bore the name of the "Military Frontier" and was probably as near a parallel as modern times can show to the Roman wall across Northumberland.

And, even apart from the Turkish question, the Habsburg rule, until the nineteenth century, was of unquestionable economic advantage to the peoples under it. The Slav and Rumanian peoples of Central Europe, and the Hungarians, except for a few noble families, had never risen

[1] Scheinauer, *Two Sieges of Vienna* (English translation).

above or had relapsed into the state of barbaric peasant nations to which the superior German civilisation brought little but good. Even at its lowest, the standard of learning, efficiency and honesty of the German race, whether as merchants, administrators or otherwise, is many hundred per cent. higher than that of its Eastern neighbours; and as a civilising force the Catholic Church has been one of the greatest of the world.

Thus, while some provinces, like Dalmatia or the Bukovina, were obvious excrescences, the rest gained by their position and knew it, and the ingenious Napoleon, who cut up the Empire in a very slapdash fashion, may well have been surprised at the energy with which it pieced itself together again.

It was not till the nineteenth century that matters changed. As the non-German races of the Monarchy one by one rose above the peasant state, and produced middle classes and an independent economic life of their own, so in one after the other the movement for national autonomy grew; grew and spread until at last it embraced them all, not least, be it remarked, the Germans. For the government of the Habsburgs, in its ideology, had never moved far beyond the days of the Turkish sieges. Its guiding principles were still clerical, military and dynastic. If one takes the history of the internal government of the Empire in the nineteenth century, sets aside the comparatively few changes or measures which were directly based on the will of the peoples, and analyses the rest, there are few behind which one does not find one of the three motives: the glory of Mother Church, the aggrandisement of the House of Habsburg, or the professional needs of the army. The central provinces of German Austria, Hungary, Bohemia and Moravia, with the port of Trieste, did indeed really form a very close "economic unity" had they been governed with a view to taking advantage of the fact; but they were not.

The system of government had little interest in or understanding for economics. Not only was the whole financial administration bad, the State debts crushing and the currency unstable, but the Habsburgs could never—until October 1918—reconcile themselves to the idea of giving the separate nationalities elbow-room and liberty. They moved slowly from despotism to constitutionalism, from a single to a dual control, but always too late. The nations, herded together, their national passions kept at boiling point largely by the policy of their rulers, succeeded in making life impossible for one another. The substance was sacrificed to the shadow. A form of unity was preserved, but there was probably a great deal less of its reality than the nations concerned would have had and will in the future create for themselves, unhampered by extraneous considerations. When the Monarchy finally broke up, its inhabitants, blinded with exasperation, made haste to "pour the child out with the bath-water" as the Germans say, and constitute themselves so many self-supporting, self-contained units.

Although their birth-pangs have been severe, there is no intrinsic reason why Poland, Czechoslovakia, Hungary, Rumania, and Yugoslavia should not, after the passage of a few peaceful years, the acquisition of a little political and common sense and possibly a few frontier corrections, become perfectly stable and prosperous States. In all of them it is only a minority which holds any other view. The case of Austria is somewhat different. Few of her inhabitants wanted her, few believed at first in her practicability. The first year or two of the peace were distracted with schemes for altering her in every imaginable way.

One of these various schemes possesses already no more than a historical interest. Not many, even among the most loyal followers of the Habsburgs, dreamed it possible to restore the Monarchy on its old scale. There were some who still, in the face of its reception, believed that Kaiser Karl's last manifesto could be accepted and a federal State of Central Europe set up under a Habsburg. Others saw the impossibility of this, but believed that a small State, consisting of Austria, Hungary and Croatia, might be formed. It is difficult to think that any couple which had got safely divorced from the appalling union which bound Austria and Hungary would desire to re-enter that state of conjugal jealousy and bickering. But there were some such. The great obstacle to this plan, apart from the veto of the Entente, was the existence of Vienna, about whose Republican sentiments there could be no doubt. Accordingly, another, or rather two other ideas were bruited.

These were the establishment of a Catholic *bloc* along the Danube. In its more modest version, it was to consist of Bavaria and the western provinces of Austria; in the more comprehensive, Hungary and perhaps a part of Croatia were to be added. In both, Vienna and the neighbouring industrial districts were to be left to form an independent free State, so that, in the narrower scheme at least, the population would have been remarkably homogeneous in race, manner of living and above all in religion, although one may have one's doubts as to the stability of its finances.

The newspaper revelations which have since been made on this subject have not gone very deeply into detail, but

it is known that the throne was to be offered to a Wittels-
bach of Bavaria. There is no reason to suppose that the
Austrian mountaineers would have raised much objection
to the change of dynasty, since their personal loyalty had
largely died with the death of Franz Josef, and conservative
Bavaria is far nearer to them in every way than Socialist
and atheist Vienna.

It was in 1922 that this plan reached the height of its
popularity. Just at this moment the situation in Austria was
at its most critical stage, while relations between Bavaria
and the industrial North and Central Germany were also
uncommonly strained. The granting of a credit to Austria,
as well as the influence of the Clerical Minister Dr Seipel,
was the first blow to it; the second came when the leaders
of the Bavarian separatist movement lost much of their
influence in the following years, and North and South
Germany again patched up a peace.

The feeling that Austria, as a whole, should join Germany
was much more widely spread and much more deeply
rooted. There are indeed two currents of opinion here also
—the "All-German" and the "Great German," of which
the one is federalist, the other centralist. The difference
is, however, a minor one. The general idea is common to
two of the three large political parties in Austria, and just
after the war was almost universal. Indeed, the first Assembly which constituted the new Republic proclaimed it
to be a part of Germany, and the veto of the Entente was
called in, first to suppress this idea, secondly to change the
actual name of the Republic from "German-Austria" to
"Austria."

Temporary and very contradictory political motives
played a part in the very general desire for union with

Germany. The political parties were so evenly balanced in Austria that each hoped that the move would reinforce it. While the Catholics desired a close federation with Bavaria, the whole of the anti-Catholic parties hoped that the influence of North Germany would go far towards breaking the clerical predominance in Austria. The chief guiding impulse was, however, economic. At a time when the Succession States had erected almost impenetrable barriers round all her Eastern frontiers, Austria had indeed no breathing space except towards the West, where alone she found a neighbour to look kindly on her. Furthermore, in comparison with the krone, the mark was at the time a miracle of stability, and it was very generally believed that in five years at the most it would recover its old value. Thus voices were loud for the introduction of a common currency for the two countries, which, it was believed, would restore economic stability in Austria. At that time there was a very general idea that the wealth and prosperity of any country is in direct ratio to the value of its currency, the awkward effects of one's money being too good not having yet been realised.

Dr Bauer in Austria and later Stinnes in Germany made repeated attempts to make the union real. But for the Entente it would have become so *de jure*, and *de facto* it almost was so. In most of the regulations issued by both countries at the time, the subjects of each were treated by the other not as foreigners, but natives, and the preference holds good to-day in many cases. The fraternal feeling began to pale a little when living in Austria became very cheap and the Germans swarmed across the frontier to enjoy it; and grew a little paler still when the position was reversed later, and the Austrians began to eat Germany out of hearth and home. So destructive are the fluctuations of paper money on all the better feelings.

Union with Germany became a catchword. It was looked on as an universal panacea, the effects of which many who called for it had not stopped to consider. It was not, however, ever without its opponents. Most obvious among these were of course the conservative circles, dynastic or clerical, which still hoped for a revival of Austria's hegemony in Central Europe. But there were others to whom that lost hegemony had brought an advantage less directly political; notably the big business men with branches and connections all through the Succession States. It was true that they were brought to the verge of ruin after the war by the frontiers and tariffs which each of these erected; but it was obvious that this state of things could not continue for ever. Sooner or later, the mania for self-sufficiency would pass, and people would turn naturally again to Vienna, their old centre. If Austria had a value at all, it was not that of a mere distant oriental province of Germany, but of a centre of supply in every way, intellectual as well as industrial, for the Danube basin and the Balkans.

And there were others also who saw that the geographical position of Austria had after all its political and military advantages.

Three combinations were disputing in Central Europe; the Slavonic of the Little Entente—Yugoslavia and Czechoslovakia, supported by France; the Italian-Hungarian; and the German. Among these three, Austria occupies a neat central position, and weak as she is, it will always be worth while bidding for her favour so long as she is not definitely committed to any particular group.

In fact, since the decree went out that Austria was to

remain independent, she has preserved the balance quite adroitly. Racially, she is most nearly allied with Germany; economically perhaps with Czechoslovakia. Her financial situation is most nearly akin to that of Hungary. She has no enemies now; the vivid hatred felt against her in 1919 has burnt itself out; she fulfils her function of a centre where the merchants, financiers and politicians of so many contending States can meet on neutral ground. It is by her services in this capacity that she has been able, so far, to maintain herself, and at one time even to give the appearance of universal prosperity. It must, however, be admitted that her position has been precarious, not only in the moments of crisis when everyone perceived this fact, but all along.

Immediately after the war, the whole country was dependent, more or less, on charity. Vienna was hardest hit; but the country districts were not in a very much better state. These conditions were, however, abnormal, the result of the war. In the years which have supervened, the Austrian farmers have been able to make good the ravages of war, to replenish their livestock, and to face the world afresh. In spite of the vanishing of their mortgages, their condition is still none too good. None of the provinces, except Lower Austria, is self-supporting throughout the whole year with its present population and its present methods of cultivation. The deficit is, however, gradually being made up. A comparison with Switzerland goes to show that the disadvantage of Austria is due far more to backward methods and to ingrained stupidity than to any necessary economic cause. The incurable conservatism of the peasant, fostered by the Church, shuts him off from modern methods, which might increase his production by a large percentage. There are also, besides agriculture, other sources of wealth in the Austrian Alps which have not hitherto been fully exploited. The yield from the State forestries, which are already admirably managed, cannot be expected to be increased greatly, although they will probably rise in value with the growing shortage of timber in the world. But there are certainly mines and mineral deposits which have never yet been fully exploited, and above all, there is one great source of income which could be had for the price, almost, of a little politeness. This is the tourist traffic. There are few countries in Europe so beautiful or so suitable for holiday-making as Austria, very few which so neglect their beauties. The inns and hotels, with very few exceptions, are primitive, dirty and uncouth, having indeed deteriorated vastly since the war. The cooking is flavourless and monotonous to a degree, the service usually beneath contempt. It is difficult to obtain information, and there is a take-it-or-leave-it idea about the whole thing which drives anyone accustomed to the twentieth century to distraction. I myself was foolish enough to spend a recent summer holiday in Carinthia. On my journey down from Vienna I stood for six hours in the corridor, because there were no seats in the train. There was room in the first class, but then I should have had to pay double, the excuse that the second class was full up not being accepted. In the first hotel in which we stopped, the host was a vegetarian. All the guests were therefore vegetarians too, perforce. The food was disgusting, but to make up for it the walls were placarded with manly German mottoes such as:

In der Beschränkung zeigt sich erst der Mensch,

or   Der beste Arzt ist jederzeit
            Des Menschens eigene Mässigkeit[1].

In the next place we asked for rooms; they wanted to know if I was a Jew. I am not one, nor do I look like one, but the question so annoyed me that I told them I was a Wunder-Rabbi from Lemberg, and went further. The next place, seeing that we were tired, asked a perfectly preposterous price for the rooms. At last we found a lodging and the next day took the steamer on the lake. On the way back, the wind was high and the steamer, with no warning, passed our landing-stage and made for the opposite side of the lake. When I asked what travellers to my destination were to do, I got for answer:

"There is nothing to be done."

And the return steamer, later, tried to make us pay excess fares for having gone on beyond our destination.

When these things are altered, the country has sufficient beauties to make the tourist traffic highly profitable, and by its help the western provinces ought to be able to make up their deficits.

The question of the towns and the industrial districts is different, and much more serious. It has yet never been really faced in its entirety, for one circumstance or another has always arisen to mask the real issue.

The first year or so after the war were altogether abnormal. During the beginning, at least, of that period, much machinery was worth no more than so much scrap-iron, and the complicated modern apparatus of Vienna was not only no asset, but a heavy drawback. But after a little while

---

[1] A man reveals himself in continence alone. The best doctor is always one's own moderation.

the barriers to international intercourse were partly re-moved, and the krone started sinking in earnest.

The falling currency brought cheap labour and low prices, unemployment ceased, the factories were fully employed and Austrian industry enjoyed a boom so long as the deficiencies remained to be made up; in Austria it lasted longer than elsewhere, owing to the cheapness of production. Just when it showed signs of flagging, the French occupied the Ruhr, the German steel and iron industry was paralysed, and the Austrians profited by their rivals being out of action.

There was a simultaneous but much greater prosperity in the world of finance. International finance had suddenly become intensely complicated, and there were enormous fortunes to be made in it. The capitals of the new States did their best to divert the stream of wealth to themselves, but it was too early. Vienna remained the centre, and a great centre, or clearing-house, was more necessary than ever. While industry did no more, as a rule, than work up to its pre-war capacity, and shortage of capital made it impossible to found any new enterprises except on a small scale, finance expanded enormously. A vast host of small banks and exchange offices sprang into being and did a roaring trade.

Trade, too, held its own and prospered. Both sellers and buyers were more numerous than in normal times; the former, because the pinch of poverty forced them to part with their old possessions; the latter, because it was no use saving money which became worthless next day.

The State was in a less satisfactory position. If private individuals kept going, it was after all on quick turnover and not on taxable accumulation. The capital was there to start with: the machinery, the shops, the railways, the business connections, the established reputations. These, combined with cheap production, could support the producer; but they could not bring in wealth to the State, whose capital was costly to maintain and whose sources of income were almost nil. During this first period, the State lived from hand to mouth on loans, and by inflating the currency.

In the autumn of 1922 the krone was stabilised and prices began to rise. The State got a loan to carry on while it put its finances in order, but the private producers found themselves in difficulties.

For a while they carried on on credit. Every company made enormous issues of new shares; the public bought; the shares boomed; speculators still made incomes. But export was dwindling, unemployment increasing, real capital getting ever shorter. Industry became more and more dependent on loans from the banks. Foreign capitalists looked askance on the situation; the local banks demanded enormous rates of interest.

At this moment the banks, with few exceptions, chose to speculate the wrong way on the French franc. They called in their loans to cover their losses; one business after another went bankrupt. Shares were thrown on the market in enormous packets; one middle-class speculator after another lost his investments. In spite of all efforts, the smaller banks were unable to meet their obligations, and became insolvent.

The summer of 1924 was a tragic but inevitable period of bubble-pricking. The unsound banks, businesses and industries, most of them the new creations which had absorbed the energies of the middle classes, vanished one after the other, and with them some firms which deserved a better fate. People cannot go on for ever living by taking in one another's washing.

The State meanwhile was putting its finances in order. Subsidies had vanished, the number of officials had been reduced, the deficit on the railways diminished. It is true that it was being done on borrowed money, but at the same time a genuine and very successful effort was being made to balance the budget by taxation.

For the first time for four years, Austria has begun to realise how impoverished she really is. The question begins to be heard again—is the State of Austria capable of existence, and in what form?

The question of external form has been definitely decided, for years to come, by international authority. There is to be no union with Germany. Nor is it easy to see how such an union would help Austria materially, apart from questions of sentiment. If, on the one hand, it brought a breath of modernity, more up-to-date methods and greater efficiency, this would certainly not penetrate Austria without difficulty and friction, and might land her in international complications which she could ill afford to face. Vienna is situated almost on Austria's eastern frontier and it is towards the East that her face is turned. Her economic future certainly depends on her position as purveyor of Western goods, Western methods and Western thought to the less civilised peoples beyond her. In that respect the centuries have brought no change. Her ideal would be, not a political union with any neighbour or a group of neighbours—the nations which knocked their heads together under the last of the Habsburgs have had enough of that—but a closest possible economic union.

And little by little the nations of Central Europe, Italy included, are moving in this direction. There is already a network of commercial agreements, extending in some cases to defensive military treaties, which has brought about far more real harmony and unity than existed when most of them were grouped together under one sceptre. The lessons of the years immediately preceding and following the war have been salutary. They have not been assimilated particularly quickly; some of the Austrians and a few of the Czechs were the only people who did not have to have them driven in "with hobnails, not tintacks." But the years are bringing an increasing understanding of them even in Hungary, that most *difficile* of all nations.

In this group of nations—this time to exclude Italy—Austria holds a position quite apart. She is much the poorest of them in natural resources; much the richest in accumulated capital. It is a dangerous situation; for national pride and economic rivalry can build banks and railways; but it cannot make trees grow much quicker, nor induce the sugar-beet and the maize to flourish on the top of stony mountains. Austria can certainly improve her resources; with more rational farming she can increase agricultural production; with better hotels and better management she can attract more foreign visitors; and, above all, she can turn to use her natural riches in waterpower, which are among the greatest in Europe.

When these are fully utilised, her coal bill, which is responsible for much of her deficit, will be enormously reduced, and both communications and industry be cheaper and better.

But meanwhile she has to live on the accumulated capital, material and spiritual, of Vienna. Of these the latter is by far the more important. The former has already suffered a severe diminution; we shall never know the value of the objects which were bought up by foreign purchasers in the great bargain years when the krone was worth next to nothing. And apart from this, the loss on depreciation, when so little has been renewed since 1914, in every variety of object from railway termini to tenement houses, must be enormous.

There still remain advantages, and great ones, over any near neighbour in the shape of buildings, factory plants and railways. But they are growing relatively less. Austria can afford little new building or construction—has ado to keep up what she has—and another fifteen or twenty years will see at least Prague equalling her in this respect and probably Belgrade.

The more material the advantage, the sooner it is likely to go. It is very doubtful indeed whether Austrian industry will be able long to maintain its present lead. Natural disadvantages—the cost of coal and transport—weigh heavily against it. If these can be counteracted to some extent by the use of waterpower, yet Vienna as a centre of delivery can hardly hope to keep its present importance, and the competition, especially of German firms, can hardly fail to reduce Austrian industry. The process is already being felt. At the time of writing, the Austrian employers suffer under a double disadvantage since the taxation and work-men's insurance, and the like, which they have to pay are much heavier than in Germany, which in addition is not bound by the eight-hour day. Thus Austrian Socialism, unless its admirable social legislation is extended inter-nationally, is likely to have to confine itself more than ever to the municipality of Vienna, for the number of private industrial undertakings, and thus of industrial workmen, can hardly fail to diminish in the future.

The position is not so bad as it would have been but for the fact that the Austrian industry is highly skilled. It consists largely in the working up of imported half-finished materials, and selling them further. In these branches the Austrians are uncommonly fine and skilful workers; in some of them, specialists whom it is hard to match in the world, and who can more or less defy competition for many years to come. Most especially is this the case in trades which are directly artistic; in much of the leather work, the porcelain factories, the furniture and the decorations of firms such as the Wiener Werkstätte.

The same can probably be said of both trade and finance. Both may seem, according to Western notions, to be run on clumsy, antiquated and insecure lines; but they still preserve relics of a tradition, are still easily the foremost in Central Europe. Vienna is not likely to be displaced for a long time as either a buying or a financial centre. It is from these sources that most of her present taxation is drawn, and everyone in the country is alive to the necessity of keeping up the Austrian supremacy. It is far more deeply grounded than most of Austria's industry, reaches back far longer. It is a thought not without irony that, after all, republican Austria owes most of her assets of to-day to the Habsburgs; that her financial mainstays are the descendants of the milliners and jewellers who adorned the Empresses of bygone days, or of moneylenders who pulled the Emperors out of financial tight corners. Another thought, from which one may draw what conclusions one will, is this: that agriculture, which is stationary, industry which if anything is retrogressive, are mostly in Aryan hands; while trade and finance, which have developed since the war and are well able to hold their own in modern conditions, are overwhelmingly Jewish.

But certainly, the longest-lived advantage which Austria possesses, and one more enduring than brass, is purely artistic and intellectual. Although in artistic matters the Viennese lack both the fire and the depth of the pure Slavs, the German strain in them has endowed them with an infinitely greater capacity for the practical application of their talents. Vienna remains a great intellectual centre for an enormous and desolate tract which needs intellectual leadership far more than it does machinery or blankets. The doctors, the lawyers and above all the University, together with the concerts and opera, are to-day the most valuable things which Austria can offer to the world. And as time goes by, their value will be seen more clearly. It is not likely to be reduced; in comparison with other things it will certainly stand out far more prominently.

For, after all, Austria has always been an idea, and her message to the world has been ideal. Since earliest times an odour of the unpractical and paradoxical has clung about her. Her rulers, various as they have been, have all had the same curious knack of incorporating ideas, often disastrous in their political application, but great in themselves. For many centuries Austria civilised Eastern Europe, and for all her faults, she is still doing so to-day. Through all the injustice, laziness and dishonesty which infest Vienna, there has always cropped out something from which others can learn, and the city herself seems destined to be the home and the symbol of ideas. As men and manners change, so do their judgements on those ideas, but even if they are condemned, it is better to have produced them than to have lain altogether fallow. Doubt-less, it was the natural advantages of Vienna's position on a junction of important trade routes which first gave her her greatness, and made the Habsburgs choose her for their capital. Yet it was because that Dynasty represented a magnificent idea—although one which is to-day lying low in the dust—that they grew and prospered, and in their shadow there grew up all the great complexity of modern Austria. Now the Habsburgs are gone, and she is left to face the world alone. And strangely enough, as it seems at first sight, are entrenched in the very stronghold of the rulers of the Holy Roman Empire some of the most careful and impassioned upholders of that one idea of modern times which, in the widespread enthusiasm which it can evoke, equals the mystic devotion of the Middle Ages. The incorporators of Socialism conceive themselves as the builders of a new and sublime Empire of thought on the ruins of the old. It is not for us to pass a judgement on their ambitions, only, with what fairness we can, to point out, how far and how wisely, they have achieved them. But it is at least worthy of notice that they are working them out in that city which is the capital of one of the smallest, weakest, poorest States in Europe, yet still —Vienna.

APPENDIX

THE AGRARIAN PROGRAMME OF THE AUSTRIAN SOCIAL DEMOCRAT PARTY

M OST of the preceding chapters had already been written when the Austrian Social Democrat Party took steps to supplement the most important deficiency in its programme. The Annual Congress of 1924 passed the following resolution:

"The Party Committee is instructed to appoint an agrarian-political commission to examine the different problems of Social Democratic agrarian policy, to further it by literary publications and to prepare a Social Democratic agrarian programme."

A certain number of such publications have already appeared, the most important being a study by Dr Otto Bauer entitled *Der Kampf um Wald und Weide* (the struggle for wood and pasture). The programme has also been completed and passed by the Congress of 1925. As the programme is mainly the work of Dr Otto Bauer, it is not unfair to consider it together with his book; the one embodying rather the practical suggestions, the other their theoretical basis.

The programme is a great advance on all previous Socialist efforts in this direction which have come under the present writer's notice. The general problem of the relations between landed capital and the anti-capitalist system is left, as far as possible, aside; and a scheme is worked out, which takes careful account both of the historical development of the land question in German-Austria and of its present economic possibilities. These are ingeniously combined to give as strong a Socialist colouring to the final result as will satisfy the demands of the present Party members without frightening the peasants more than necessary.

The flat corn-growing districts are dealt with in a summary fashion. The interest of the scheme centres round the mountainous, forest-clad regions which make up far the greater part of the present surface of Austria, and where the land—except for the great forests—is almost entirely in the hands of small peasant proprietors, who depend for their livelihood on cattle-breeding and dairy-farming.

Dr Bauer points out that, contrary to the expectations of the agricultural theorists of the last century, small holdings have by no means always vanished before the advance of large estates. Admitted that the large proprietor has the advantage of economic working, especially where machinery can be used on a large scale and man-power saved; the small holder, on the other hand, gives greater intensity of production, and can therefore hold his own in many branches of agriculture. The Alpine farms of Austria are an instance in point; if it is true that many of the mountain settlements have vanished in the last half century, yet these small holdings have given way, not to larger farms, but to persons who used the land either for exploiting its forests, or for preserving game, or for a combination of both. As cattle-breeder and dairy-farmer the small peasant has not been ousted.

Bauer proposes then to preserve and increase this class. If intellectually and economically developed, it can increase its production of meat and dairy produce sufficiently to compensate for the importation of cereals which will then be more than ever necessary.

To leave this class as it is at present constituted presents, however, economic difficulties, as the fate of the peasants since 1848 has shown; and no less political difficulties, since the peasant proprietors are staunchly anti-Socialist. It is proposed therefore to adapt present conditions by an ingenious method both sanctioned by tradition and agreeable to Socialists.

The early chapters of Bauer's *Der Kampf um Wald und Weide* are devoted to a detailed history of the land question in Austria; and form an exposition which would be of the utmost value, if only in the cause of history. It has, however, a further aim.

Bauer points out that the original German settlers lived in communes—"Gemeinde"—among the forest-clad Austrian mountains. Each peasant took up agricultural land according to his powers and needs, and this became his private property. Outside the village stretched the pasture and forest land, which —land being ample for all and timber practically valueless— was used by all in common. A settler was at liberty to found a new homestead on it; and the whole commune used it as common land—"gemain"—where each gathered wood for fuel, fencing and building, brushwood for stedding, wood-mould for fertiliser; grazed his cattle on it; and hunted his game as he required.

With the increase of population it became necessary to draw certain limits, and each commune received a definite tract of common land for these purposes. The members of the commune depended for their existence at least as much on their rights as commoners as on their private fields.

But as time went by, first of all the feudal system developed, later the forests acquired a new value with the development of the Austrian mining industry. The liege lord and his vassals asserted claims over the forests. Beginning with the sole right of hunting big game, they extended their claims step by step —the struggle lasted for centuries—until the whole of the forest land was in their possession outside the arable land of the peasants and the remnants of the "gemain," which was, however, greatly restricted in extent. If in many cases the peasants still retained certain old rights in the royal and feudal forests, these were yet much reduced and tended ever to diminish.

The restricted common land had, moreover, now grown too small to satisfy the needs of the communes, as their population increased. A further social struggle was fought out in the commune itself, in which two classes grew up: the wealthier yeomen, who not only owned farms sufficient for their needs, but in many cases further divided the commoners' rights exclusively among themselves, and the poorer "village proletariat," whose members either retained cottages with strips of land insufficient for their needs, eking out their existence by hiring themselves out to their wealthier neighbours; or else sank to be country labourers pure and simple, living in the houses of their employers and altogether dependent on them. Others again, especially after Josef II removed the restriction which kept them "adscriptus glebae," went to the towns and mines, and formed the industrial proletariat proper.

The present state of affairs in the Austrian country, after 1848 and 1918, is thus as follows:

Large tracts of forest land (and a few large agricultural estates in the Danube valley), some of which are State-owned, others the property of private individuals.

Numerous small peasant properties, the owners of which are engaged essentially in cattle-rearing and Alpine dairy-farming.

Some of these farms are at least tolerably prosperous and self-supporting. The owners of these, the peasant proprietors proper, are the backbone of the Christian Socialist Party.

Besides these, there are the cottagers and labourers, who are either wholly or partly dependent on hiring out their labour to their richer neighbours; and are thus either wholly or partly proletariat, in the strict sense of the word. This is the class which the present Social Democrat programme sets out in the first instance to capture, with a frank and perhaps slightly repellent insistence on the importance of its votes. It must be said that Social Democracy has already made considerable progress among this class.

Regarding the relative numbers, these are fairly equally divided. Of the—roughly—million and a half persons engaged in agriculture or forestry in Austria, about half are independent peasants with their families; about one-third labourers; the remainder cotters whose independence is only nominal. A very small number are great proprietors and their higher employees.

The programme proposes to expropriate the large properties altogether, whether these be forest or agricultural. The moral argument in favour of this move is that which is everywhere brought forward—that the people are only taking back what was stolen from them. No mention is made in the programme of the fact that the owners of landed property to-day have usually acquired it by legal purchase; as a matter of fact, the number of estates in Austria which still remain in the hands of descendants of the first baron who removed it, by force or Royal consent, from the people is unusually large. The question of compensation is left untouched.

The outlying portions of the great estates are to be used to increase the common lands with which they march—of this more later. The remainder is dealt with as follows:

In the case of agricultural estates, which are few in number, any small tenants of old standing keep their land as tenants of the commune. The remainder of the estate is administered as a model estate, the occupant being pledged to use modern methods as an example to the surrounding peasantry, to carry out experiments and to supply his peasant neighbours with seeds, stud stock and machinery on favourable terms. As an ideal, these estates are to be conducted on co-operative lines by the persons working on them; where this proves impossible, they are to be rented to farmers of known intelligence and experience. In the case of forests, these are to be united with the existent State forests and administered as "Socialist welfare forests."

This last proposal has met with much sympathy, even from non-Socialist critics. It is not necessary to go deeply into the question here. Every State has passed through a period of allowing its capitalists a free hand to buy up and make what they could out of the forests, and each has regretted it. The growth of timber is slow, and a capitalist who exploits his forests without diminishing them to future generations cannot hope to get a return from his money comparable to that to be got in trade or industry; least of all in a country like Austria, where the bank rate must be kept abnormally high to attract foreign capital. On the other hand, forests have an enormous climatic influence on the whole countryside, affect the entire community, and are therefore an obviously proper subject for State control.

The "Socialist welfare forest" is not to aim at making the highest direct profit on the forests themselves, which must involve their impoverishment, but at turning them to the best advantage for the welfare of the community. As the peasants of the surrounding communes are deeply interested in them, the peasants as well as the foresters and the representatives of the State are to have a voice in their administration. Whenever the interests of the forest allow it, the open spaces are to be at the disposal of the communes for grazing; and arrangements are to be made—rotation of clearing and plantation, etc.—to allow the communes all possible benefit without damaging the forests. The forest authorities are responsible for satisfying the just needs of the peasants regarding wood, stedding, etc., and for carrying through such improvements as will reduce those needs within the narrowest possible limits.

So much for the great properties—it may be mentioned in passing that the dividing line between a "great" and a peasant's property is nowhere defined. Is the distinction purely one of size? Without regard to the fertility of the land? Or of income derived from it? If so, this is a poor inducement to develop a property! Or of social standing, which has been technically abolished since 1918? Anyway, "great properties" are expropriated, but peasants are not.

The programme states, in a phrase which possibly sounds better than it bears analysis, that "Socialism is against property derived from robbery, of the ruling classes, but not against property derived from work, of the peasants." The latter will be fortified, not weakened, by the socialisation of the former (we have spoken before of the danger of letting Socialism degenerate into a mere campaign against wealth). "Peasants will continue to live on their soil as free owners within the Socialist state of society."

The peasants' existence is to centre round the commune, which is to be both extended and reformed. The outlying portions of the expropriated great estates are to be added to the common land. All land which was common before 1848 and has since passed under any other control is to be restored to the commune. The commune has the right to take up an option on any land coming into the market, and may bid for it at public auction. It is proposed that, when the scattered properties are rounded off, the commune take advantage of this process to increase its property.

No member of the commune is to have a right of priority in the usufruct of common land; all old privileges are abolished. The common land is treated as common property, is indivisible and inalienable.

Rights of pasturage, wood-cutting and pannage are not granted to those who possess enough pasture and forest of their own, but are equal for all other commoners, so far as they need them for their own domestic purposes (these distinctions seem to the lay mind positively to bristle with difficulties).

Meadow and arable land, where the commune possesses such, is to be divided into plots, and leased by the commune on long lease to small peasants and cottagers.

The commune must provide teams for the use of the small peasants and cottagers who do not own teams of their own. In this regard, the co-operative system is to be encouraged and subsidised from public funds.

Hunting and fishing rights will pass to the commune.

The commune will thus be enlarged and democratised at the expense both of the great landowners and of the richer peasants. It is hoped that in its new form it will both support and attract a larger class of cottagers and labourers, thus putting a stop to the growing danger of rural depopulation. This "back to the land" problem is to be solved by a large resettlement scheme. Labourers are to be settled at the public expense on small plots, which they will hold as tenants of the commune. These plots are to be large enough to enable them to keep their own cattle, which will be grazed on the common land. Further, the common meadow and arable land will be divided into plots, and each married cottager will have a claim to one such plot. He will thus have more land during the period when his family is growing up, and will relinquish it when he gets past work. As the commune will not profiteer on the land, nor constant buying and selling drive up its price, it is hoped that one of the great causes of rural distress, the disproportionately high price of land, will thus be partly removed.

The process of carrying through this expensive plan will admittedly be a slow one. The programme allots it one generation. Whether Austria will find the money for it within a generation remains to be seen.

Not only the commune, but also the State, is allotted a much larger liberty of control in agriculture than has hitherto been the case. A number of measures are here envisaged which are generally welcomed by non-socialist critics, while in some instances such critics have declared that the Socialist programme does not go far enough.

The most general, but perhaps the most important, of all these provisions deals with education. Primary education in country districts is to be extended and reformed. Compulsory extension classes are to be introduced for all persons from fourteen to eighteen years of age engaged in agriculture, who will receive general instruction in them for the first two years, specialist instruction in the last two. Secondary schools in agriculture and forestry are to be established throughout the country, with a system of scholarships. Higher education is to be extended. Then come travelling teachers, winter courses, model farms, exhibitions, conferences, etc.

Chapter vii has been written to little purpose if the reader does not realise the enormous benefits which such a programme could bring. Unfortunately, besides being costly, it will meet with much opposition from the peasants themselves as well as their spiritual fathers. Nothing short of rigorous compulsion will persuade the peasant to forgo the whole-time services of his sons during the four years of the extension classes, while the priest will naturally oppose "reform," as the Socialists understand it, of primary education.

Furthermore, the principle is laid down that it is the duty of the community to see that the soil is properly utilised. The State and the provinces are required to interest themselves, technically and financially, in necessary improvements as regards roads, regulation of streams, the use of fertilisers,

sound stud animals, etc. Many of these provisions have long
ago been adopted in Austria, as in every other civilised country.
The Socialist programme, however, gives the State the right
to carry through such improvements on private land, even
against the will of the proprietor, and at his expense. Among
such definitely authoritative measures may be mentioned: the
compulsory assembling of scattered farms; the confiscation of
land which is not cultivated by its owner, such land to be
handed over to communes, co-operatives or efficient farmers;
the killing off of game, if its increase prove harmful to agriculture, without regard to the wishes of the holder of
shooting rights.

The forest lands now in possession of peasants are to be re-
afforested and administered by communes or districts, or by
compulsory co-operative bodies representing the owners. In
any case such forests, like the State forests, are to be under
strict control.

A separate long section of the programme is devoted to the
special needs of the country labourers. The social legislation
now enjoyed by the industrial proletariat is to be extended
with, one must think, insufficient modifications, to the country
labourers. A number of old friends make a reappearance: the
Works Councillors, an average eight-hour day, collective agreements, insurance, inspectors, sanitary dwelling-rooms. All
these measures are preliminary to the final grand settlement
scheme described above.

It must be said at once that the need of social legislation in
favour of the country labourers is a very urgent one. Their
wages are miserable, their hours long, their amusements nil,
their housing conditions worse than bad. On the other hand,
in the present condition of agriculture, few peasants can afford
much improvement. If the spirit of class warfare, as it rules
in industry to-day, be fostered to an equal extent in agriculture,
the result will be the ruin of the proprietors, and must result
in an inverse form of depopulation, the labourers stopping
behind, but the peasant proprietors disappearing.

So much for the internal organisation of socialised agriculture in Austria; the forests and large estates under State control, the peasants centred round the commune. Those who believe in Socialism will agree heartily with most of its proposals.

Now for the proposed relations between the peasant and the outer world.

Two sections of the programme deal with "the protection of agriculture from exploitation through trading capital" and "the prevention of accumulation of debt in agriculture" respectively.

The former paragraph adopts the proposals made by President Hainisch on the basis of measures taken during the late war, and suggests that the import and export of cereals, flour and clover be made a State monopoly, in the hands of a Committee composed of representatives of the State, the farmers and the consumers' co-operative stores. Trade in home-grown cereals and their products within the frontiers of Austria remains free, but the monopoly must buy any quantity of home-grown cereals offered it at its fixed price.

This price is to be fixed independently of the world's quotations, and is to secure the maintenance of Austrian corn-farming without imposing unnecessary burdens on the consumer—*o si sic omnes!*

The monopoly buys abroad at the world price, at home at its fixed price, and sells at a combined price without profit.

For the rest, every encouragement is to be given to the co-operative movement in order gradually to eliminate the middleman. Producers' and consumers' co-operatives are to be linked up and, when sufficiently developed, will take over the monopoly under State control.

The measures for avoiding indebtedness are perhaps the least satisfactory of the whole programme. The abolition of entails on great estates and the transference of hunting and fishing rights to the commune are measures which can bring only a very limited relief. Their real effect is to strengthen the commune; but while the communal organisation may bring relief to the cottagers, largely at the expense of the yeomen, general experience, at least in Austria, has not to my knowledge shown that communities run into debt much less easily than individuals.

Obligatory insurance against hail, fire and loss of cattle, compulsory old-age pensions for all cottagers and labourers, and security of tenure are recommended.

Cheap credits for agriculture are to be obtained by fostering savings banks, co-operative credit associations, etc., and breaking the power of the present banks.

Only one of the provisions regarding taxation need be mentioned here: the land-tax is to be replaced by a tax on the produce of the land. When the value of the produce acquired by the peasant and his family from his own soil does not exceed what they would earn as labourers, it is treated as wages of labour and exempt from any taxation except income tax. The surplus produce alone is taxed on a sharply rising scale, the average value of the land being taken as the basis of taxation. This idea is taken from one recently evolved in Germany, and has much to recommend it, although only feasible if supplemented by the widest insurance. It may be well to illustrate its working.

A peasant has five acres on which he produces for the market. The average produce of each acre is worth—say—£10. He pays taxation on £50, say £5. If he has cultivated the land successfully, and got £70 for his crops, £65 remain to him, if badly, so he gets only £35, then £30 remain to him.

A second peasant, with ten acres of better land, is assessed at £150. Taxation being "sharply progressive" is £25. If he cultivates well, he may realise £200 − £25 = £175, if badly, perhaps £100 − £25 = £75.

The last section of the programme assures the peasant in the words quoted above that Socialism fortifies rather than weakens his property. When Socialism will have assumed control of banking and industry, the alternations of stagnation and soaring prices will cease. The position of the peasant in Society will be regulated. Secondly, the new security which the workman will enjoy will remove the great advantage which a peasant's life has over an industrial workman's; the price of land will no longer be beaten up by the desire to enjoy security at all costs. The price of land will fall; with high prices will vanish the necessity of mortgages, and the land will be freed from debt. Finally, the spread of the social idea will lead the peasants to wider and wider use of co-operative methods, so that the combinations of small proprietors will work with as much science and economy as the present large estates.

These somewhat utopistic thoughts conclude what is in many points a thoroughly practical, in all a most interesting, scheme.

BIBLIOGRAPHY

CHAPTER I

The literature on this subject is so rich that it is useless to attempt a bibliography. I shall therefore confine myself to recommending the best single work that I know:

KLEINWÄCHTER. Der Untergang der österreichisch-ungarischen Monarchie. Leipzig, 1920.

CHAPTER II

CHARMATZ, R. Deutschösterreichische Politik. Leipzig, 1907.
BRÜGHEL. Geschichte der österreichischen Sozialdemokratie. 5 vols. Vienna, various dates.
—— Geschichte der sozialen Gesetzgebung in Österreich.
DEUTSCH. Geschichte der Gewerkschaftsbewegung in Österreich.
—— Geschichte der deutsch-österreichischen Arbeiterbewegung. Vienna, 1922. (Good short account.)

CHAPTER III

HÖTZENDORF, CONRAD VON. Aus meiner Dienstzeit. 5 vols.
CZERNIN. Im Weltkrieg. 1920.
NOVAK. Der Sturz der Mittelmächte. Munich, 1921.
—— Chaos. Munich, 1923.
ADLER, FRIEDRICH. Vor dem Ausnahmegericht. Vienna, 1919.
KIRCHENAWE. Der Zusammenbruch der österreichisch-ungarischen Wehrmacht. Munich, 1921.
REDLICH, JOSEF. Österreichs Regierung und Verwaltung im Weltkriege. Vienna, 1925.

CHAPTER IV

BAUER, OTTO. Die österreichische Revolution. Vienna, 1923. See further to Chapter x.

CHAPTERS V AND VI

A mass of literature issued by the Wiener Volksbuchhandlung; the most important is summarised by Bauer, *op. cit.* See further the series of Protocols of the Social Democrat Party, the series "Tätigkeit der sozialdemokratischen Abgeordneten im Nationalrat."

GLÖCKEL. Die österreichische Schulreform.

ANON. Rätediktatur oder Sozialdemokratie?

BAUER. Der Kampf um die Macht.

ADLER, MAX. Demokratie und Rätesystem.

ELLENBOGEN. Sozialisierung in Österreich.

—— Die Fortschritte der Gemeinwirtschaft in Österreich.

CHAPTER VII

STRAKOSCH. Grundlagen der Agrarwirtschaft in Österreich. Vienna, 1916.

BAUER. Der Kampf um Wald und Weide. Vienna, 1925.

ROSEGGER. Jakob der Letzte.

HAINISCH. Die Landflucht. Jena, 1924.

GRÜNBERG. Studien zur österreichischen Agrargeschichte. Leipzig, 1921.

SCHIFF. Österreichs Agrarpolitik.

CHAPTER X

TOYNBEE. Survey of International Affairs. Oxford, 1925.

MACARTNEY, M. H. H. Five years of European chaos. London, 1923.

Reports of the General Commissioner, the various Experts, etc.

Studies on the Reconstruction plan, which really come outside the scope of this work, have been recently published in considerable numbers.

APPENDIX

BAUER. Der Kampf um Wald und Weide.

DIE ARBEITERZEITUNG: for September 27th and November 17th, 1925.

INDEX

For EU product safety concerns, contact us at Calle de José Abascal, 56–1°,
28003 Madrid, Spain or eugpsr@cambridge.org.

www.ingramcontent.com/pod-product-compliance
Ingram Content Group UK Ltd.
Pitfield, Milton Keynes, MK11 3LW, UK
UKHW012329130625
459647UK00009B/173